Europe and the MENA Region

"This book is designed to be a friendly reference guide on the subject incorporating analytical lenses and policy guidelines. It will be of good use to under and post graduate students and to those engaged in National Dialogues and policymakers at the national, regional, and international levels."
—Prof. Hamid Ali, *Dean of School of SEAPP, Doha Institute for Graduate Studies, Qatar*

Moosa Elayah

Europe and the MENA Region

Media Reporting, Humanitarianism, Conflict Resolution, and Peacebuilding

Moosa Elayah
School of Public Administration
and Development Economics
Doha Institute for Graduate Studies
Doha, Qatar

ISBN 978-3-030-98834-0   ISBN 978-3-030-98835-7 (eBook)
https://doi.org/10.1007/978-3-030-98835-7

© The Editor(s) (if applicable) and The Author(s), under exclusive license to Springer Nature Switzerland AG 2022
This work is subject to copyright. All rights are solely and exclusively licensed by the Publisher, whether the whole or part of the material is concerned, specifically the rights of translation, reprinting, reuse of illustrations, recitation, broadcasting, reproduction on microfilms or in any other physical way, and transmission or information storage and retrieval, electronic adaptation, computer software, or by similar or dissimilar methodology now known or hereafter developed.
The use of general descriptive names, registered names, trademarks, service marks, etc. in this publication does not imply, even in the absence of a specific statement, that such names are exempt from the relevant protective laws and regulations and therefore free for general use.
The publisher, the authors and the editors are safe to assume that the advice and information in this book are believed to be true and accurate at the date of publication. Neither the publisher nor the authors or the editors give a warranty, expressed or implied, with respect to the material contained herein or for any errors or omissions that may have been made. The publisher remains neutral with regard to jurisdictional claims in published maps and institutional affiliations.

This Palgrave Macmillan imprint is published by the registered company Springer Nature Switzerland AG
The registered company address is: Gewerbestrasse 11, 6330 Cham, Switzerland

Preface

In any given conflict, National Dialogues present a valid way to transcend internal factions and to rebuild relations between the state and different groups in conflicted and fragile counties. Over the years, National Dialogues have been considered important in state-building because they are designed for peaceful transformation. Many National Dialogues throughout history have been supported by the UN, US, and European Union; the recent ones being Yemen and Tunisia, regardless of the outcomes of each dialogue.

The Tunisian National Dialogue in 2013 is described as an ideal example of a successful National Dialogues, in the country where the Arab uprisings started. "The Quartet" was behind the Tunisian National Dialogue receiving the Noble Peace Prize for reshaping the political processes and reshaping the country's constitution, whereas the Yemeni National Dialogues failed to bring the internal warring parties to a consensus. The situation worsened by due to the regional and international military intervention called to solve Yemen's internal affairs and to install legitimacy in the state. Furthermore, the social fabric of the society was ruptured.

This book is doubly effective due to the concerns of the authors and their belief in the need for conflict resolution processes to be as inclusive as possible, involving a broad range of political actors and extending beyond a limited set of political players to include society at large.

This book contributes to a better understanding of the nature of National Dialogues of different regions: the commonalities and differences, challenges, and lessons learned. This book is designed to be a friendly reference guide on the subject incorporating analytical lenses and policy guidelines. The authors hope it will be of good use to those engaged in National Dialogues and policymakers at the national, regional, and international levels.

Results indicate that during the two years of this study, the Yemen war did not have receive adequate news coverage, especially the humanitarian side of the war as compared to the Syrian conflict which gained huge international coverage. The Conflict and Consequence frames were the most prominent frames in both cases. The four media outlets relied more heavily on presenting violence, air strikes, death, and injuries caused due to the action of the opposing party. Although it is not the focus of this study, it is found that in the case of Yemen these platforms portrayed the conflict as a sectarian issue, framing it as a Shia-Sunni conflict or proxy war between Iran and Saudi. To sum up this study, it is without a doubt that the war in Yemen and the crimes committed by both warring sides were underreported or ignored by the media although the atrocities were as serious as the conflict in Syria.

In other words, what went wrong in the Yemeni National Dialogues that could not prevent the later outbreak of a war, compared to successful dialogues in other countries such as Tunisia post-2011? This book provides empirical evidence that helps those engaged in the implementation of these processes to understand whether National Dialogues have only delayed the outbreak of civil wars like in Yemen or reached an agreement to end the state of chaos and advancing to the state-building processes as in other countries. This book starts out by providing relevant information about the roots of the Yemeni and Syrian conflicts. It presents the literature review, theoretical framework using media framing theory, and identifies the primary frames that are used in reporting the Yemeni and Syrian conflicts and whether these media outlets differ in their news coverage of both conflicts.

It also goes beyond the traditional exploration of political and social conflicts by adding a rich theoretical layer of analysis of Humanitarian Aid and its contribution to war economies in the Arab region. The situation is examined through an empirical analysis of HA organisations during the war. Furthermore, the book presents a radical contrast between the on-ground reality of the conflicts in the region, distinguished by various social, political, economic, geographic, and humanitarian factors, and the portrayal of the suffering and challenges faced by the people in European online media. This demonstrates that the chapter on media framing is working against the preceding chapters proving that European media fails to provide a true depiction or representation of the conflict in the Arab region, and devotes negligible coverage especially to the conflict and violence in Yemen. With its unique and comprehensive analytical approach, the book presents deep insight and greater understanding of the situation in Yemen, the accurate reality versus the abstract and distorted portrayal in European media.

Doha, Qatar   Moosa Elayah

Contents

1 Introduction National Dialogues Backed
by EU-International Interventions in Conflict-Torn
Countries 1
Moosa Elayah

2 Theoretical, Conceptual, and Methodological
Frameworks 47
Moosa Elayah

3 Wars and EU's Peace Interventions in the International
Setting: Yemen Versus Afghanistan and Ethiopia 93
Moosa Elayah and Bakeel Alzandani

4 Wars and EU's Peace Interventions in the Regional
Setting: Yemen Versus Iraq and Tunisia 119
Moosa Elayah

5 EU's Peace Interventions in the Regional Setting
(MENA) and the Effectiveness of Humanitarian Aid
in Arab Region 149
Moosa Elayah and Qais Jaber

6 Framing Conflict in the Middle East: Yemen and Syria
in European Media 173
Moosa Elayah and Fatima Al Majdhoub

7	Conclusion	201
	Moosa Elayah	

References 215

Index 251

LIST OF FIGURES

Fig. 1.1 Defining characteristics of and differences between negotiation, mediation, and National Dialogue (*Source* Blunck et al. [2017]) 14

Fig. 2.1 Peace process cycle 56

Map 1.1 Well-known National Dialogues (1990–now) (*Source* Paffenholz et al. [2017]) 3

List of Tables

Table 2.1	Lederach's model: explanations and hypotheses	59
Table 2.2	Cash as Aid advantages and disadvantages	72
Table 2.3	Sample and responses	75
Table 2.4	Framework for selecting the National Dialogue cases	77
Table 2.5	Media outlets & countries	80
Table 3.1	Strength Points (DP) in the Yemeni and Afghanistan cases	98
Table 3.2	Weak Points (WP) in the Yemeni and Afghanistan cases	99
Table 3.3	The core working groups within the Yemeni NDC 2013	101
Table 3.4	Important lessons (IL) from the Yemeni and Afghanistan cases	105
Table 3.5	Dynamic Points (DP) in Yemen-Ethiopia comparative case study	107
Table 3.6	Weak Points (WP) in Yemen-Ethiopia comparative case study	109
Table 3.7	Important lessons (IL) from Yemen-Ethiopia comparative case study	112
Table 4.1	Strength Points (SP) in Iraqi-Yemeni comparative case study	121
Table 4.2	Weak Points (WP) of Iraqi-Yemeni case study	123
Table 4.3	Important lessons from Iraqi-Yemeni case study	125
Table 6.1	The amount of coverage on the Yemeni and Syrian crises by European media outlets	181
Table 6.2	The amount of coverage of Yemeni and Syrian crises by European countries	182

Table 6.3	News frame used for the coverage of Saudi-Yemen war by European countries	182
Table 6.4	News frames used for the coverage of Syrian Civil war by European countries	183

CHAPTER 1

Introduction National Dialogues Backed by EU-International Interventions in Conflict-Torn Countries

Moosa Elayah

Human conflict, an ancient phenomenon, is almost as old as the first human. It is a reflection of human's innate nature, theorised by many political thinkers, including Socrates, Plato, Machiavelli, Ibn Khaldun, Thomas Hobbes, John Locke, and Rousseau. This phenomenon is often a consequence of the inability of two or more groups to coexist peacefully (Wolff, 2007). Many domestic conflicts from the Global South are missing or misrepresented in international media reportage, wherein "many policy makers, academics and members of the media believe that they are religious fundamentalism and religiously driven ethnic conflicts" (Fox, 1998). In this book, we argue that wars occur when one group or party attempts to take control of the overall social, economic, and political aspects of life—where the other parties essentially receive nothing (Kacowicz, 1997) and that the role of religion in domestic conflicts has weakened throughout history, which is slightly different from how Western media frames it (Price et al., 2009). Historically, the absence of the notion of justice in society, along with unparalleled distribution of authority and wealth, has led to military confrontations, where the winner takes all (Acemoglu & Robinson, 2012). In the modern era, such disagreements bring about the downfall of the concept of nation state and transform it into a group of fragmented antagonistic entities that cannot exist for long periods of time (Stavenhagen, 2016). They can assume ethnic, religious, or regional shapes, but in essence, they are quests for power and wealth (Loh, 2021).

Over the last fifty years, the world has witnessed several conflicts in different countries, and millions of innocent people have lost their lives without a holistic media coverage. There have been many internal wars, genocides, and human rights violations, in countries such as South Africa, Mali, Nigeria, Rwanda, Sierra Leone, Uganda, Congo, Somalia, Ivory Coast, Croatia, Bosnia, Yugoslavia, Ethiopia, Afghanistan, Iraq, Lebanon, Argentina, Georgia, and Yemen (Pettersson & Wallensteen, 2015). These countries entered into civil wars and in some cases the conflicts resulted in the collapse of the state (Papagianni, 2014a). Although each case is characterised by its own political and social circumstances, the cause, in reality, is the poor and unjust distribution of authority and the country's resources (Rotberg, 2010). Consequently, corruption deepens, and citizens lose their rightful part in the state. This creates a sense of revolution or political movement to destabilise the status quo (Rose-Ackerman & Palifka, 2016). In the absence of social equality, this unjust situation generates hatred within society and sparks deadly conflicts, where each side attempts to take down the other often under wrong and false justifications (Kriesberg, 2007). Ultimately, behind these conflicts stand a group of warlords and/or militia whose quest is to gain power and enforce their political ideologies (Acemoglu & Robinson, 2012).

The continuation of these wars and civil conflicts not only affects countries' internal matters but can extend to influence regional and international security (Turkoglu, 2021). Therefore, peacebuilding and resolution of conflicts, National Dialogues and conventions are not merely a national gain but have become a matter of the international community to mediate and, when needed, intervene to end such clashes (Annan, 2004). However, to resolve conflict, end wars, and begin peacebuilding, the international community must incorporate information on local drivers, processes, and complexities of wars (Millar, 2021). Empirical research and professional media that reflect reality beyond the drama are the main sources of deep knowledge about world conflicts, which this book attempts to provide (Vladisavljević, 2015). Information on the local knowledge of wars can help decision-makers in Western countries determine how to prevent wars or how to solve them through

Map 1.1 Well-known National Dialogues (1990–now) (*Source* Paffenholz et al. [2017])

peacebuilding processes, including National Dialogues (Mikha'el et al., 2009). National Dialogues are negotiating mechanisms supported by international communities, including the EU and are intended to expand participation in political transitions beyond the political and military elites (Alsoswa & Brehony, 2021). Often, dominant elite groups impede the process of conflict resolution by excluding other actors from the participatory processes. The aim of National Dialogues is to move away from elite-level deal-making by allowing diverse interests to influence the transitional negotiations (Papagianni, 2014b). Over the past decade, the world and specifically the Middle East and North Africa (MENA) region have witnessed several EU-supported National Dialogues, which have gained considerable importance as platforms for peaceful transformation (Helfer 2017). EU Bilateral and multilateral donors have supported National Dialogues in a number of countries as shown in Map 1.1, which includes Namibia (1990), South Africa (1993), Ethiopia (2000), Afghanistan (2010), Bahrain (2011), Iraq (2004), Jordan (2011), Lebanon (2008/2014), Sudan (2014/2016), Tunisia

(2013/2014), and Yemen (2013/2014) (Blunck et al., 2017; Paffenholz et al., 2017).

There are three regular components in the above-mentioned National Dialogue processes. First, dialogue was used as a tool to oversee complex change processes. Second, during the dialogue process, an extensive scope of national stakeholders was incorporated to address an extensive scope of issues contrasted with the elite agreements common at that time (Murray & Stigant, 2021). Although each process reacted to a special arrangement of difficulties, they all offered the promise of a change that was far from elite deal-making towards progressively comprehensive and participatory governmental issues (Planta et al., 2015). Third, there are no blueprints, formats, or tool compartments accessible to plan each of these National Dialogue processes. This is because each conflict transformation tool and its objectives must be modelled to suit the setting in which it seeks to support change (Elayah et al., 2020b). In each case, there are factors that either strengthen or weaken its chances of success (Elayah et al., 2020b). However, with any National Dialogue, the ultimate goal is to reach an agreement to end the state of war and chaos, especially in countries with internal social, ethnic, and religious divisions, which we illustrate via the cases chosen for this book (Paffenholz et al., 2017).

Some of the aforementioned National Dialogues have been used as instruments to resolve political crises and pave the way for political transitions and sustainable peace (Ndekwo, 2020). The others sought social harmony on the essential standards to overcome the divisions (Magure, 2008). Some seek to establish a new power-sharing process in society by building a new constitution that reorganises societal structure, fortifies a unified sociopolitical fabric, and advances a national culture of peace and a new "Social Contract" (Blunck et al., 2017). However, observations about preparing, conducting, and implementing these National Dialogue processes can draw attention to very interesting common grounds for research and investigation for the international knowledge outreach. While most of these National Dialogues came to an agreement, only 50% of these agreements were executed (Pettersson et al., 2019). At the point when National Dialogues brought about manageable changes and sustainable transformations, there was an ideal agreement among elites, notwithstanding worldwide help and public purchasing (Hartmann, 2017). National Dialogues have regularly been utilised by national elites to acquire or recover political authenticity and legitimacy, which has restricted their potential for transformative change (Elayah et al., 2020a). Measures for planning and actualising National Dialogues, specifically selection and basic leadership rules, assume a definitive job in whether processes are seen as representative, legitimate, and authentic (Avis, 2020). Meanwhile, National Dialogues have possessed the capacity to reduce violence by transferring grievances from the avenues into formalised procedures (Siebert, 2016). In cases with progressing and ongoing violence, National Dialogue results were sometimes constrained, but no clear pattern was found in the other studies (Paffenholz et al., 2017).

The EU-international interventions for peacebuilding and ending wars through National Dialogues are not only based on humanitarian considerations (Avis, 2020), but also strategic economic, political, military, and security drivers that work against achieving tangible results for peacebuilding. These aspects have been discussed by many researchers (Ayoob, 2002; Barnett & Snyder, 2011; Binder, 2015), but the diplomacy in resolving conflicts and the role of media framing have not been deliberated, especially how the content of conflicts is presented, which eventually moulds public opinion on issues of peaceful or military interventions by Western countries in conflict states. This book fills the lacuna by mapping out this missing pattern in past studies in both theoretical and policy discourses by providing a background based on specific past and present case studies, wherein wars and peacebuilding processes occurred, namely National Dialogues for EU efforts of reconciliation and state-building. It also covers the main research between the conflict and the international media. It is noticed that there is little empirical data, and only a few studies available on the media coverage of the Saudi-Yemen war, and it is assumed that the Yemeni war is underreported as compared to the case of Syria. Therefore, the following contribution comprises empirical observations that allow explorative assumptions as a starting point for future research. This book initiates research into the nature of news coverage of conflicts in the Middle East, by examining and comparing the amount of news coverage devoted to the two deadliest conflicts in the Middle East, in Yemen and Syria. With this the author can prove whether the Saudi-Yemen war is underreported by foreign media and whether it should be considered a serious crisis similar to the situation in Syria.

This text also closely investigates the commonalities between the Yemeni situation and four other National Dialogue cases—Afghanistan,

Ethiopia, Tunisia, and Iraq—in terms of their strengths and weaknesses, along with the lessons learned from their EU-backed National Dialogues and reconciliations. As a powerful tool for peacebuilding, National Dialogues have been used in one form or other for several centuries (Siebert, 2014), but recently the concept has also emerged within the scientific arena (Murray, 2017). Providing a space for joint reflection on the emerging trends and concept of the National Dialogue is a new addition to the literature of peacebuilding and conflict transformation (Collén, 2014). Accordingly, the overarching objective of this book is to contribute to the controversial and theoretical debate on National Dialogues, addressing past and recent cases from fragile and conflict-ridden countries for more insight. This can improve the quality of EU and international peacebuilding interventions and give deep local insights, which are not available in scientific dialogue or media reports, for meaningful, situation sensitive, and sustainable transformation processes.

This book is ground-breaking as the insights presented on National Dialogues uniquely analyse the international community's implementation of peaceful mechanisms, such as National Dialogues, and how they work to end wars and sustain peace in fragile and conflict-ridden countries. In this regard, this book is useful for peacebuilding scholars, practitioners, political organisations, policymakers, brokers, civil social organisations, media establishments, and other groups interested in peace and state-building to comprehend and deal with the challenges and learn from the past or other's experiences and design the most appropriate solution for their respective settings. It can also help graduate and undergraduate students deepen their knowledge of contemporary international peacebuilding interventions and the local generative machines of wars and conflicts in fragile countries.

Using a straightforward approach, this book seeks to provide well-founded reflections on designing a National Dialogue in fragile settings and an overview of National Dialogue processes at the national, regional, and international levels, by comparing and contrasting different cases and drawing inferences for future dialogues. The main aims of the book are: (1) to offer a multi-level analytical framework for National Dialogues in fragile settings; and (2) to provide empirical evidence that helps those engaged in the implementation of these processes internally and externally. Furthermore, this book uniquely integrates a media lens by analysing the extent of media coverage devoted to the Yemeni and Syrian wars and peacebuilding processes by four prestigious European online

English news outlets, The Independent, France24, SWIswissinfo.ch, and NRC Handelsblad. This book examines the news frames used in the coverage of the two cases. The second level of agenda setting is used as a theoretical guide to understand the news frames used to report on both wars. Through analysing the content of non-US media, four European media were selected to answer the following questions: (1) How much coverage is devoted to the Saudi military intervention in Yemen and the Russian military intervention in Syria by the online news platforms of The Independent France24, NRC Handelsblad, and Swissinfo.ch? (2) How do these European media outlets frame both conflicts? (3) Does the online news coverage of these outlets differ in their approach to the Saudi military intervention in Yemen from the Russian military intervention in Syria? To which extent the media reporting in Western countries related to the motives of these countries themselves towards the various conflicts in the world? To what extent is the media covering the reality of the conflicts and their complexities, as well as the peace processes that are supported and mobilised by Western countries?

This book's distinctive analytical approach supplements the empirical contribution to the Saudi-Yemen war. In this book, researchers argue that the ongoing geopolitical game in Yemen constitutes a significant threat not only to the country or the Gulf states but to the whole world. The main reason being Yemen's location that controls maritime routes, especially the Red Sea strait of Bab-el-Mandeb, which is considered one of the world's most strategic waterways and important chokepoints for international shipping. Not to mention al-Qaeda has continued to expand its reach due to the political and security vacuum in some provinces and threatened to carry out terror attacks in and outside Yemen. Therefore, it is believed that these relevant issues justify more attention and coverage either from regional and international media as well as international policymakers. However, the contrasting reality has motivated the researchers to examine the media coverage, particularly by Western media in Europe, of the recent war in Yemen, since the main role of the media is setting the agenda for the public.

Before we dive deeper into conflicts selected as case studies in this book, it is important to provide a definition of National Dialogues and other tools of conflict transformation.

What is a National Dialogue?

A distinct definition of the concept of National Dialogue will help the readers understand its processes and differentiate it from other utilised conflict transformation mechanisms as National Dialogues are always supported by the international community including the EU (Estefan et al., 2019). However, National Dialogue is not a polysemic term; it is a vague concept that has have several possible meanings (Siebert, 2014). "Diálogos" is etymologically derived from the Greek word "dialegesthai," which means through (*dia*) and the word (*logos*) or reason. Dialogue as a verb means "to discuss areas of disagreement frankly in order to resolve them" and as a noun is a category or a quality of the "exchange of ideas or opinions on a particular issue, especially a political or religious issue, with a view to reaching an amicable agreement or settlement" (Dictionary.com).

In the post-cold war context, this concept was used to describe a passive form of communication that used words to convey meaning or a kind of participatory process—one that was particularly well suited to addressing societal needs (Pruitt & Thomas, 2007). It emerged with the historical waves of political transition or what is called the Third wave of democracy (Blunck et al., 2017). The definition of National Dialogues is evolving, but they are essentially inclusive negotiation processes designed to expand participation in political transitions beyond the incumbent elite to a wide array of political, military, and, in some cases, civil society groups (Papagianni, 2014a).

National Dialogue, which is also known as dialogue roundtable, national forum, or presidential commission, is a peace mechanism designed as a political solution to protect national sovereignty and to question the regional and international interventions in conflicted or war-torn parts of the world (Francis, 2017). Some National Dialogues have succeeded in initiating genuine change while others have failed and been followed by armed violence or civil wars (Paakkinen & Turtonen, 2017). This definition will be used as the touchstone guiding the theory and empirical findings in this book. It will be elaborated and built upon based on the findings from the cases selected for this study.

The Institute for Multi-Track Diplomacy has defined dialogue as "a fundamental component in the process of peacebuilding. When people are divided by their differences, the patterns of relating tend to reinforce separation, fragmentation and divisiveness" (Wils et al., 2006). They also define it as a way of creating bridges across the chasms of our differences. Dialogue generates pathways for developing trust, changing old habits of thought and action, and stimulating new behaviour (Gaston, 2014). The Berghof Foundation (2017) directed a project titled "National Dialogue Handbook: A Guide for Practitioners" and defined National Dialogues as "nationally owned political processes aimed at generating consensus among a broad range of national stakeholders in times of deep political crisis, in post-war situations or during far-reaching political transitions." However, a National Dialogue cannot replace the need for democratic tools of acquiring legitimacy of ruling that is based on an effective constitution. It simply provides a normative and practical outline for building trust and instilling confidence in the conflict-stricken state (Miller & Aucoin, 2010). The main aim of a National Dialogue is to carve a creative space by bringing in the various and divergent interests of all stakeholders during processes of political transition, within which ideas of national unity, reconciliation, and peacebuilding can prosper (Elayah et al., 2020a; Planta et al., 2015). Ideally, a National Dialogue should "serve as a common platform for trust-building, learning, reflection and decision-making with the aim of developing a new social contract."

In the OECD arena, there is a less comprehensive definition of "National Dialogue," which has been utilised progressively among the international donors' organisations circle. OECD perceives a National Dialogue as a reaction that is required, relating for the most part to specific issues of public policy, which influence an extensive gathering of stakeholders, e.g. in the segments of health, finishing, business, education, transport, and so forth. The purpose of National Dialogue here is to unite all stakeholders for a specific timeframe to improve the odds of an agreement with an extensive broad-based ownership.

The UN defined National Dialogue as a dynamic system of related structures, instruments, assets, qualities, and abilities which, through dialogue and consultation, enhance to struggle and conflict prevention and peacebuilding in societies. A National Dialogue can create foundations, which can be considered as constituting a society's collaborative capacity, can help a fragile, divided, or post-conflict society, or a society in rapid transition, to make and sustain peace and harmony by:

- managing recurrent conflicts over land, natural resources, apportioning of mineral wealth, and contested elections, especially where development itself has exacerbated these conflicts.

- finding internal solutions, through a mediated consensus or a multistakeholder dialogue, to specific conflicts and tensions, especially in circumstances where concerns over sovereignty are paramount.
- complementing external mediation targeted at the primary parties with internal negotiations that bring together actors at different levels of the society and polity, often inaccessible to itinerant external mediation, or a wider group of stakeholders, including civil society, thus broadening the base for peace; and
- Negotiating and implementing new governing arrangements in an inclusive and consensual manner, especially after periods of turbulent political or socioeconomic transition (Kumar, 2012).

National Dialogues commonly depend on a blend of entire sessions and working groups. They are based on a clear structure, characterised standards, and procedures for discourse and decision-making (Elayah et al., 2020a). They may last from just a few days to a significant span of time, and their size can change impressively, from a hundred members to a few thousand (M'rad, 2015). National Dialogues are ordinarily accompanied by more extensive societal consultations intended to convey the consequences of arrangements and channel people's requests into the procedure (Dessu & Yohannes, 2020). These may appear as consultations, commissions, abnormal state critical-thinking workshops, and referendums (Unruh, 2015). This vast consideration of society within the ambit of a National Dialogue produces ownership and social responsibility for enhancing the sustainability of implementation (Paffenholz et al., 2017).

According to Odendaal (2011), National Dialogues constitute a combination of four types:

- The **first** one is a Summit Dialogue, which can be either initiated or driven by external or internal actors at the highest level of authority. For the most part, this type is used to defuse a national political crisis, normally initiated by incumbent presidents or governments, as tentative efforts to move towards increased political representation and liberalization, or to manage transitional periods. It can be exceedingly successful when the key decision-makers are set up to truly engage in this unique circumstance. It may likewise undermine political legitimacy when there are questions about the political will driving the initiative of a Summit Dialogue.

- The **second** type is the Civil Society Generate-Dialogues or Track Two dialogues that run from community-level interventions to interventions in multinational conflict, which can take different forms like: think tanks, workshops, discussion groups, seminars, or conferences where participants are representative of the conflict spectrum. This type of dialogue has no official status, mostly initiated in a discreet manner by civil society organisations or individuals. This type presents low-risk opportunities to establish more reliable channels of communication between groups, to develop trust, and to obtain greater clarity on preparatory steps that have to be taken to initiate a peace process. In addition, Track Two dialogue may engage actors that may have been excluded from the main process: and those with an interest in subverting the official processes. The advantage of a Track Two dialogue is its informality, but it can be unproductive when discussions take place in a manner that is too disconnected from political reality. For example, if the participants are too distant from the centres of power, a dialogue may end up in futile "talk shop."
- The **third** type is the Issue-fixated Dialogue that is centred on developmental planning processes, at different levels of society and not only between local stakeholders, but also with donors. The endeavour is to set development priorities, for instance in the short- or medium-term aftermath of violent conflict or political crisis and to coordinate all partners into a joint procedure of basic leadership with the point of expanded proprietorship and cooperation. Such procedures have much potential incentive as dialogue opportunities. They depend for progress on a well-structured design and talented facilitation. Since the pertinence of political dialogue for arranging is underestimated right now, it is regularly managed in a bureaucratic way.
- The core type, especially in this book, is the **fourth** one, Multilevel Dialogues. It is a support process for new "Social Contracts." They involve broader society in a dialogue, as opposed to exclusive elite-driven processes and relying on civil society capacity to facilitate such processes. The objective is to address issues of horizontal divisions and vertical legitimacy between communities as well as the vertical challenges between the citizens on the ground and the political elite. The strongest contribution is in the area of vertical legitimacy, this is dependent on the confidence of citizens in state institutions. The

greatest challenge, however, is to guarantee that there is linkage and coherence between the procedures, that they feed into and expand on one another, and that they prevail with regard to tending to the political reality.

The aim of this variation among different types of political dialogues, and more on the concept and other related concepts, which will be presented in detail in Chapter 2, is to understand that the purpose of a dialogue is to discuss deep-rooted conflicts. Furthermore, to seek other viewpoints from various stakeholders in the society other than political elites, to facilitate respect and understanding through communication, and work hand in hand for effective outcomes to stabilise the state (Haider, 2019). National Dialogues provide an inclusive, broad, and participatory official negotiation framework, which can resolve political crises and lead countries into political transitions (Paffenholz & Ross, 2015). With mandates that include political reforms, constitution-making, and peacebuilding, National Dialogues are convened to address issues of national concern, typically longstanding causes of conflict that have been brought to the fore by political protest or armed insurrection (Blunck et al., 2017). Dialogue is an inclusive process, entailing learning, not just talking, recognising one another's humanity, and stressing a long-term perspective (UNDP, 2009). The dialogue, as a tool in peacebuilding and conflict transformation, requires knowledge of what dialogue is, competence of how to employ dialogue, and adherence to the use of dialogue (Incerti-Thery, 2016).

NATIONAL DIALOGUES AND OTHER TOOLS FOR CONFLICT TRANSFORMATION

Dialogues are one of the approaches to dealing with conflicts. As part of the basic repertory of management in international relations, two skills are important: negotiation and dialogue (Ropers, 2004). Ropers (2004) defines negotiation as a face-to-face communication approach that takes the shape of organised group encounters with individuals below top-leadership positions. These negotiations are generally managed (initiated, organised, and directed) by a third party (Ropers, 2004). Dialogue projects are important tools of conflict resolution approach. The main objectives of dialogue projects are the reciprocal clarification of views and relations as well as improvements in communication processes (Ropers, 2004). Although dialogue projects are generally brief and difficult to maintain over a long period, when successfully managed, they usually increase the possibility that the process will lead to the formation of a group of people with the skills and experience needed for dialoguing and closing links with the other parties involved (Ropers, 2004).

Mediation has also been defined as an approach to managing conflict. It is peaceful, non-coercive, and non-binding (Fisher, 2001). All concerned parties can enter the agreement freely, while at the same time maintaining control over the terms of the agreement (Joenniemi, 2015). Essentially, mediation is a method oriented towards resolving disputes between involved parties rather than an approach that concerns the nature of the relationship of the parties involved. Mediation also aids cooperation and constructive behaviour among conflict parties (Dessu & Yohannes, 2020). It is not commonly considered a tool for forging formal agreements but rather creates perspectives for resilient and transformed relationships between the parties in conflict (Giessmann & Wils, 2011). As a political process, in mediation, parties in conflict concede to accept one or more third actor(s) who are not affiliated to the conflict, but are trusted by the disputants, and who are considered supportive in finding a solution to the stalemate in the conflict (Giessmann & Wils, 2011).

Negotiation is universal but it varies depending on different cultural contexts (Planta et al., 2015). Negotiations (formal talks) can be considered one of the components of mediation (Lehti, 2019). Mediation focuses on influencing the views and attitudes (behavioural change) of the conflict parties by exploring opportunities for change for either of the parties involved (Giessmann & Wils, 2011). Mediation (as a means to facilitate the negotiation process) should also be practised within the traditions and norms of any cultural or subcultural context (Fisher, 2001). Mediation can be wielded during bilateral or multilateral forms of disputes; it is an important mechanism for settling complex multilateral negotiations (Fisher, 2001) (Fig. 1.1).

Dialogue, in this sense, is different from other conflict resolution processes such as negotiation and mediation. Dialogue is a particularly revealing and familiar way of outlining a party, without an exigency to reach an agreement with the "other," and without a specific timeframe (Paffenholz & Ross, 2015). Negotiation is based on prior knowledge of what the other wants in the context of consultations that are later aimed at obtaining gains, on the one side, and concessions, on the other. In

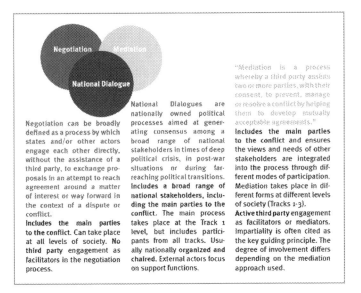

Fig. 1.1 Defining characteristics of and differences between negotiation, mediation, and National Dialogue (*Source* Blunck et al. [2017])

each negotiation, all conflicting parties win and waive at the same time. The difference, in this regard, is the range of profit and loss accounts by the conflicting actors (Incerti-Thery, 2016). The dialogue has no gains or concessions. It is a cognitive interaction in which there is a need to clarify the other's opinion without the stipulation of acceptance or a common result (Murray & Stigant, 2021). Dialogue is not a tool to resolve an existing problem, but it is being employed to prevent future or potential future problems or conflicts (Castaneda, 2012). Dialogue is an expression of the recognition of the existence of "another opinion within a society" and the right to express this opinion and belief without distortion or pressure (Zachariassen et al., 2016). Dialogue is a revealing, familiarising, and defining method of a conference for exchanging ideas. Both parties share their ideas and are free to continue upholding their stance even after the finishing stage of a dialogue unless they are convinced to accept another shared idea (Krause, 1998). Dialogue can broaden debate regarding a country's trajectory beyond the usual elite decision-makers; however, it can also be misused and manipulated by leaders to consolidate their power. Dialogue, as an interchange of ideas without the pressure of commitment, is a very important first step towards the more demanding process of negotiation (Zachariassen et al., 2016). However, the official negotiation process can be an alternative to armed resistance or conflict, but not peace. To build peace, we need an inclusive dialogue and a smart mediation to have deeper peacebuilding and state-building interaction (Giessmann & Wils, 2011; Ropers, 2004).

The concept of National Dialogues is not intended to challenge mediation, but to reinforce it. Traditional third-party mediation is frequently vital in supporting the dialogues (Visoka & Doyle, 2016). Generally, mediation is a standout amongst the most omnipresent ways of assisting conflict resolution in a wide array of social arenas (Rodt & Okeke, 2013). At its core, mediation is a political procedure in which conflicting factions' consent to acknowledge at least one or more third-party actors who are not faction to the conflict, who appreciate the trust of the disputants, and who are considered possibly supportive in overcoming the deadlock triggered by a stalemate in the conflict (Giessmann & Wils, 2011). The stakeholders, including the conflicting factions and mediators, must plan methodologies that address wide constituencies affected by the conflict. National and local dialogues are essential as they complement traditional third-party mediation in an important way (Collén, 2014). Mediation is a pacific, non-coercive, and non-restricting way to deal with peace-making that is gone into unreservedly by the concerned parties, who in the meantime keep up power over the substance of the agreement. Therefore, mediation is basically an undertaking orientated technique, coordinated towards handling a common issue of the conflicting factions; it isn't straightforwardly worried about the idea of the relationship and connection between the factions (Potter & Centre for Humanitarian Dialogue, 2005). Mediation can be coordinated between two bilateral factions in its reciprocal structure, but it can include various factions when it is called upon to assist in complex multilateral negotiations (Kestemont, 2018). In mediation, mediators are characterised by not having a similar identity as either of the conflicting factions, nor do they have any direct interest in, or any immediate enthusiasm for the dispute. However, it is not necessarily the case that mediators are impartial, or that they have no substantial interests to be served by entering the area of the conflict (Pearson, 1997). Notwithstanding, mediators require the imperative information, local knowledge, and skills to appropriately satisfy their job and roles (Donais & McCandless, 2017). This implies a careful comprehension of factions, the substantive issues that separate them, the arrangement procedure and negotiation itself, and the more extensive framework in which it is embedded (Fisher, 2011).

The nature of media framing in mediating countries undergoing peacebuilding processes is important in shaping the nature of external pressure on the conflicting parties to accept peaceful settlements (Donais & McCandless, 2017). However, regarding domestic media policy in Western countries, actors from interest groups to governments themselves use political means, such as media, to control, manipulate, and to influence external decision-making processes and the multi- diplomacy tracks for peacebuilding (Ginsberg, 1999; Higgins, 2011). Media outlets seek to create local support to deal with external conflicts as well as the nature and level of mediations. Western media greatly respects the political elites, and in many cases, they follow them to serve the national interest that these elites claim they seek to fulfil (Gilboa et al., 2016). Therefore, they are used in elite campaigns and populist propaganda, in addition to ideological influences on public opinion of conflicts around the world (Crocker et al., 1999; Gilboa et al., 2016). The media often acts as a critical tool in increasing the frequency of interference in foreign diplomatic mediation or even provoking conflicts through the intervention of states and external parties in favour of a conflicting party on ground (Deng et al., 2010). Thus, this section presents a deeper conceptual part to examine the roles that the media plays and their influence on a Western government's response to a conflict in a southern country. Much of what has been written so far has highlighted the significant influence of political elites on media coverage, and the conditions in which the media can play a more independent role during conflicts in the world (Brown, 1996; Burton, 2010; Gilboa et al., 2016; Tidwell, 2001). In some cases, the media can play a more divisive role than a constructive one during critical moments and intensify conflicts and wars (Cottle, 2006). Competing actors in Western countries can influence international media coverage to support local conflict parties, from setting the agenda and framing to facilitating diplomatic and military assistance to the conflicted parties in the Southern countries (Gilboa, 2006; Saleem & Hanan, 2014).

Mediation processes can be official or unofficial and they may also complement one another (Alexander, 2009). While, as a general rule, mediation is frequently a joined exertion by official and informal performers, there is little evidence so far of working deliberately with and in intercession with groups (Unger, 2010). This is due to the insufficiency of research and clear media reports that prevent intervening parties in armed conflicts from obtaining full knowledge of the nature of conflicts (Yawanarajah, 2021). Western countries often become the negotiators themselves. Negotiations, along these lines, are just a single component of official mediation (Lempereur et al., 2021). Official mediation needs to happen behind the scenes. For example, mediators go into consultations on either side about how the procedure can be expedited, and their mediation endeavours may incorporate a few components of control to help the struggling parties by sorting out and organising talks or negotiations (Clapham, 1998). Many conflicts can be avoided or averted from the beginning, but the ineffectiveness of the media to act as a means of early warning or prevention has hindered it (Boutros-Ghali, 1992). Media tends to focus on the sensational aspect of conflict. They generally avoid covering situations that have not yet reached the point of disaster. Coverage of conflicts is selective and major violent conflicts are often ignored, as seen recently in Yemen and other countries, such as Sudan (Spencer, 2005). The international community and its media tools are indifferent to conflict prevention and peace building, as many writings have shown the failure of humanitarian responses and the failure of many journalists, humanitarian agencies, and decision-makers to understand the needs of people in war-torn societies (Fahmy, 2020; Trotskovets, 2021). Thus, there is a clear failed relationship between media and human responses in war-torn and conflict-ridden regions (Autesserre, 2017).

Even more vitally, mediation must affect the positions and viewpoints of the warring factions, but when it is part of the conflict itself, it will not achieve this end and its impartiality. Bearing in mind that Western mediations consider the reality of open doors for change on either side, because they are not bound by a media reality that reflects the on-ground reality. Therefore, mediations seek results to achieve certain domestic political gain in Western countries more than behavioural changes. Official brokers are clearly bound by the mandate offered, specific compliance guidelines and rules of engagement, and fixed plans and timeframes. In the event that they neglect to make unambiguous progress within an agreed timetable, the mediation procedure turns out to be briefly stymied or may be rescinded without solid results (Giessmann & Wils, 2011).

Theoretical research and results of intergroup and national conflict resolutions and management are still incomplete (Ropers, 2004). There is also a lack of a sharp distinction between "wars of national interest" as in Afghanistan, and interference in "wars of others" as has been the case in

Sudan, Yemen, and other countries or those wars that are covered by the media as wars of national interest but are frequently in the context of the human narratives (Winright & Johnston, 2015). Although many important questions have naturally arisen from practical experiences regarding related strategies in conflict situations, these questions remain largely ignored or unexplained in the geopolitical context of media-conflict interactions (Taylor & Bean, 2019). The matter of media in Western countries and their coverage of conflicts in southern countries needs to be refocused. Similarly, specific recommendations based on empirical evidence that explores the relationship between foreign policy and the media on Western issues, especially the European Union, are needed. This is due in part to the renewed recognition of the importance of the local/domestic dimension of conflicts, and the need to move beyond research that assumes that Western media and foreign policy are the beginning and end of the story (Gilboa et al., 2016). Fisher and Ury's (1981) concepts of "interest-led conflict resolution" are the most obvious methods in this environment, and a sharp distinction must be made between "ours" and "others' wars" or "national interest" and "humanitarian" wars (Urlacher, 2007). Comparative case studies (qualitative analysis) of the components of conflicts that appear to have been peacefully resolved or that have not been resolved are of great importance. These will be presented in the next section: Yemen and Afghanistan, Yemen and Ethiopia, Yemen and Iraq, Yemen and Tunisia and in the coming chapters, as well as the selection of studies in the framework of the media dimension in the penultimate chapter of this book between Yemen and Syria.

It is noticeable that the issue of peacebuilding operations, supported by the European countries in places of conflict in the Arab region, was also associated with Humanitarian Aid that targeted, at least on paper, the groups most affected by conflicts. Thus, it became important to investigate whether the EU Humanitarian Aid employed achieves its goals of alleviating the suffering of the disadvantaged people and reducing hunger, or if it is causing harm by exacerbating the conflicts in the Arab region and causing the so-called war economy, the failure of peace processes, and European interventions. This is, despite the European media, through our observations, covering the human suffering in the Arab countries, which in turn urges European societies to provide aid and relief in times of disasters and wars. Developing this argument, this book also offers food for thought for the EU donors to take alternative solutions in delivering and distributing HA in fragile states, as their funds have inadvertently become entangled in a highly problematic war economies' dynamic. As for the NGOs, on which the EU is relying to deliver the Humanitarian Aid during the war, they are unable to provide the conditions needed to bear their success or deliver HA to those who are in need (Elayah & Verkoren, 2020). The main takeaway is that even though HA has the potential to have a net positive effect by alleviating suffering of the population and rebuilding failed states, this is often not the case in areas of high political instability.

CASE SELECTION CONSIDERATIONS AND DATA COLLECTION

This book focuses on the Yemeni context and employs a multi-level analysis approach (international, regional, and local levels within the media outlets in selected EU countries), zeroing in on the Yemeni and Syrian wars, which have had a devastating impact over the years following the Arab Spring in 2011 (see Chapter 5). The international intervention in these two cases can be assumed to be the reason for media attention on wars between the Saudi-led coalition and Houthi militias in the case of Yemen, with al-Assad forces and the forces of the opposition parties backing the two sides with international military intervention. These wars have drastically pushed the two countries towards social, economic, and institutional collapse as the world keeps ignoring the severity of the crisis. The aim of this book is to identify and analyse the amount of coverage devoted to the Yemeni and Syrian wars by four prestigious European online news publications, The Independent, France24, SWIswissinfo.ch, and NRC Handelsblad. This book also examines the news frames used in the coverage of the two cases. The second level of agenda setting was used as a theoretical guide to understand what news frames were used to report on both wars (see Chapter 2).

The author looks closely at the commonalities shared by the Yemeni situation and the other four cases—Afghanistan, Ethiopia (Chapter 3), Tunisia, and Iraq (Chapter 4)—in terms of strengths and weaknesses, along with the lessons learned from their National Dialogues and reconciliations. There are other National Dialogues that have not been covered, including more recent ones, such as the Sudan and South Sudan National Dialogues, and prominent older cases, such as South Africa, where local knowledge was incorporated for the international media, policymakers, and academics. The conflict in Sudan has ethnic and Christian-Muslim-religion dimensions and it has, therefore, been excluded because it does not conform to the Yemeni situation, which is the main case under investigation in this book. The National Dialogue in South Africa is one of the most studied and debated case by many scientists and researchers in the world, and it has therefore been excluded in order to introduce new cases in the global trend of National Dialogues keeping in mind the dramatic changes brought on by the Arab Spring. National Dialogues became a prominent tool proposed by the ruling elites of the old Arab regimes as well as Arab Spring activists to establish common frameworks for peaceful transformation in the Arab societies. However, a closer look at these proposals reveals that they are obviously driven by quite different motives. For the one side, it is a mechanism to slow down the transition process and to safeguard as much as possible from the former regime. For the other side, it is a mechanism to ensure a peaceful, but nevertheless radical regime change towards a more democratic arrangement (Ropers, 2011). Tunisia and Yemen, which are selected for this book, are the first two Arab countries that were engulfed with unrest in 2011, followed by the National Dialogue Conferences (NDCs) that were designed to break the political deadlock and to solve conflicts peacefully. The NDC in Tunisia is recognised as a successful example in the Arab world, whereas the Yemeni one failed to bring the warring parties to a consensus and ended with civil war and regional military intervention. In Yemen, the NDC has been classified as a successful experience that can be used as a positive model for transition in other places (Gaston, 2014). Still, the outbreak of conflict in Yemen has resulted in a questioning of the Yemeni NDC's effectiveness. As a result, one section of this book will respond to a key inquiry: Why has National Dialogue succeeded in moving Tunisia towards stability but failed in Yemen when both countries spent significant time and resources to ensure the National Dialogues' success?

On the basis of the comparison between different cases, different settings, and also different experiences based on their success, the author investigates the strengths and weaknesses as well as the lessons learned from each process. This can be utilised in the future construction of any peace processes in fragile contexts like Yemen.

There are other varied considerations and lines for selecting the cases (for further information see the methodology section):

- The tribal line: The Afghanistan (2002) case was considered as Afghanistan has a similar social setting as Yemen characterised by strong tribal organisation. The conflicts in both countries are along ethnic/tribal lines.
- The issue line: Ethiopia has gone through a political crisis that needed comprehensive political dialogue to bring about national consensus, manage, and resolve the conflict among the political parties by also creating a space for other actors in the Ethiopian society. The author thinks that the case of Ethiopia is a good lesson to learn from not only among African countries, but it could be for any other country that has a similar political crisis. The Ethiopian case is very interesting because it dealt with an issue of federalism, which is also one of the debated issues in Yemen.
- The ethnic/religion lines: Although the case of Iraq (2008) is not recent and was before the Arab Spring wave that hit the region, Iraq is culturally not that different from Yemen. Furthermore, conflicts in both countries have been fought along similar ethnic/religion lines.

The book is leading the contemporary vanguard because it addresses and analyses the local-level perspectives on the EU NDC interventions by focusing on the Yemeni Syrian case and specifically the views of the EU media outlets. This book contributes to a better understanding of the nature of wars and National Dialogues based on different geographical cases, and it also examines the news frames that were used to present conflicts in MENA by the European media outlets. As this book argues that the success of the National Dialogue should be an internal affair and not external, the interventions of third parties do not serve the national interest. External parties work to dismantle the social fabric in different conflict countries by using the media outlets, and all parties must be aware of the dangers of such tactics, which will not end before reducing countries to a non-state phase. Therefore, this book aims to help the readers better understand the history of Yemeni NDCs and whether these dialogues have succeeded in actuating political transformation and stability in the country.

This book is designed to be a friendly reference guide on the subject of National Dialogues incorporating media analytical lenses, lessons learned, and policy guidelines. The author hopes it will be of good use to those engaged in National Dialogues, media outlets, and policymakers at the national, regional, and international levels. This book serves as an empirical contribution to the Saudi-Yemen war, but it uses a different analytical approach. The researchers argue that the geopolitical game happening in Yemen constitutes a significant threat, not only to the country and the Gulf states, but also to the whole world. The strategic location of Yemen that controls maritime routes, especially the Red Sea Strait of Bab-el-Mandeb, is considered one of the world's most strategic waterways and important chokepoints for international shipping. Besides, al-Qaeda has continued to expand its reach due to the political and security vacuum in some provinces, threatening terror attacks in and outside Yemen. Therefore, these issues warrant more attention and coverage either from regional and international media as well international policymakers. However, the reality might tell otherwise, and this is what has motivated the researchers to examine the media coverage of the recent war in Yemen, particularly by Europeans for the reasons provided in the methodology section.

The qualitative approach adapted in this book is based on a comparative, descriptive, and analytical tools containing many of the curriculum and feeder roads to the study of peacebuilding phenomena. The qualitative descriptive analytical approach focuses on the characteristics of the phenomena and interprets their occurrence and the relationship between variables, as well as the results of the analysis. Analytical methodology, by comparing cases in places that have similar components, helps policymakers adapt strategies that work well in similar environments. For instance, there are many post-civil war societies that became interested in going through National Dialogues to cease wars and rebuild their countries. Breslau states that "investigators of natural science disciplines have shown that methodological positions, which specify the relevant objects, questions, and techniques for an area of study, are also political arguments that implicitly specify who can legitimately produce authoritative knowledge in the field in question, and under what conditions" (1997). Thus, political scientists use scientific methods to answer questions about political phenomena that can happen anywhere and at any time.

Profiles of the Selected Cases

The 2011 Arab Spring uprising that swept nearly all Arab countries is defined as an epoch-making event when anti-regimes protests demanded reorganisation and the ouster of the long authoritarian regimes. The ongoing conflict in Yemen and Syria is part of the wide wave of 2011 that was inspired by the successful uprisings in Tunisia and Egypt and is a symbol of hope for Syrian and Yemeni pro-democracy activists to demand similar changes.

YEMEN

The uprising in Yemeni was emboldened after the former presidents of Tunisia and Egypt were toppled in 2011. Several dozen students, civil society, and political opposition groups and activists attended a rally in Sana'a, the capital city of Yemen (Elayah & Verkoren, 2020). The protesters chanted pro-democracy slogans and condemned poverty and official corruption. The protests all over the country reached their peak following the resignation of Mubarak, the former president of Egypt, and protesters called for the similar change in Yemen (Durac, 2012). The vast majority of the anti-regime protesters who camped at the crossroad outside Sana'a University represented Yemen's youth movement, a group of young, pro-democracy activists who present themselves as unaffiliated to any traditional political alliance (Nevens, 2011).

This movement had formed an umbrella group—the Civil Coalition of Revolutionary Youth—which brought together Yemen's four main youth organisations, the Alliance for the Youth's Revolution; the Alliance of the People's Youth Revolution; the Alliance of Youth and Students for a Peaceful Revolution; and the Coalition of Change Leaders (France 24, 2011). Later, the Civil Coalition released its overall vision of the protesters which was:

> to lay the ground for a civic, modern and democratic state which can interact with the realities of the modern world on the basis of equal citizenship, human rights, social justice, a plural political system, and the freedom of expression and opinion. (Elayah & Verkoren, 2020)

The protesters were supported by the Houthi movement in the north of Yemen and al-Hirak in the south, as well as the opposition parties and the Joint Meeting Parties, who condemned the attack on protestors by the regime's security forces and called on their supporters to join the protests (Durac, 2012; Nevens, 2011).

The political unrest resulted in a security vacuum in the north and south of the country, where terrorist elements and militia have taken advantage of the situation to fill the vacuum (Kronenfeld & Guzansky, 2014). The US, EU, Saudi Arabia, and other members of the international community attempted to broker a political compromise. A transition plan was brokered, and in 2012 former Vice President Abd-Rabbu Mansour Hadi became president (Juneau, 2013). With the support of the US, Saudi Arabia, and the United Nations Security Council, President Hadi attempted to reform Yemen's political system. Throughout 2013, key players convened a National Dialogue Conference aimed at reaching broad national consensus on a new political order (Elayah et al., 2020b). However, in January 2014 it ended without an agreement (Sharp, 2017). In other words, Yemen has been engulfed by many challenges prior to 2011. However, it was the year of the Arab Spring when the Arab nations erupted to end long-term dictatorships (Edwards, 2019; Hill et al., 2013). Yemen was facing popular protests, a secessionist movement in the south, a spiralling security crisis, and a deep fracturing of political factions. That situation led Yemen's political elite to agree on the Gulf Initiative in 2011, which established a caretaker transitional government. The agreement signed in Riyadh stipulated a two-year transitional period and created a National Dialogue Conference (NDC) as a forum involving delegates from all parts of the country to solve the country's political problems (Kestemont, 2018). The results of 10 months of talks were expected to form the basis for a new constitution, and Yemenis would then elect a new government and conclude the transitional period (Eshaq & Al-Marani, 2016). Some groups occasionally suspended attendance or boycotted the NDC due to some grievances, such as the Houthi movement located in the north of Sana'a and the southern movement known as Al-Hirak Al Janubi (Garallah, 2013).

One group in particular, the northern Yemeni Houthi movement, a religious group that began as "Believing Youth Forum," affiliated with the Zaydi sect of Shia Islam, maintains a stronghold in the northern province of Saada. It is involved in six wars with the former regime (Al Batati, 2015) and sought to use military force to reshape the political order. On 4 March 2015, Houthi militants raided the NDC's secretariat in Sana'a, thereby suspending its activities. This act of violence was perhaps the most tangible sign that the broad National Dialogue initiated in 2013 had failed to set Yemen on the path out of conflict and nudge it towards a citizen engagement process to build a more just, equitable, and prosperous land (Elayah et al., 2020b). Instead, the country plunged back into full-blown civil strife, as Houthi rebels conquered large parts of the country and its institutions. The Saudi-led military intervention in support of the exiled President Hadi, which was launched in the same month as the NDC became dysfunctional, further escalated the conflict. Two years into the war, the country has faced a humanitarian calamity (Ghafarzade, 2015). In early 2017, international agencies monitoring the conflict confirmed a death toll exceeding 10,000 with another 40,000 wounded and estimated the number of IDPs at three million. Moreover, there was warning of an impending famine, with approximately five to eight million people facing acute malnutrition, of which a quarter are estimated to be in a state of "emergency" (FEWS Net). The Houthis were joined by the forces that were still loyal to former President Saleh, creating an alliance that was a great opponent to President Hadi and his allies. In 2014, Houthi militants took over the capital, Sana'a, and violated several power-sharing arrangements. In 2015, Houthi militants placed President Hadi and his cabinet under house arrest. Hadi was able to escape to Aden in southern Yemen, as Houthi forces advanced from the capital all the way to Aden. In March 2015, after President Hadi, who had fled to Saudi Arabia, appealed for international intervention, Saudi Arabia and regional and international coalition launched a military offensive aimed at restoring Hadi's rule and removing Houthi fighters from the capital and other major cities. The Saudi-led coalition launched air strikes in response to a specific request from President Hadi to the moment of writing this paper (Durac, 2012; Sharp, 2017).

This level of human suffering, combined with the grim outlook of protracted conflict, contrasts sharply with the optimism that reigned in international policy circles at the outset of the National Dialogue Conference (NDC) in 2013. The NDC was a much-touted event that The Economist (29 May 2013) referred to as "quite a novelty." EU media and policy praised the NDC as a positive and constructive tool to follow up on the Yemeni Arab Spring (Zyck, 2014). It was hoped that the Yemeni NDC would present a promising model for other Arab Spring countries of what could be achieved through (inter)national consensus on resolving armed conflict. Hopes of improved living standards and security were also high among Yemeni citizens (Brehony, 2015). The NDC was propagated through television, radio, and newspapers, and developments at the conference received daily coverage in the news (Yadav, 2015).

The NDC was the most important element of the Gulf Cooperation Council (GCC) Initiative, signed in November 2011 by the EU, Saudi Arabia, the Gulf Countries, and the US. This initiative aimed to persuade the conflicting Yemeni parties to enter into peace talks, following international concern that growing instability would leave Yemen exposed to al-Qaeda and other extremist organisations (Elayah et al., 2020b). The NDC would run for a two-year period of political transition after President Saleh "agreed" to step down (after 33 years) and Hadi was installed as Interim President. Backed by a UN Security Council Resolution (2051), the NDC commenced on 18 March 2013, assembling no less than 565 participants from a wide array of political factions and civil society representatives (Elayah et al., 2020b). Nine Working Groups were set up covering both the critical political dilemmas, such as the Southern issue and the Sa'ada (Houthi) issue, as well as issue-related development. It is worth mentioning that women and young people were effectively empowered in the NDC (Laub & Robinson, 2016).

Four months after the NDC began, an Outcomes Document was signed on 25 January 2014. It contained a roadmap for a new territorial division and the setup of more inclusive institutions (Elayah et al., 2020b). Although the political issues on the table were not fully resolved, the initial reaction to the agreement was positive, and the NDC was heralded as a success by most national and international stakeholders. However, when political realities on the ground conflicted with the roadmap, the optimism did not last (Yadav, 2015).

The apparent ineffectiveness of the NDC agreement triggered many critical assessments of its design and implementation. Many foreign political analysts, scholars, activists, donor agencies, and academic institutions pointed out flaws in the NDC, to which they attributed its eventual failure. It is believed that the NDC had a long list of mistakes ranging from content issues (e.g. mix up of political and developmental goals) to more process-oriented critiques (e.g. timing and scale of conference or the selection procedure of selecting delegates) (Elayah et al., 2020b). It comes to the researchers' mind that it is important to check with those actors who were involved in the NDC and have been less vocal until now about whether they have the same reading of the NDC experience, or whether they bring different narratives to the table about the failure of NDC (Elayah et al., 2020b). Since Yemeni society focuses more on civil society in interpreting political processes in the country, the researchers expect them to have information about international commentators, at least on some counts (Elayah et al., 2020b).

AFGHANISTAN

The downfall of the Taliban by the US after the events of 2001 led to a political gap in Afghanistan, which had to be filled to ensure that the Afghani government was one that the international community could communicate with—and also to make the NATO and American military operations lawful (Jones, 2008). Therefore, the US, accompanied by international support, pushed heavily for national reconciliation, inclusive of all political and civil sectors—including military groups, except the Taliban (Masadykov et al., 2010). This had a negative effect on the future political stability of the country, seen through the constant warring between the Taliban and the new government, lasting until 2010 when President Karzai headed a peace conference which the Taliban and a number of warlords, who fought the US and NATO for more than 9 years, attended and agreed to participate in national reconciliation (Kamal, 2021). This reconciliation effort failed to accomplish what the people had anticipated, for it followed a policy of excluding a certain group, holding it back from reaching a level of National Dialogue (Mubarak, 2020). In reality, the post-Taliban fall cannot be described as a phase of National Dialogue, for it was rather a reconciliation due to the absence of vital societal components such as the Taliban and other military movements that had a major influence on the people of Afghanistan (Quie, 2012). This is evidenced by the remarks of the UN envoy to Afghanistan: It is no one's benefit to prevent a big portion of the population from participating in the elections, in which case the results would not be a reflection of the people's will (RT Arabic, 2009).

ETHIOPIA

In the case of Ethiopia, a one-party dominant state, the elections between 1992 and 1995 were boycotted by the opposition parties, as they were considered in favour of the ruling party (Aalen, 2006). In 2000, the opposition parties agreed to participate in the elections but won only 12 out of a total of 540 seats (Lyons, 2006). In fact, there was no real confidence from either the opposition parties or the people that they would play an effective role in a democratic transformation through their participation in the elections, for the ruling party of Zenawi was in total control (Aalen & Tronvoll, 2009). The Ethiopian people had suffered for a long time due to the ruling party's authoritative practices. Thus, there was a need for an egress that would guarantee fair participation of people, without the exertion of force by the ruling party (Wodajo & Mengesha, 2021).

Potentially, the constant struggle and challenges faced by Ethiopia would have turned it into another Somalia (Gedamu, 2021). With international and internal pressure, the ruling party agreed to enter into a dialogue with the opposition based on a guarantee of participation in all societal sectors and their right to determine Ethiopia's fate and transform it into a federal state that would represent all spheres and ethnicities (Habtu, 2003). Thus, this dialogue presented solutions to deep problems that agonised the society for many decades (Svensson & Brounéus, 2013). The situation in Ethiopia was not mere political reconciliation, for it proved its failure in the past and, therefore, there had to be rooted solutions (Dessu & Yohannes, 2020). Ultimately, the case of Ethiopia presented a good example for a federal system in a region that is enduring numerous ethnic conflicts (Bélair, 2016). The success of Ethiopia's experiment with multinational federalism depends on the ruling party's willingness and ability to disengage itself from democratic centralism, extend and consolidate the democratisation process, reduce poverty, ensure a sustained economic growth rate, and expand educational coverage (Weldemariam, 2009). Many experts have stated that the Ethiopian National Dialogue is a case worth studying to understand similar situations in the region (Mengistu, 2015).

TUNISIA

After the overthrow of Ben Ali, the first election was held on 23 October 2011. It was won by the Islamic Renaissance Party that, jointly with two secular parties (Conference for the Republic Party and Takatol Party), formed the so-called ruling troika, which led to power-sharing, and serious disagreement over the new constitution within the Constituent Assembly (Lamont & Boujneh, 2012). In 2012, protests renewed, accusing the Renaissance Party of moving towards a radical Islamic State (Sukhoparava, 2014; Lerougetel & Stern, 2013).

The political crisis ensued mainly after the assassination of leftist politician Shokri Belaïd on 6 February 2013, and when the ruling troika refused to form a "non-partisan" government of national competencies (Resta et al., 2018). The conflict intensified after the resignation of Mohamed Jebali and the formation of the Ali Alaridh government, which included a number of non-partisan ministers, in addition to the failure of political and community components, especially the ruling troika and opposition parties, from sitting down at the collective or bilateral negotiating table with different pretexts (Andrieu, 2016). The Ennahda party and People's Congress rejected direct dialogue with the Nidaa Tounes party and refused to sit with them at the same table, considering it as an extension of the dissolved former ruling party, Rally Constitutional Democratic (RCD) (Haugbølle et al., 2017). Dispute continued between the opposition and the ruling troika amid exchanges of charges and insults, despite everyone's inclusion in the dialogue of "Guesthouse at Carthage." In this atmosphere, Mohammed Barhimi, Member of the National Constituent Assembly, was assassinated on 25 July 2013, worsening the political crisis (Kohler, 2015).

Consequently, the opposition parties pressurised the Government of Tunisia to take political and moral responsibility for the assassination, followed by several field movements to achieve several objectives, in particular the overthrow of Ali Alaridh's government (Abdelaty, 2021). These movements reached a peak with the sit-in called "Leave," organised in a yard in front of the Constituent Council's headquarters, which resulted in the withdrawal of most opposition representatives from the Council, together with absence from its sessions for a few weeks (Tamburini, 2021). Then, confrontation between the ruling troika and opposition parties became aggravated in a way that foreshadowed serious repercussions (Mia, 2016). Therefore, civil society had to act in order to absorb the tension and identify compromising solutions between the disputing parties to save the country from any possible negative repercussions. Accordingly, the Tunisian General Union, in agreement with the Federation of Industry and Commerce, the Deanship of lawyers, and Tunisian Human Rights League (called Quartet's Dialogue Sponsor), submitted an initiative with a blueprint including several procedural points and basic principles for the dialogue and its objectives (Bellin, 2013).

All parties accepted this role, but the trust of some in the neutrality of these organisations was weak due to a dispute that had occurred in the last two years between the Renaissance and the Tunisian General Union leadership (Hamidi, 2015). Nevertheless, the trust gradually strengthened among the parties amidst the complex and profound crisis threatening the stability of the country, which pushed the political actors to find solutions (Ben Salem, 2016). Although that required a lot of effort and time, all parties were convinced that they had to ignore the minor issues, think of the big picture, accept the "Four Sponsors Dialogue Initiative," and sit together at the table of dialogue (AbdelMoula, 2013).

An initiative was agreed upon that included a roadmap containing the main goals to terminate the crisis: (1) Accelerating the ratification of the Constitution; (2) Resignation; (3) Reaching consensus on a new technocrat government. Thus, Tunisia was able to complete the transitional specified stage (from the end of 2014 until 2015) through the election of the People's Congress which began operation on 2 December 2014, the election of the President who assumed office on 31 December 2014, the appointment of the new government on 6 February 2015, and this finally created new Constitutional Bodies in 2016 besides the Constitutional Court (Redissi & Boukhayatia, 2016).

In the legislative elections held on 26 October 2014, Tunisia's appeal won by an absolute majority, followed by Renaissance Movement party. The President of Nidaa Tounes, Beji Qaid Sebsi, won the presidential election with 55%, against the outgoing President Moncef Marzouki, who received 45% of votes (Battera & Ieraci, 2019). The Ennahda Movement had not nominated any candidate in this election and did not support any of the candidates. Consensus was the solution at this stage, as Nidaa Tounes, the election winner, submitted an independent figure as Prime Minister and conducted consultations with several parties to form a governmental coalition of four parties: Nidaa Tounes, Ennahda Movement, Free National Union, and Afaqh Tounes, which won big approval in Parliament after the elections of 2014. Nidaa Tounes, the secular leftist-oriented party, showed flexibility during this time by accepting to share government with the right-oriented Islamic Ennahda Movement, and two secular parties (Garrett, 2019).

The president of Ennahda Movement, Rashid Ghannouchi, participated in the first Congress of the party of Tunisia Call on 9 January 2016 in the presence of President Beji Qaid Sebsi, a moment which has been described as historical (Grewal & Hamid, 2020). In his speech to the Congress, Ghannouchi emphasised that his presence among them was the result of consensus and compromise, and it consolidated the principles of democracy and coexistence. He said that Tunisia is a bird with two wings, namely Nidaa Tounes and Ennahda, and it is a ship that bears all parties and sensitivities of the people of Tunisia (Shuker & Alrdisi, 2015).

IRAQ

After the fall of Saddam Hussain in 2003, the US primarily focused on ending his Ba'ath party once and for all. According to US and Iraqi leaders, this was a strategic mistake that contributed to security and political turmoil (Sassoon, 2012). The consequence was societal division among the three main Iraqi sectors: the Sunnis, the Shiites, and the Kurds (Kirmanc, 2013). Each sector attempted, unsuccessfully, to secure itself a place in post-Saddam Iraq (Katzman, 2004). This led many analysts to consider Iraq's need for a National Dialogue that includes all political sectors, with no exclusions, in order to reach an agreement followed by free and transparent elections (Abdul-Muna'im Ibrahim, 2019). However, this was not fulfilled because the ruling powers, backed by the US, preferred to take on a political reconciliation rather than a National Dialogue—which ultimately led to military conflicts between these powers (Papagianni, 2006). This is discernible through Steele's remark that the absence of security and the presence of poor economic and political conditions, along with the policy of exclusions, increased the degree of conflict (Steele, 2008).

The divisions and conflicts among the different powers, where each one attempted to exclude the other, proved the ineffectiveness of the reconciliation process. This called for an immediate National Dialogue after the invasion of Iraq to avoid the fight for power and to preserve the country's institutions (Alshamary, 2021). Some experts viewed "fighting in southern Iraq and in Shiite sections of Baghdad in late March 2008 as a setback to the assertions of progress on political reconciliation" (Steele, 2008).

SYRIA

As the Syrian crisis enters its tenth year, it is estimated that more than 835,000 Syrians have been killed in the strife, more than a million injured, over 12 million Syrians have been displaced from their homes, and 13.1 million people require humanitarian assistance (Elayah, 2021; OCHA, 2017). As is the case in all Arab countries, the common causes for revolutions are a lack of freedom, economic grievances, and political marginalisation. Anti-Assad regime groups took to the street after 15 boys were detained and tortured; one of them was killed simply because they supported the Arab uprising. Shortly after, Assad's forces responded harshly to the protests by killing hundreds of demonstrators and imprisoning many more (Blanchard et al., 2014). High rank military officials defected and announced the formation of the Free Syrian Army, a rebel group aiming to overthrow the government, and this group was joined by many Islamist movements that opposed Assad's rule. The unrest in Syria started as non-sectarian but when the armed conflict led to the emergence of severe sectarian divisions, the country began to slide into civil war (Al Jazeera, 2018). Most Syrians are Sunni Muslims, but Syria's security establishment has long been dominated by members of the Alawite sect, of which Assad is a member (Steenkamp, 2017). Minority religious groups tend to support the Assad government, while the overwhelming majority of opposition fighters are Sunni Muslims (Phillips, 2016). The sectarian split is reflected among regional actors' stances as well. The deteriorating situation in Syria led to international involvement. Foreign backing and open intervention have played a large role in Syria's civil war. Russia entered the conflict in 2015 and has been the Assad government's main ally since then (Al Jazeera, 2018).

From the aforementioned cases, it is clear that with different approaches, dialogue is a tool of governance that can foster representative and participatory forms of democracy. Regardless of whether they are called dialogue, roundtables, presidential commissions, or national forums, they are in essence political dialogue processes in which governments, political parties, and organised civil society come together to re-establish democratic order, addressing deep-rooted conflicts in a society.

The Anatomy of the Book

This book is split into seven chapters. This introduction, or this chapter, has provided a background of past and new case studies wherein peacebuilding processes took place, namely National Dialogues for reconciliation and state-building. It also covers the main research between the conflict and the international media by examining and comparing the amount of EU news coverage devoted to the most two deadliest conflicts in the Middle East, in Yemen and Syria. Chapter 2 explains the relevant concepts and theories, as well as the data collection and analysis methods. Theories of agenda-setting, media framing theory, peacebuilding, and conflict transformation models are used as the main concepts. These key concepts and theories provide direction for the data collection and analysis process in this book. Through this lens, a multi-level analytical approach is adopted to reflect on and compare the different process designs and external support provided by the EU in selected cases from different regions and levels. The Conflict Transformation School or the change peacebuilding theory is the most interesting because of its main transformation and premise of how to tackle the differences between long-term and short-term conflict management resolution, and how to deal with the underlying causes of the conflicts to build sustainable peace in a divided society. The main synthesis of the change peacebuilding theory is the need for behavioural, structural, and cultural transformation of violence, especially in post-conflict transition, from violent dynamic conflict to constructive social change. The change peacebuilding theory argues that the transformation process can only be achieved through a combination of integrated security, social, political, development, media and judicial peacebuilding strategies, and coordination among involved actors at the local and international levels. Then, the chapter moves on to compare and contrast the practice through reflections on process design and external support by analysing, in detail, cases from different regions and levels by adopting a multi-level analytical approach.

Chapter 3 provides a comparative analysis of Wars and EU's peace interventions providing a comparative analysis at the international level by examining the Yemeni NDC 2013 with those of Afghanistan and Ethiopia. The chapter also stresses on the lessons gleaned from these dialogues that are essential to state-building and highlights the local realities from these dialogues, as core elements of state-building in fragile states, to work against international media outlets. By doing so, this chapter contributes to the existing concepts of National Dialogues in peacebuilding literature that have remained under-theorised. In fragile states, dialogues have been defined as efforts by national actors and the international community to respond to violent conflict to build a national vision in fragile contexts. From an international comparative perspective, this chapter also contributes to understanding political reconciliation and National Dialogue processes of countries with different ideological parties and ethnic backgrounds, such as religious and tribal systems.

Chapter 4 analyses the Wars and EU's peace interventions in the regional setting (MENA), focusing on cases such as Iraq, Tunisia and comparing some of these to the Yemeni NDC. The success or failure of the National Dialogues in selected countries are discussed and four main aspects are underlined—the tribal variable, the issue variable, the

Arab Spring variable, and the ethnic/religion variable. The Arab Spring variable (good example): Tunisia and Yemen are the first two Arab countries that were engulfed with unrest in 2011. This was followed by the National Dialogue Conferences (NDCs), which were designed to break the political deadlock and to resolve the conflicts peacefully. The NDC in Tunisia is recognised as a successful example in the Arab world, whereas the Yemeni NDC failed to bring the warring parties to consensus, and this ended in civil war and regional military intervention. The final variable is the ethnic/religion variables: Iraq is selected because it is culturally similar to Yemen. As per one of the main arguments, conflicts in both countries have similar ethnic/religion variables. This chapter argues that the success of the National Dialogue should be an internal affair and not external. The interventions of third parties do not serve the national interest. The external parties are working to dismantle the social fabric in different conflict countries through media, and all parties must be aware of the dangers of such tactics, which will not end before rendering countries to a non-state phase. Therefore, to help the readers better understand the history of Yemeni NDCs and whether these dialogues have succeeded in bringing political transformation and stability in the country, the following chapter addresses the conflicts and civil wars in Yemen that ended with dialogues. This is one of the core subjects of this book.

Chapter 5 deals with the EU's peace interventions in the regional setting (MENA), and the effectiveness of Humanitarian Aid. This is due to food-aid, which is delivered by the NGOs, being vulnerable to looting by the conflicting factions, enabling funds to be inadvertently captured into the highly problematic war economy dynamic. In the "neo-humanitarianism" period following World War II, the number of humanitarian and intergovernmental agencies grew rapidly. In the four years succeeding the war over 200 new NGOs were formed globally and the UN grew in both size and significance (Rysaback-Smith, 2016). The UN's progress led to the conclusion of the Universal Declaration of Human Rights in 1948, and the formation of many organisations under the auspices of the UN such as the WHO (1948), UNICEF (1946), and UNHCR (1950) (Paulmann, 2013). Randolph Kent argued that this was a turning point for HA as "it was only in the midst of World War II that governments began to fully appreciate the need for greater international intervention in the plight of disaster-stricken people" (Kent, 1987). The relief effort became increasingly international due to advancements in technology, transport, and communication and this resulted in a shift of focus from Europe to less developed countries, thus laying the foundation for the international HA network we have today. This chapter investigates the impact of HA on war economies by offering a brief overview of the history of HA in the Arab World and in Yemen, followed by an explanation of how HA has impacted the war. The situation will then be explored through an empirical analysis of HA organisations operating during wartime.

Chapter 6 paints the full picture of framing conflict in the middle east by European media. This chapter compares the media coverage of wars in Yemen and Syria by European media (the selection of these media is discussed in the methodology part). The researchers examined how the online news of leading newspapers (The Independent, British, NRC Handelsblad, the Netherlands) and international broadcast news (France24, Franc, and Swissinfo.ch, Switzerland) report on both wars. The aim of this chapter is to compare the amount of the coverage devoted to the deadliest conflicts in Yemen and Syria over two years by four prestigious European media outlets. This chapter also examines the four online English news media frames used in the reporting of the two cases, and whether they significantly differ in their news coverage. This chapter works against the third and fourth chapters in terms of the nature of the conflicts and how the European media presented them in light of contradictory or incomplete facts.

Finally, Chapter 7 provides conclusion, recommendations, and well-founded reflections on the design of a hypothetical National Dialogue in a fragile setting. It provides the Western reader, media outlets, and decision-makers with important information about the nature of conflicts and peace processes and how media should avoid simplifying the realities on ground when covering devastating humanitarian cases in the MENA region.

References

Aalen, L. (2006). Ethnic federalism and self-determination for nationalities in a semi-authoritarian state: the case of Ethiopia. *International Journal on Minority & Group Rights, 13*, 243.

Aalen, L., & Tronvoll, K. (2009). The end of democracy? Curtailing political and civil rights in Ethiopia. *Review of African Political Economy, 36*(120), 193–207.

Abdelaty, M. (2021). *Democratization and extremism: The case of Tunisia* [Master's Thesis, the American University in Cairo]. AUC Knowledge Fountain. https://fount.aucegypt.edu/etds/1671

AbdelMoula, L. (2013). Spotlight on Tunisia's experience in democratic transition. *Al Jazeera Center For Studies.*

Abdul-Muna'im Ibrahim, T. (2019). The dialectical relationship between human and cultural diversity in building a civil state in Iraq| research in cultural anthropology on the possibility of presenting a strategy of national dialogue and peaceful coexistence. *Journal of Al-Frahedis Arts/* مجلة آداب الفراهيدي, *11*(39 I), 519–548.

Acemoglu, D., & Robinson, J. A. (2012). *Why nations fail: The origins of power, prosperity, and poverty.* Crown Publishers

Al Batati, S. (2015, March 29). Who are the Houthis in Yemen. *Al Jazeera.* https://www.aljazeera.com/news/middleeast/2014/08/yemen-houthis-hadi-protests-201482132719818986.html

Alexander, N. M. (2009). *International and comparative mediation: Legal perspectives* (Vol. 4). Kluwer Law International BV.

Al Jazeera. (2018). *Syria's Civil War.* https://www.aljazeera.com/program/featured-documentaries/2018/3/15/syrias-war-seven-years-seven-documentaries

Alshamary, M. R. (2021). Religious peacebuilding in Iraq: Prospects and challenges from the Hawza. *Journal of Intervention and Statebuilding*, 1–16.

Alsoswa, A. A. A., & Brehony, N. (Eds.). (2021). *Building a new Yemen: Recovery.* Bloomsbury Publishing.

Andrieu, K. (2016). Confronting the dictatorial past in Tunisia: Human rights and the politics of victimhood in transitional justice discourses since 2011. *Human Rights Quarterly, 38*, 261.

Annan, K. (2004). The causes of conflict and the promotion of durable peace and sustainable development in Africa. *African Renaissance, 1*(3), 9–42.

Autesserre, S. (2017). International peacebuilding and local success: Assumptions and effectiveness. *International Studies Review.*

Avis, W. (2020). *International actors' support on inclusive peace processes.* K4D Helpdesk Report. Brighton, UK: Institute of Development Studies.

Ayoob, M. (2002). Humanitarian intervention and state sovereignty. *The International Journal of Human Rights, 6*(1), 81–102.

Barnett, M., & Snyder, J. (2011). 6. The grand strategies of humanitarianism. In *Humanitarianism in question* (pp. 143–171). Cornell University Press.

Call, C. T., & Cousens

Battera, F., & Ieraci, G. (2019). Party system and political struggle in Tunisia. Cleavages and electoral competition after the transition to democracy.

Bélair, J. (2016). Ethnic federalism and conflicts in Ethiopia. *Canadian Journal of African Studies / Revue canadienne des études africaines, 50*, 295–301. https://doi.org/10.1080/00083968.2015.1124580

Bellin, E. (2013). Drivers of democracy: Lessons from Tunisia. *Middle East Brief, 75*, 1–10.

Ben Salem, M. (2016). The national dialogue, collusive transactions and government legitimacy in Tunisia. *The International Spectator, 51*(1), 99–112.

Binder, M. (2015). Paths to intervention: What explains the UN's selective response to humanitarian crises? *Journal of Peace Research, 52*(6), 712–726.

Blanchard, C. M., Humud, C. E., & Nikitin, M. B. D. (2014). Armed conflict in Syria: Overview and US response. Library of Congress Washington DC Congressional Research Service.

Blunck, M., Vimalarajah, L., Wils, O., von Burg, C., Lanz, D., Mubashir, M., Prinz, V., & Denkovski, D. (2017). National dialogue handbook. *Berghof Foundation Operations*.

Boutros-Ghali, B. (1992). An agenda for peace: Preventive diplomacy, peace-making and peace-keeping. *International Relations, 11*(3), 201–218.

Brehony, N. (2015). Yemen and the Huthis: Genesis of the 2015 crisis. *Asian Affairs, 46*(2), 232–250.

Breslau, D. (1997). The political power of research methods: Knowledge regimes in U. S. labor-market policy. *Theory and Society, 26*(6), 869–902.

Brown, M. E. (1996). *The international dimensions of internal conflict* (No. 10). MIT Press.

Burton, J. W. (2010). *Systems, states, diplomacy and rules*. Cambridge University Press.

Call, C., & Cousens, E. (2008). Ending wars and building peace: International responses to war-torn societies. *International Studies Perspectives, 9*(1), 1–21.

Castaneda, D. (2012). *The European Union in Colombia: Learning how to be a peace actor*. L'Institut de Recherche Stratégique de l'École Militaire.

Clapham, C. (1998). Rwanda: The perils of peacemaking. *Journal of Peace Research, 35*(2), 193–210.

Collén, C. (2014). *National dialogue and internal mediation processes perspectives on theory and practice*. The Ministry for Foreign Affairs.

Cottle, S. (2006). *Mediatized conflict: Developments in media and conflict studies*. McGraw-Hill Education (UK).

Crocker, C. A., Hampson, F. O., & Aall, P. R. (1999). *Herding cats: Multiparty mediation in a complex world*. US Institute of Peace Press.

Deng, F. M., Kimaro, S., Lyons, T., Rothchild, D., & Zartman, I. W. (2010). *Sovereignty as responsibility: Conflict management in Africa*. Brookings Institution Press.

Dessu, M. K., & Yohannes, D. (2020). National dialogues in the Horn of Africa: Lessons for Ethiopia's political transition. *ISS East Africa Report, 2020*(32), 1–24.

Dialogue. Dictionary.com. https://www.dictionary.com/browse/dialogue

Donais, T., & McCandless, E. (2017). International peace building and the emerging inclusivity norm. *Third World Quarterly, 38*(2), 291–310.

Durac, V. (2012). Yemen's Arab spring-democratic opening or regime maintenance? *Mediterranean Politics, 17*(2), 161–178.

Edwards, A. (2019). Yemen: Civil War and humanitarian catastrophe. *Political Insight, 10*(2), 14–16.

Elayah, M. (2021). Arab conflicts today: Statistics and trends. In I. Fraihat (Ed.), *The rooting and marketing of conflict science in the Arab world*. Arab Center for Research and Policy Studies.

Elayah, M., Schulpen, L., van Kempen, L., Almaweri, A., AbuOsba, B., & Alzandani, B. (2020a). National dialogues as an interruption of civil war–the case of Yemen. *Peacebuilding, 8*(1), 98–117.

Elayah, M., van Kempen, L., & Schulpen, L. (2020b). Adding to the controversy? Civil society's evaluation of the national conference dialogue in Yemen. *Journal of Intervention and Statebuilding, 14*(3), 431–458.

Elayah, M., & Verkoren, W. (2020). Civil society during war: The case of Yemen. *Peacebuilding, 8*(4), 476–498.

Eshaq, A., & Al-Marani, S. (2016). Assessing the EU's conflict prevention and peacebuilding interventions in Yemen. *WOSCAP Case Study Report*.

Estefan, L. F., Armstead, T. L., Rivera, M. S., Kearns, M. C., Carter, D., Crowell, J., & Daniels, B. (2019). Enhancing the national dialogue on the prevention of intimate partner violence. *American Journal of Community Psychology, 63*(1–2), 153–167.

Fahmy, S. S. (2020). Virtual theme collection: Journalism and mass communication research in the MENA region. *Journalism & Mass Communication Quarterly, 97*(3), 590–593.

Fisher, R. J. (2001). *Methods of third-party intervention*. Available at: https://www.berghof-foundation.org/fileadmin/redaktion/Publications/Handbook/Articles/fisher_handbookII.pdf

Fisher, R. J. (2011). *Methods of third-party intervention*. Available at: https://www.berghof-foundation.org/fileadmin/redaktion/Publications/Handbook/Articles/fisher_handbookII.pdf

Fisher, R., & Ury, W. (1981). *Getting to yes: Negotiating agreement without giving in*. Houghton Mifflin.

Fox, J. (1998). The effects of religion on domestic conflicts. *Terrorism and Political Violence, 10*(4), 43–63.

Francis, D. J. (2017). *Uniting Africa: Building regional peace and security systems*. Routledge.

Garallah, M. A. (2013). *Successful separationists in a unity fan society: Al-Hirak Al-Janubi social movement in the Republic of Yemen*. Naval Postgraduate School Monterey, CA, Defense Analysis Dept.

Garrett, S. (2019). *Tunisia's Ennahda Party: Developing a framework for interpreting political decision-making in historical context*. Undergraduate Dissertation, Georgetown University.

Gaston, E. (2014). *Process lessons learned in Yemen's national dialogue*. US Institute of Peace.

Gedamu, Y. (2021). *The politics of contemporary Ethiopia: Ethnic federalism and authoritarian survival*. Routledge.

Ghafarzade, B. (2015). Yemen: Post-conflict federalism to avoid disintegration. *NYU Journal of International Law and Politics, 48*, 933.

Giessmann, H. J., & Wils, O. (2011). Seeking compromise? Mediation through the eyes of the conflict parties. *Berghof Foundation*.

Gilboa, E. (2006). Media and international conflict. In *The Sage handbook of conflict communication: Integrating theory, research, and practice* (pp. 596–626).

Gilboa, E., Jumbert, M. G., Miklian, J., & Robinson, P. (2016). Moving media and conflict studies beyond the CNN effect. *Review of International Studies, 42*(4), 654–672.

Ginsberg, R. H. (1999). Conceptualizing the European Union as an international actor: Narrowing the theoretical capability-expectations gap. *JCMS: Journal of Common Market Studies, 37*(3), 429–454.

Grewal, S., & Hamid, S. (2020, January). *The dark side of consensus in Tunisia: Lessons from 2015–2019* (Brookings Report). Available at https://www.brookings.edu/research/the-darkside-of-consensus-in-tunisia-lessons-from-2015-2019

Habtu, A. (2003). Ethnic federalism in Ethiopia: Background, present conditions and future prospects. *International Conference on African Development Archives, 57*. https://scholarworks.wmich.edu/africancenter_icad_archive/57

Haider, H. (2019). *National dialogues: Lessons learned and success factors*. K4D Helpdesk Report, Institute of Development Studies, Brighton, UK.

Hamidi, H. (2015). A comparative analysis of the post-Arab spring national dialogues in Tunisia and Yemen. *African Journal on Conflict Resolution, 15*(3), 11–35.

Hartmann, H. (2017). National dialogues and development. *National Dialogue Handbook Background Paper, 3*.

Haugbølle, R. H., Ghali, A., Yousfi, H., Limam, M., & Mollerup, N. G. (2017). *Tunisia's 2013 National dialogue* (Berghof Foundation Report, Şubat).

Higgins, J. W. (2011). Peace-building through listening, digital storytelling, and community media in Cyprus. *Global Media Journal: Mediterranean Edition, 6*(1).

Hill, G., Salisbury, P., Northedge, L., & Kinninmont, J. (2013). *Yemen: corruption, capital flight and global drivers of conflict*. Chatham House.
Incerti-Thery, I. (2016). *Dialogue as a tool in peacebuilding: Theoretical and empirical perspectives*. UiT The Arctic University of Norway.
Joenniemi, P. (2015). *Russia's approach to arms control, peace mediation and national dialogues*. Tampereen yliopisto.
Jones, S. G. (2008). The rise of Afghanistan's insurgency: State failure and Jihad. *International Security, 32*(4), 7–40.
Juneau, T. (2013). Yemen and the Arab Spring: Elite struggles, state collapse and regional security. *Orbis, 57*(3), 408–423.
Kacowicz, A. M. (1997). 'Negative' international peace and domestic conflicts, West Africa, 1957–96. *The Journal of Modern African Studies, 35*(3), 367–385.
Kamal, O. (2021). *After the collapse of the Taliban: A study of the US statebuilding failure* (Doctoral dissertation, Webster University).
Katzman, K. (2004). Iraq: US regime change efforts and post-Saddam governance. Library of Congress Washington DC Congressional Research Service.
Kent, R. C. (1987). *Anatomy of disaster relief: The international network in action* (pp. 137–138). Pinter, 36.
Kestemont, E. (2018). *What role(s) for the European Union in national dialogues? Lessons learned from Yemen* (EU Diplomacy Paper 05/2018).
Kirmanc, Ş. (2013). *Identity and nation in Iraq*. Lynne Rienner Publishers.
Kohler, M. H. (2015). *Agents of democracy: Political parties in the success and failure of Tunisia and Egypt*. Western Illinois University.
Krause, K. (1998). Cross-cultural dimensions of multilateral non-proliferation and arms control dialogues: An overview. *Contemporary Security Policy, 19*(1), 1–22.
Kriesberg, L. (2007). *Constructive conflicts: From escalation to resolution*. Rowman & Littlefield.
Kronenfeld, S., & Guzansky, Y. (2014). Yemen: A mirror to the future of the Arab Spring. *Military and Strategic Affairs, 6*(3), 79–99.
Kumar, C. (2012). *Building national infrastructures for peace: UN assistance for internally negotiated solutions to violent conflict*. Available at: http://www.pnud.org/content/dam/undp/library/crisis%20prevention/UNDP_BCPR_Chetan%20Kumar_UN%20Support%20to%20internal%20solutions.pdf
Lamont, C. K., & Boujneh, H. (2012). Transitional justice in Tunisia: Negotiating justice during transition. *Politička misao: časopis za politologiju, 49*(5), 32–49.
Laub, Z., & Robinson, K. (2016). Yemen in crisis. *Council on Foreign Relations, 19*, 1–7.
Lehti, M. (2019). Inclusivity in track one mediation and national dialogues. *The Era of Private Peacemakers* (pp. 165–177). Palgrave Macmillan.

Lempereur, A., Salzer, J., Colson, A., Pekar, M., & Kogan, E. B. (2021). *Mediation: Negotiation by other moves*. Wiley.
Lerougetel, A., & Stern, J. (2013). *Tunisian political parties organize national dialogue*. https://www.wsws.org/en/articles/2013/10/15/tuni-o15.html
Loh, F. K. W. (2021). Ethnic diversity and the nation-state in the 21st century: Lessons from Malaysia and Myanmar. *International Journal of Asian Christianity*, 4(1), 28–49.
Lyons, T. (2006). Ethiopia in 2005: The beginning of a transition? *CSIS Africa Notes*, 25.
Magure, B. (2008). The state, labour and the politics of social dialogue in Zimbabwe 1996–2007: Issues resolved or matters arising? *African and Asian Studies*, 7(1), 19–48.
Masadykov, T., Giustozzi, A., & Page, J. M. (2010). *Negotiating with the Taliban: Toward a solution for the Afghan conflict* (Crisis States Research Centre Working Paper 66, Series 2). London: London School of Economics.
Mengistu, M. M. (2015). Ethnic federalism: A means for managing or a triggering factor for ethnic conflicts in Ethiopia. *Social Sciences*, 4(4), 94–105.
Mia, M. (2016). National dialogue Quartet in democratic transition of Tunisia: An analysis. *Asian Studies, 19781*, 125.
Mikha'el, K., Michael, K., Kellen, D., & Ben-Ari, E. (Eds.). (2009). *The transformation of the world of war and peace support operations*. Greenwood Publishing Group.
Millar, G. (2021). Trans-scalar ethnographic peace research: Understanding the invisible drivers of complex conflict and complex peace. *Journal of Intervention and Statebuilding*, 1–20.
Miller, L. E., & Aucoin, L. (2010). *Framing the state in times of transition: Case studies in constitution making*. US Institute of Peace Press.
M'rad, H. (2015). *National dialogue in Tunisia: Nobel Peace Prize 2015*. Éditions Nirvana.
Mubarak, S. (2020). *Political settlement and national reconciliation: The right diplomacy for ending the war in Afghanistan* (Doctoral dissertation, Indiana University).
Murray, E., & Stigant, S. (2021). *National dialogues in peacebuilding and transitions – Creativity and adaptive thinking*. United States Institute of Peace, June 2021, No. 173. https://www.usip.org/sites/default/files/pw_173-national_dialogues_in_peacebuilding_and_transitions_creativity_and_adaptive_thinking.pdf.
Murray, C. (2017). *National dialogues and constitution making* (National Dialogue Handbook Background Papers, 2).
Ndekwo, R. (2020). *National dialogue as a strategy for intra-state conflict resolution in Africa: The case study of Anglophone Cameroon* (Doctoral dissertation, University of Nairobi).

Nevens, K. (2011). Yemen's Youth Revolution. In *The Arab Spring: Implications for British policy* (pp. 24–27). Conservative Middle East Council. https://cmec.org.uk/sites/default/files/field/attachment/October%202011%20CMEC-Arab-Spring.pdf

OCHA. (2017). *Humanitarian needs overview: Yemen.* New York. https://www.unocha.org/sites/dms/Yemen/YEMEN%202017%20HNO_Final.pdf

Odendaal, A. (2011). The role of political dialogue in peacebuilding and state-building: An interpretation of current experience. *Working group on political dialogue of the international dialogue on peacebuilding and state-building.*

Paakkinen, E., & Turtonen, O. (2017). *National dialogues conference: The third conference on national dialogues.* http://nationaldialogues.fi/wp-content/uploads/2017/09/NDC-2017-Conference-Report-final.pdf

Paffenholz, T., & Ross, N. (2015). Managing complexity in negotiations: All inclusive national dialogues: The cases of Congo and Egypt. In *Conference paper for Academic Conference on International Mediation.* Pretoria (pp. 2–4).

Paffenholz, T., Zachariassen, A., & Helfer, C. (2017). *What makes or breaks national dialogues?* Inclusive Peace & Transition Initiative, Graduate Institute of International and Development Studies.

Papagianni, K. (2006). National conferences in transitional periods: The case of Iraq. *International Peacekeeping, 13*(3), 316–333.

Papagianni, K. (2014a). Civil Society Dialogue Network Discussion, Paper No. 3 National Dialogue.

Papagianni, K. (2014b). *National dialogue processes in political transitions.* Geneva and Brussels: Centre for Humanitarian Dialogue and European Peacebuilding Liaison Office.

Paulmann, J. (2013). Conjunctures in the history of international humanitarian aid during the twentieth century. *Humanity: An International Journal of Human Rights, Humanitarianism, and Development, 4*(2), 215–238.

Pearson, J. (1997). Mediating when domestic violence is a factor: Policies and practices in court-based divorce mediation programs. *Mediation Quarterly, 14*(4), 319–335.

Pettersson, T., Högbladh, S., & Öberg, M. (2019). Organized violence, 1989–2018 and peace agreements. *Journal of Peace Research, 56*(4), 589–603.

Pettersson, T., & Wallensteen, P. (2015). Armed conflicts, 1946–2014. *Journal of Peace Research, 52*(4), 536–550.

Phillips, C. (2016). *The battle for Syria.* Yale University Press.

Planta, K., Prinz, V., & Vimalarajah, L. (2015). Inclusivity in national dialogues. *Guaranteeing social integration or preserving old power hierarchies.*

Potter, A., & Centre for Humanitarian Dialogue. (2005). *We the Women: Why conflict mediation is not just a job for men.* HD Centre for Humanitarian Dialogue.

Price, M. E., Al Marashi, I., & Stremlau, N. A. (2009). Media in the peace-building process: Ethiopia and Iraq. *Departmental Papers (ASC), 149*.
Pruitt, B., & Thomas, P. (2007). *Democratic dialogue—A handbook for practitioners*. International IDEA.
Quie, M. (2012). Peace-building and democracy promotion in Afghanistan: The Afghanistan Peace and Reintegration Programme and reconciliation with the Taliban. *Democratization, 19*(3), 553–574.
Redissi, H., & Boukhayatia, R. (2016). *The national constituent assembly of Tunisia and civil society dynamics* (No. 2) (Working Paper).
Resta, V., Cavatorta, F., & Storm, L. (2018). Leftist parties in the Arab region before and after the Arab uprisings: unrequited love? In *Political parties in the Arab world. Continuity and change* (pp. 23–48).
Rodt, A. P., & Okeke, J. M. (2013). AU-EU "strategic partnership": Strengthening policy convergence and regime efficacy in the African peace and security complex? *African Security, 6*(3–4), 211–233.
Ropers, N. (2004). From resolution to transformation: The role of dialogue projects. In *Transforming ethnopolitical conflict* (pp. 255–269). VS Verlag für Sozialwissenschaften.
Ropers, N. (2011). *A systemic approach: Reflections on Sri Lanka*. Handbook article. Berghof Foundation.
Rose-Ackerman, S., & Palifka, B. J. (2016). *Corruption and government: Causes, consequences, and reform*. Cambridge University Press.
Rotberg, R. I. (2010). One. The failure and collapse of nation-states: Breakdown, prevention, and repair. In *When states fail* (pp. 1–50). Princeton University Press.
RT-Arabic. (2009). July 29th Afghanistan and the Taliban. Prepping for elections.
Rysaback-Smith, H. (2016). History and principles of humanitarian action. *Turkish Journal of Emergency Medicine, 15*, 5–7.
Saleem, N., & Hanan, M. A. (2014). Media and conflict resolution: Toward building a relationship model. *Journal of Political Studies, 21*(1), 179.
Sassoon, J. (2012). *Saddam Hussein's Ba'th Party: Inside an authoritarian regime*. Cambridge University Press.
Sharp, J. (2017). Yemen: Cholera Outbreak. *CRS INSIGHT*. https://fas.org/sgp/crs/mideast/IN10729.pdf
Shuker, H. & Alrdisi, H. (2015). Presidential elections in Tunisia between competition and consensus. Arab Reform Web, Political Alternatives. Available at: www.arab-reform.net/sites/default/files
Siebert, H. (2014). National dialogue and legitimate change. *Accord, 25*, 36.
Siebert, H. (2016). Beyond mediation: Promoting change and resolving conflict through authentic national dialogues. In *Interventions in conflict* (pp. 153–162). Palgrave Macmillan.

Spencer, G. (2005). The media and peace. In *From Vietnam to the war on terror*. Palgrave.
Stavenhagen, R. (2016). *Ethnic conflicts and the nation-state*. Springer.
Steele, D. (2008). Reconciliation strategies in Iraq. Institute of Peace. Available at: http://www.usip.org/sites/default/files/sr213.pdf
Steenkamp, C. (2017). The crime-conflict nexus and the civil war in Syria. *Stability: International Journal of Security and Development*, 6(1).
Sukhoparava, I. (2014). *Tunisia: Success story?* Available at: www.rt.com/opedge/tnisia-arab-spring-democratic-transition-579
Svensson, I., & Brounéus, K. (2013). Dialogue and interethnic trust: A randomized field trial of 'sustained dialogue' in Ethiopia. *Journal of Peace Research*, 50(5), 563–575.
Tamburini, F. (2021). The Ghost of the constitutional review in Tunisia: Authoritarianism, transition to democracy and rule of law. *Journal of Asian and African Studies*.
Taylor, B. C., & Bean, H. (Eds.). (2019). *The handbook of communication and security*. Routledge.
Tidwell, A. (2001). *Conflict resolved? A critical assessment of conflict resolution*. A&C Black.
Trotskovets, I. V. (2021). *The role of media in hybrid wars: Ukrainian experience* (Doctoral dissertation, National Aviation University).
Turkoglu, O. (2021). Supporting rebels and hosting refugees: Explaining the variation in refugee flows in civil conflicts. *Journal of Peace Research*, 0022343321989786.
UNDP. (2009). *Why dialogue matters for conflict prevention and peacebuilding*. Available at http://www.undp.org/content/dam/undp/library/crisis%20prevention/dialogue_conflict.pdf
Unger, T. (2010). *The European Union and transitional justice*. TMC Asser Institute.
Unruh, J. D. (2015). The structure and function of keywords in the development of civil wars: Opportunities for peace building? *Peace and Conflict: Journal of Peace Psychology*, 21(4), 621.
Urlacher, B. (2007). *Third parties and the tacit mediation of intra-state conflict: Negotiating with an elephant in the next room*. University of Connecticut.
Visoka, G., & Doyle, J. (2016). Neo-functional peace: The European Union way of resolving conflicts. *JCMS: Journal of Common Market Studies*, 54(4), 862–877.
Vladisavljević, N. (2015). *Media framing of political conflict: A review of the literature*. Media, Conflict and Democratisation (MeCoDEM).
Weldemariam, A. (2009). *Conflict management in the Ethiopian multi-national federation*. European University Center for Peace Studies. Available at: http://epu.ac.at/fileadmin/downloads/research/Weldemariam.pdf

Wils, O., Hopp, U., Ropers, N., Vimalarajah, L., & Zunzer, W. (2006). The systemic approach to conflict transformation. Concept and fields of application. *Berlin, Berghof Foundation for Peace Support Krisenprävention, Zivile Konfliktbearbeitung, Friedensförderung.*

Winright, T., & Johnston, L. (2015). *Can war be just in the 21st century?* Orbis Books.

Wodajo, M. R., & Mengesha, O. (2021). Contested politics in Ethiopia, Post of 2018: Challenges and prospects of the ruling party. *SSRN Electronic Journal.* https://doi.org/10.2139/ssrn.3829270

Wolff, S. (2007). *Ethnic conflict: A global perspective.* Oxford University Press on Demand.

Yadav, S. P. (2015). The "Yemen Model" as a failure of political imagination. *International Journal of Middle East Studies, 47*(1), 144–147.

Yawanarajah, N. (2021). Informality and the social art of mediation: How pure mediators create conditions for making peace. *New England Journal of Public Policy, 33*(1), 10.

Zachariassen, A., Ross, N., Paffenholz, T., & Hawana, F. (2016). *Dialogues in peace and mediation processes: definitions, types, goals, and success factors for sustainability.* Geneva, Inclusive Peace and Transition Initiative (IPTI). https://www.inclusivepeace.org/content/dialogues-peace-and-me-diation-processes-definitions-types-goals-and-suc-cess-factors

Zyck, S. A. (2014). *Mediating transition in Yemen: Achievements and lessons.* International Peace Institute.

CHAPTER 2

Theoretical, Conceptual, and Methodological Frameworks

Moosa Elayah

The sphere of conflict and peacebuilding requires a great degree of particular delineation. Over the last few decades, new ideas and concepts have emerged with the non-conventional employment of acknowledged terminology and theories in the peacebuilding field (Boege, 2011; Maweu & Mare, 2021). In addition to the concepts that have been operationalised in Chapter 1, the objective of this chapter is to briefly elaborate and discuss the key concepts and peacebuilding and conflict terminology (Mwagiru, 2016). These definitions are important to enhance the valuable analysis propounded in this book. This chapter will lay out and define a few key concepts that are either combative in their scope or overlapping in their implications and meanings. The essential terms for this book that need exploration are conflict, peacebuilding, peace-making, peace enforcement, dialogue, political dialogue, agenda setting, and media framing.

Many scholars have theorised and posited an explanation or definition of the notion of conflict, mainly after the end of World War II. Some explain it as an introduction of interests over political and economic priorities (Ballentine & Nitzschke, 2005; Humphreys, 2003; Khan, 2021; Vahabi, 2009); others described it as a fight over regional, ethnic, or religious safeties (Korostelina, 2007; Paden, 2015). Pia and Diez (2007) note that "Conflict is a struggle or contest between people with opposing needs, ideas, beliefs, values, or goals." The overall interest behind all conflicts is to motivate people to demand their rights at all costs. It can be said that the "aim justifies the means," otherwise they will live in injustice forever. Also, in some cases, there are groups who have tried to impound other people's rights for their own benefit (Smet, 2010); as a result, civil conflict arises within society (Matanock, 2017).

The cause of conflict varies, but in the end, it always becomes a threat to society, security, and stability (Mukhammadsidiqov, 2020; Liotta & Owen, 2006). Pondy identified three types of conflicts among the subunits of formal organisations:

"(1) bargaining conflict among the parties to an interest-group relationship;
(2) bureaucratic conflict between the parties to a superior-subordinate relationship; and (3) systems conflict among parties to a lateral or working relationship". (Pondy, 1967)

In each of the three cases, conflict is treated as a series of episodes, each episode including stages of latency, feeling, perception, manifestation, and aftermath. The idea of excluding some parties in any society will often end in armed conflict, regardless of how long that exclusion takes. Thomas defined conflict as "The process which begins when one party perceives that another has frustrated, or is about to frustrate, some concern of his" (Thomas, 1992). However, we believe that conflicts or fights between groups start when there is a great feeling that one of them will exclude the other from participating and representing themselves in political and economic life (see, e.g., Elbadawi, 2000; Veneklasen, 2006).

Peacebuilding is a well-known concept, but there is disagreement about what it exactly means and entails (Llewellyn & Philpott, 2014). However, it is not vastly different in its temporal position and objectivity from the concepts of conflict resolution, National Dialogue, peacemaking, and peacekeeping. Peacebuilding bridges these four concepts, and elaborating upon its historical development builds a premise for its specific meanings (Hertog, 2010). The concept of peacebuilding first came to the spotlight more than 30 years ago through the in-depth intellectual work of Johan Galtung, who raised a call for producing peacebuilding structures that would advance a maintainable peace by addressing the underlying drivers of conflicts and supporting indigenous capacities with respect to peace management and resolution (Cheng-Hopkins, 2010). It is the outside intercession that is resolved to wipe out and keep the substance of contention and its risk in the general public through different aggressive instruments (Olaifa, 2017).

The development of the concept of peacebuilding has undergone three generations of conceptualisation (Kenkel, 2013). The first generation considered the generative mechanisms of a conflict as related to the weakness of the government. This generation of peacebuilding used more liberal goals of diffusing and managing the conflict without overt violence (Carter, 2010; Heathershaw, 2013). The peacebuilding process was reduced to peacekeeping activities that were performed by little military units to secure a specific conflict zone (Hoelscher et al., 2017). The units were reasonable, as they were permitted to use their power only in self-preservation situations; thus, their process was a non-violent one (Ramsbotham & Woodhouse, 2013). The second generation paved the way to a "win-win" peace and provided a counter to conflict resolution (Fetherston, 2000). The second-generation approach took a more goal-oriented position on the peacebuilding process, concentrating on the root drivers of conflict from the point of view of individuals, groups, and societies that engage with conflicting situations (McAuliffe, 2017).

In the second generation, traditional peacebuilding still maintained its function for inter-state conflicts, and it was adapted to domestic conflict situations (Kenkel, 2013). The peacebuilding missions were premised on the permission of the host state(s) and a mediator, such as the UN, to ensure conflicting factions cooperate, giving these factions the best way of leaving each other alone. Undeniably, the methods used are still non-offensive (Bellamy, 2004). The challenge offered by the second approach carried such discursive and normative power that might have become the requirement for more sophisticated methods in the construction of civil peace in conflicting states (Whalan, 2013). This positive peace, which has been conceptualised as a "cosmopolitan turn" in conflict resolution, also empowered non-state actors and NGOs to assist in the development of peace, based on the identification and allocation of human needs, and according to the voices of non-state and unofficial actors, such as international organisations, and the people themselves (Richmond, 2010).

The third generation re-geared the peacebuilding conception as a grassroots bottom-up process in which local consensus leads to positive peace (Kenkel, 2013). The main approach to peacebuilding has developed quickly from multidimensional peacekeeping to state-building, including different local actors and in a multilateral framework, and again without governmental consent (Caparini, 2016). In 2000, then UN Secretary-General, Kofi Annan, outlined the shift to "robust peace-building" when he recommended that the UN should abandon outdated concepts of neutral peacebuilding and replace them with a more muscular form of peace operation to avoid bad or catastrophic events of previous missions and also to deal with any circumstances of future UN missions (Bar-Siman-Tov, 2004). This paradigmatic shift to robust peacebuilding efforts worldwide, however, raises certain operational challenges since it stands in contradiction with the constitutive elements of peacebuilding, namely consent, impartiality, and the limited use of force (Nsia-Pepra, 2016). The likely repercussions and challenges include the prospects of open battles with armed groups, greater threat to non-military UN personnel, reprisals against civilian population, and a lack of consent and cooperation from conflicting factions and from extremists and spoilers (Karlsrud, 2017). Apart from these negative repercussions, the provisions of adequate resources and major participation seem problematic based on traditional rates of support and contribution (Richmond, 2008, 2010).

Based on the development of peacebuilding's concept in the second and the third generations, one can summarise two broad approaches to define the concept. The first considers peacebuilding as a coordinated process that purposefully centres around addressing the variables driving or relieving strife (Cunliffe, 2018). While applying the expression "peacebuilding" to this work, there is an explicit endeavour to diminish structural or direct violence (Schaefer, 2010). The second describes the concept of peacebuilding as endeavours to facilitate a multi-level and a multi-sectoral procedure, including guaranteeing that there is financing, legitimate government, and coordination among foreign aid components such as humanitarian help, development, security, governance, and justice. One of the main aspects is giving more legitimacy for non-state actors in the transformation process from conflict to peace (Terpstra et al., 2014). Accordingly, the peacebuilding process has to be inclusive of different segments within a conflicting society such as state actors, women, young people, NGOs, and civil society organisations, in order to ensure their right of expression in a "peacebuilding" process (Richmond, 2010; Wood, 2003). To inform our analysis by more comprehensive and normative definition, the authors use this definition of peacebuilding:

those activities and processes that: focus on the root causes of the conflict, rather than just the effects; support the rebuilding and rehabilitation of all sectors of the war-torn society; encourage and support interaction between all sectors of society in order to repair damaged relations and start the process of restoring dignity and trust; recognize the specifics of each post conflict situation; encourage and support the participation of indigenous resources in the design, implementation and sustainment of activities and processes; and promote processes that will endure after the initial emergency recovery phase has passed. (Spence, 2006)

With the increasing number of conflicts, wars and civilian war victims over the last 30 years, local and international civil society organisations, donors, EU, the United Nations and multilateral regional organisations, and diplomatic missions of democratic governments, have begun to use a common ground for peacebuilding processes to ensure the security of people, which has become the central task of international and local peacebuilding efforts (Autesserre, 2017). The peacebuilding process involves a wide range of efforts from various actors such as governments and civil society at the community, national and international levels, to address the root causes of violence and to ensure civilians have freedom from fear, want and humiliation before, during and after violent conflict. Additionally, one of the peacebuilding processes for human protection is a military model of observing ceasefires and forcing separations after inter-state wars, and one that incorporates a complex model of both militaries and civilians, working together to build and restore peace in a conflict-torn region (Cheng-Hopkins, 2010).

The concept of peace-making is a process used to bring hostile factions to an agreement, essentially through amicable means. It is a process involving any action aimed at pushing warring factions to reach a peace agreement through negotiation, dialogue, diplomacy, and mediation to address conflicts in progress, attempting to bring them to a halt (Bercovitch et al., 2009). Peace-making, in essence, is a diplomatic effort to reshape a violent situation into a non-violent dialogue, where differences are resolved using national, multinational, and supranational representatives (Richmond, 2010) to restore non-violent state of affairs. It should be noted that peace-making does not include the use of military force against any of the conflicting factions to end the conflict (Aguilar, 2021). That is the aim of peace enforcement which refers to the use of armed force or threat to compel the concerned conflicting factions to comply with decisions and sanctions imposed to maintain peace and order. Peace enforcement efforts may include non-military measures such as sanctions (Paffenholz, 2009).

The transition from peacekeeping and peace-making to peacebuilding has been a prelude for many thinkers to find a way to support peacekeeping operations and peace-making, by trying to find an alternative that enables the conflicting factions to restore confidence and to build institutional structures for peace. Peacebuilding is therefore linked to peacekeeping, as both are characterised by some common principles required for the success of a peace process. Since 1980, peacekeepers and a large number of peacebuilding activists have been deployed within countries to maintain order and help implement conventions (Wildeman & Swan, 2021). Accordingly, National Dialogues have become an integral part of the peacebuilding process in post-conflict and post-crisis countries (Richmond, 2010). While, the concept of dialogue, in general, refers to a wide range of activities, from high-level negotiations and mediation to community attempts at reconciliation, the objective of a dialogue is to devise and execute practical and peaceful solutions to problems and conflicts. At a deeper level, the aim is to address conflict drivers, build a greater national consensus and social cohesion, and define a shared vision of the future. Although dialogues are only one aspect of peacebuilding, they play an indispensable role in efforts by national actors and the international community to respond to violent conflict and to build a national vision in fragile contexts (Odendaal, 2011).

However, the concept of political dialogue is still under-theorised (Paffenholz, 2009), and the notion of dialogue within policy and academic spheres is still problematic (Pruitt & Thomas, 2007). Concepts like mediation, facilitation, preventive diplomacy, and political dialogue have overlaps and are used reasonably and reciprocally as a part of the field. Political dialogue is often utilised as part of a comparably adaptable method, yet the parameters are that the discourse must be political in nature and targeting to solve deep-rooted conflicts (Holper & Kirchhoff, 2021; Jun & Reiterer, 2021). Political dialogue is a response process by national actors and the international community to violent conflict, aiming to achieve practical and peaceful solutions by addressing conflict drivers and reconciliation, and consequently building a national vision and consensus or cohesion in fragile contexts (Van Nieuwkerk, 2021). This process alludes to an extensive variety of exercises, from abnormal state arrangements to intervention at the national, middle, and local levels within a society (Odendaal, 2011).

In complex sociopolitical and divided societies that have been assaulted by rough clashes, building adequate social cohesion is a long-term transformation of relationships and a reconciliation process (Lemay-Hébert, 2009). Multi-faceted and multi-level dialogue forms, which include all segments of society and at all levels, are the key to developing long-term infrastructures (Lederach, 1997; Odendaal, 2011; QUNO, 2015). In other words, National Dialogue in divided societies is a long-term transformation of reconciliation processes and a multi-level activity that should include all segments in a society and at all levels. Lederach (1997) regards the establishment of social cohesion for an effective peacebuilding process as multi-level reconciliations, which can be usefully viewed as the process of transforming relationships in divided societies (QUNO, 2015).

Dialogues manifest in many forms are initiated and facilitated by a variety of actors and take place at various levels of society. Odendaal (2011) identifies four main types of dialogues:

i. high-level or summit dialogues involving the top leadership of contending sections of the population, often initiated or mediated by the international community
ii. track two interventions by civil society organisations that provide discreet and relatively low-risk opportunities to explore options, and build trust and skill in the process of dialogues
iii. dialogues that are indispensable aspect of planning for peacebuilding, state-building, and development, starting from the idea that such planning has to be driven by political dialogue
iv. multi-level dialogues, where dialogue takes place at various levels of society in an effort to engage citizens in building sufficient national consensus on critical challenges.

These four types are not mutually exclusive, but instead are complementary. It is often advisable to pursue different types of dialogue parallelly, on the condition that they have the same overall objectives and are not contradictory (Odendaal, 2011). All types and forms of dialogues can be used to gather the key stakeholders once the political institutions lack legitimacy or collapse. Dialogue is also increasingly used in transitional communities to conduct collective deliberation on key issues necessary for community stability (Houlihan & Bisarya, 2021).

Revisiting Peacebuilding: The Change Peacebuilding Theory

Since the end of World War II, a number of political scholars have devised peacebuilding theories to help countries, as well as societies, to remedy their war sufferings (Heathershaw, 2013). These theories are not only to facilitate the study of civil conflicts and how to avoid wars, but also go beyond that to rebuild countries' institutions and improve their economy, as well as invest at the human level to achieve long-term peace and stability. Ultimately, to declare war is not the difficult step; the most complicated stage is how to end it, mend war's damages, and rebuild peace (Del Castillo, 2008). Doyle and Sambanis (2000) state that: "one of the most important challenges for the international community is how to rebuild stable polities in the aftermath of civil war. How can it help prevent renewed hostility? What role should it play to ensure that failed states do not relapse into chaos as soon as the peacekeepers leave?" Thus, some peacebuilding theories present a good understanding of the notion of reconstructing societies and states in the aftermath of wars.

Peace consolidation is a very exhausting process and requires time to attain its goals—to create and maintain peaceful and productive societies. It can take years as it requires reconstructing every aspect of the country's infrastructure. Not only that but it also secures citizens' rights (Sargent, 2016). Furthermore, it seeks to improve facets of human life including education, health care, and a variety of public services (Dudouet, 2006). Thus, the reconciliation strategy in any society should go hand in hand with the development process, which ultimately should ensure substantial peace in all aspects of life. To have peace, there needs to be a remedy for the roots of conflicts within society and among warring states. Essentially, we can create peace, but if we don't understand its primary causes, conflict will inevitably repeat.

Peace-promoting theories usually bet that reconciliation policy will eventually lead to democracy that guarantees all citizens the right to societal participation (Rosato, 2021). Usually, democratic states do not solve their domestic or foreign problems by going to war but rather through negotiations (Irrera, 2021). However, the international and regional organisations often play an important role in both the reconciliation and peacebuilding policies (Özerdem et al., 2021). Doyle and Sambanis confirm that: "The political strategy of a peacebuilding mandate is the concept of operations embodied in its design. Just as civil wars are usually about failures of legitimate state authority, sustainable civil peace relies on its successful reconstruction. Peacebuilding is about what needs to happen in between" (Doyle & Sambanis, 2000).

Accordingly, mediators in a peacebuilding process need to have a clear strategy from the first day of the National Dialogue until the end of the transformational period; otherwise, the dialogue can fail at an early stage (Paffenholz, 2021). Some scholars have argued that in order to have a successful peace negotiation, there are certain conditions that need to be met: (1) re-concentrate central power (the powerful must be recognised as legitimate, or the legitimate made powerful), (2) increase state legitimacy through participation (elections, power-sharing), (3) raise and allocate economic resources in support of peace, and (4) external, international assistance, or authority in a transitional period (Doyle & Sambanis, 2000). In this regard, the existence of a strong government that receives support from international society is vital to the achievement of consistent peace in societies.

For peacebuilding theories in political fields, it is a certainty that the road to peace is very intricate, especially in countries undergoing wars, where the number of casualties rises alongside the amount of hostility in their society (Barash & Webel, 2016). Consequently, we need to secure a clear strategy that helps these societies overcome such threats, which can only be done by considering all aspects of life—social, economic, and political. Fischer (2011) writes that: "In the past decade 'reconciliation' has become one of the four main categories of initiatives that receive donors' support, along with political development, socio-economic assistance and security." Neglecting this principle would sentence any National Dialogue or reconciliation to an early end.

Figure 2.1 explains how a peace process could work in the right direction, where many elements could exist in a National Dialogue. The absence of these factors could weaken a peace process. Peacebuilding processes need an appropriate environment internally (readiness of political elites to work with each other towards peace, alongside public support for national conferences), and externally (international society has to support countries involved in wars) (Elayah et al., 2020; Koser, 2007; Van Tongeren, 2013). Peacebuilding theories try to tackle these complications to create stable situations and to rebuild peace in countries facing chronic challenges. Moreover, the elimination of any political power from participation would typically weaken a peace process (Murphy, 2007).

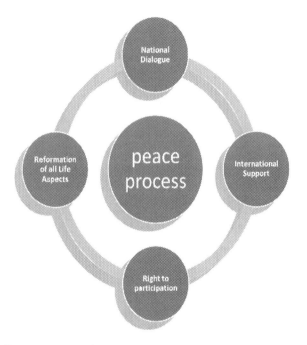

Fig. 2.1 Peace process cycle

The mainstream literature surrounding peacebuilding theory identified five schools of thought or approaches for peacebuilding in fragile contexts:

(1) The Conflict Management School
(2) The Conflict Resolution School
(3) The Complementary School
(4) The Conflict Transformation School
(5) The Alternative Discourse School of Peacebuilding (McCandless, 2013; Paffenholz, 2009, 2013; Richmond, 2013; Tschirgi, 2015).

From the aforementioned, the Conflict Transformation School or the change peacebuilding theory is the most compelling because of its main transformation and premise of how to tackle the differences between long-term and short-term conflict management resolution and how to deal with the underlying causes of the conflicts and build sustainable peace in a divided society (Lederach, 1997). The raison d'être of the change peacebuilding theory is the need for behavioural, structural, and cultural transformation of violence, especially in post-conflict transition, from violent dynamic conflict to constructive social change. The change peacebuilding theory argues that the transformation process can only be achieved through a combination of integrated security, social, political, development, and judicial peacebuilding strategies, and coordination among involved actors at the local and national levels (Aryal, 2012), as it is in Lederach's Transformation-Oriented Model of Peacebuilding. This approach constitutes assisting individuals and groups and providing them opportunities to present their views and opinions by engaging in a dialogue. This approach focuses on peacebuilding and conflict transformation, as well as instilling the skills of conflict management in a society.

In order to unpack the concept of transforming relationships in divided societies, this book uses John Paul Lederach's *Building Peace: Sustainable Reconciliation in Divided Societies* (1997), to understand and discuss transformative approaches to building peace (Paffenholz, 2013). This model is important to explain why some countries succeed and others don't in building peace after conflicts. It focuses on the systemic way of how we can build long-term infrastructure for peacebuilding by enhancing the social cohesion and potential reconciliation in divided and non-divided societies. This is because of a basic lack of sufficient social cohesion and consensus within a society. There is a need for a full awareness of the local context, mapping locally driven preconditions for successful transformation process from conflict to peace. When the peacebuilding process is backed by minimal divided social cohesion and consensus, the peacebuilding potential advances significantly. The employment of the theoretical framework of Lederach's model of a systematic conflict transformation is important for the analysis in this book, as cases like Yemen and Afghanistan face problems because of their divided societies.

Lederach's model (1997) mainly focuses on five key components or dimensions of an effective peacebuilding process:

- Structure
- Process
- Reconciliation

- Resources
- Coordination.

Lederach argues that these components must comprise any peacebuilding process in order to be effective, taking into consideration the local context in any individual country. For Lederach, truth, equity, kindness, and peace at all levels of a society form the bedrock of reconciliation. Subsequently, he focuses on the need to reconstruct decimated relationships, concentrating on reconciliation within society at every stage of peacebuilding, and fortifying its social cohesion and peacebuilding potential. It is essential to place the reconciliation dimension first as it focuses on the emotional and psychological aspects of conflict transformation and is a cogent investigation of the conflict and the involved parties' interests and fears. Reconciliation represents the process of preparation at the heart of developing long-term infrastructures for peacebuilding. The progress of subsequent stages depends on what is accomplished at this stage. Lederach emphasised the significance of pre-intervention consultations to ensure the adequate buy-in of all parties into the process. These pre-consultations can take distinctive structures like sub-dialogues at multiple levels (multi-track pre-consultations), among various fragments of societal groups, and by various issues and characters of the general public, before undertaking a comprehensive National Dialogue. During this phase, learning lessons from past encounters is significant, especially the reasons behind past disappointments (Table 2.1).

The second dimension refers to the structure, which is a crucial aspect of conflict transformation and reconciliation, involving interaction between three tracks of actors: Track I—the top leadership; Track II—the middle-range leadership; and Track III—the grassroots leadership. The types of actors at all levels are different, including powerful actors and non-powerful actors within the society. Top-level actors consist of political, military, or sometimes religious leaders. The middle range consists of people whose positions of leadership are not directly dependent on the power hierarchy of the top level, such as CSOs, NGOs, respected heads of business, education, or agriculture. The grassroots leadership operates in direct connection to the masses of people and includes local strongmen, refugee camp officials, NGO workers, and health workers. The grassroots-level leadership is an inlet for pressuring the masses and for more indigenous and customary mediations among the different groups at the local levels within the society. The main peacebuilding

Table 2.1 Lederach's model: explanations and hypotheses

Theoretical dimension	Explanation	Hypotheses. To have an effective conflict transformation in a divided society is with …
Reconciliation	A solid investigation and preparation process for the National Dialogues	• Solid investigation of the conflict and parties' interests and fears • More learning lessons from past encounters • Holding sub-dialogues at local levels • Holding sub-dialogues among different segments of societal groups (like young people and women) • Holding sub-dialogues based on the national conflict issues (like national separation issues, economic- and religion-based conflict issues)
Structure	It is concerned with the systemic components of how to address a setting of conflict inside the general public, involving interaction between three tracks of actors: the top leadership; the middle-range leadership; and the grassroots leadership	• A higher involvement of the civil society organisations as a main component of the middle-out approach of peacebuilding
Process and Efficiency	The timeframe and efficiency of a conflict transformation process	• A long-term process of conflict transformation • Talented facilitator of conflict transformation process • A peacebuilding process paralleled by economic and financial assistance

Source Author, based on Lederach's Transformation-Oriented Model on Peacebuilding approach within the grassroots track is called the "bottom-up approach of peacebuilding."

Among the three levels of initiative, or tracks, in Lederach's hypothesis, he argues that the middle-level leadership (Track II) holds the "best potential for building up a framework and an infrastructure that can manage the peacebuilding procedure over the long timeframe," notwithstanding serving as a source of practical, and immediate action, "supporting" long-term transformation in the setting. On the ground, close backing for the middle level (Track II) by the outside is expected to impact peacebuilding at both the top (Track I) and at the grassroots (Track III) levels, as they connect and coordinate with people at both levels. Lederach meaningfully said that if the actors in the middle track mobilised strategically for peacebuilding, they will be well-suited to execute the implementation of the comprehensive peacebuilding arrangements and projects. They can, moreover, establish the framework for long-term and feasible conflict transformation. These three approaches are not mutually exclusive, but rather complementary in peacebuilding interventions. It is often advisable to adopt the three approaches in parallel, on the condition we should take into consideration local knowledge in its informal aspects on the power configuration within a society, and make sure we are pursuing the same overall objectives at all levels and providing Humanitarian Aid for the needed people (Elayah, 2014).

The third dimension focuses on the long-term process of conflict transformation in divided societies. The process of transforming deep-rooted conflict, which tends to be underlying with multiple drivers, must be dealt with in the long-term. Deep-rooted conflicts are not static but rather expressive. Therefore, conflict transformation must comprise of a proper procedure, illuminating and apportioning roles of different support actors. It is important to host a talented facilitator with a deep local knowledge that all conflicted groups acknowledge and feel comfortable with, to make the process of transforming conflict as reasonable and fair as possible. The fourth dimension concerns the importance of the economic and financial support for achieving a systematic conflict transformation and building stable peace in a divided society, because in most countries facing conflicts economies are at zero level, zero growth, or at least damaged. That is why the peacebuilding process must be supplemented by economic and financial assistance to alleviate the suffering of a society, especially the majority at the grassroots level. The final dimension refers to the need for innovative mechanisms to enhance coordination and communication: setting up a strong supported structure to manage subsidising, logistical plans, and money-related administration; and planning a suitable communication strategy to deal with conflicted factions, press, and public outreach.

As we navigated Lederach's proposed three dimensions, we found them overlapping, and it is hard to have a reasonable distinction among them, so we merged them into one dimension under the heading "Process and Efficiency." In every dimension we squared rank of independent variables. Although numerous, we picked the ones that can really be behind the achievement of peacebuilding in a divided and fragile society. This was also suggested by different scholars who used Lederach's model in their work (e.g. Odendaal, 2011). Moreover, this depends on local knowledge as we have selected independent variables that are well-suited to the contexts being studied (Tunisia and Yemen).

The change process and political transition are helped by creating channels of dialogue and communication, including local elites, as well as a broad group of civil society and non-governmental organisations, such as media local and internationally, trade groups, intellectuals, local community leaders, and the promotion of multi-track diplomacy for peacebuilding, which needs media support by various outlets and channels (Heathershaw, 2008). Therefore, we argue that the media and the nature of the industry at the local or international levels within the framework of the European Union, as an example, have a role in increasing the effectiveness of diplomatic moves, especially that it may create a local public opinion in increasing the diplomatic pressures in order to end conflicts and build peace in fragile countries, most of which are suffering from many disadvantages. But the question is, how are media materials produced and how do they frame conflicts in the countries sponsoring peace, and are these materials realistic in support of diplomatic moves for peacebuilding? This question lies at the core of this book, which links the peacebuilding process and how the media can be supportive of or opposed to diplomatic moves aimed at making peace in fragile states.

MEDIA AND DEEP-ROOTED CONFLICTS IN THE INTERNATIONAL SETTING

Much of the existent research has examined the media coverage of international news that either gains a great deal of media attention or not (Rozanov et al., 2021). It is believed that there are some factors that determine the way international media report issues especially with the level of public concern towards international problems such as terrorism or international conflict (Arafat et al., 2021; Mohammadi, 1997). Shoemaker and Reese (1995) proposed that domestic factors influence media reporting. They suggested that media coverage is encased in layers of influence. The outer layer consists of a country's historical and cultural characteristics which may differ according to national traditions of journalism, geographical, or linguistic particularities, religious differences, or the different value systems of political elites (Lee & Maslog, 2005). The next layers of influence consist of country specific, structural, institutional, and organisational characteristics such as economic factors, technological influences, or typical working processes in newsrooms (Doll, 2021). The inner layer comprises of the sociodemographic characteristics, attitudes, self-perceptions, and motivations of journalists. Scholars assumed that the characteristics and relevance of these factors vary from country to country, and that coverage on external or transnational issues, such as international terrorism, and international crises are shaped by them into a specific, domestic view (Gerhards & Schäfer, 2014; Shoemaker & Reese, 1995). Some other scholars think that the difference in media reporting across nations might be subjected to regional and global factors. These assumptions would help this study to guide the interpretation of the findings (Camaj, 2010).

Many researchers have pointed at the lack of balance in news flow and coverage (Masmoudi, 1979; Sobel & Riffe, 2015) as a select number of nations are consistently covered while most nations receive limited to no coverage (Chang, 1998; Harvey, 2012). In this context, media researchers have tried to identify the key variables that influence international news selection processes. Some of the findings point at several key variables that are associated with the newsworthiness of nations and global events. These include deviance (Shoemaker et al., 1986), relevance (Chang et al., 1987), cultural affinity (Hester, 1973), and position in the hierarchy of nations (Chang, 1998; Harvey, 2012). It is also suggested that the newsworthiness of the international events may result from inter-media agenda process (Vicente, 2013). In other words, the coverage of international news might be influenced by the international news agendas of other media sources (Golan, 2006).

Ryan (1991) believed that there is one aspect that unites all the different views of news values or news criteria. It is combining their complete and accurate list although it seems impossible. Pavelka (2014) stressed that when an event has been successfully covered on the news, a combination of various news values always occurs. At the same time, there are also a number of internal and external factors and pressures that play their part. Regardless of the type of news value, emphasis is always laid upon attracting the attention and interest of the target audience (Pavelka, 2014). Also, there is a contradiction among the interests of the audiences, media owners, mediators (editors), politicians, and advertisers (Regan, 2002).

A media person selects a tiny fraction of a great amount of the existing news being offered. The person selects only some of the news available, that is, she/he decides which of the topics will become a subject of mass communication and consequently a matter of public interest, suppressing the rest of the topics (Axelrod, 2009). The Persian Gulf War in 1991 (Summers, 1995) is an example of such gatekeeping activities and censorship. When the war broke out, there were probably about 96 more war conflicts going on in other parts of the world. Despite this, it was the Iraq war that featured on major international news (Rantanen, 2004). CNN even broadcast it live—for the first time in the history of news (Smith, 1991). Another example is the Rwanda genocide. It was one of the most devastating human crises in history that claimed as many as a million lives. On the one hand, Rwanda's media coverage instigated such horror while on the other it was ignored by most international media (Boone, 2011).

Many studies on the international news coverage proved the lack of balance in the coverage (Jost & Koehler, 2021). It is noted by Chang (1998) that American coverage of international news often focuses on select nations while abandoning coverage of most nations around the world. Some scholars argue that several factors influence whether a conflict gets covered in the media, including its political and economic significance and its proximity, both geographically and culturally, to the nation covering it (Nohrstedt & Ottosen, 2014). Most importantly, the conflict has to be of national and political interest (Wolfsfeld & Gadi, 1997). The idea of national interest includes strategic military and economic concerns—"are they a military or terrorist threat; do they have oil?" along with how interesting the nation is (Harvey, 2012).

The first study on media framing theory in the MENA was during the Arab–Israeli conflict in 1973 when the Western media framed Arabs as extremists and unpeaceful nations who are controlled by Islamic militant groups (Asim, 2015). Kaid et al. (2005) examined the coverage of the 2003 Iraq War on the home pages of some 246 international news websites. This study found that there was a significant difference between the frames that appeared in the USA and non-U.S. media. US media frames focused more heavily on the military conflict and human interest, while the responsibility frame was more common for international sites. Above all, the news coverage in countries officially supporting the war was more positive than in the countries opposing the war. These examples indicate that framing of the news is likely to be expected differently depending upon the national interests and direct involvement in a certain conflict or war. However, there is not much evidence available, in which a military conflict is framed based on indirect involvement by a third party.

A recent study used inductive approach to analyse the coverage of Saudi-Yemen conflict by some of the most prominent newspapers (online news content) originating from various key Sunni (Saudi, UAE, and Egypt), Shia dominated countries (Iran and Iraq) in the MENA region and online news content originating from UK and US (Asim, 2015). The researcher studied the most prevalent frame associated with the Saudi-Yemen conflict, the tone and approach in headlines and the news body used while covering the conflict by the regional Western media firm. He found that regional newspapers did not considerably rely on the sectarian frames to invoke the emotions of their audiences as he assumed. Instead, they rely more on blaming the actions of the opposing party that caused the humanitarian crisis. This triggered the already existing inter-sectarian differences and misunderstandings. Looking at the Western media, they portrayed this conflict as a sectarian issue, while framing this as a Shia-Sunni conflict. In his study, Asim (2015) proved that affective agenda setting role of media engages its audiences in an in-direct fashion to trigger emotions to form opinions based on their existing beliefs and convictions.

Agenda Setting and Framing Theory in the Media

According to McCombs and Shaw (1972), media plays an important role in shaping the political reality and diplomatic moves by selectively displaying the news coverage of a certain event/issue that enables the public not to learn only about a given issue but how much importance to attach to that issue from the amount of information in a news story and its position. In this context, some scholars suggest that the media performs its agenda setting function at different levels. The first-level agenda setting suggests that the media selects certain issues that the public should be aware of and decides the amount of coverage to be devoted to the issue (Rosenthal, 2015). The second-level agenda setting suggests the media also frames certain attributes of these issues, thus affecting how the issue is defined (McCombs & Valenzuela, 2020). Strong evidence is available to suggest that the affective attributes about any newsmakers or an event reported in the media influences the attributes the public associates with those events or newsmakers (McCombs et al., 1997).

The media frames an issue by selecting certain attributes about ongoing issues and packaging it a certain way (Entman, 1993). As schemata of interpretation, Goffman (1974) also highlights the way the media reports an event allows consumers to understand the event. The concept of framing involves both inclusion (emphasising) and exclusion (de-emphasising) and media news outputs can prioritise some aspects over others, therefore intentionally or unconsciously promoting one particular interpretation of events over another (Li & Khalaf, 2012). Media frames according to Kinder (1998) seek to capture the essence of an issue. They define what the problem is and how to think about it; often they suggest what, if anything should be done to remedy it.

There are a considerable number of definitions of news frames in both theoretical and empirical contributions. Gitlin (1980), for instance, defines frames as "persistent patterns of cognition, interpretation, and presentation of selection, emphasis and exclusion by which symbol handlers routinely organise discourse." Gamson and Modigliani (1989) refer to frames as "interpretative packages" that give meaning to an issue. At the core of this package is "a central organizing idea, or frame, for making sense of relevant events, suggesting what is at issue." By virtue of emphasising some elements of a topic above others, a frame provides a way to understand an event or issue. In this vein, Cappella and Jamieson (1997) suggest that frames activate knowledge, stimulate "stocks of cultural morals and values, and create contexts." In doing so, frames "define problems," "diagnose causes," "make moral judgments," and "suggest remedies" (Entman, 1993). He (Entman) also noted that frames have several locations, including the communicator, the text, the receiver, and the culture. These components are integral to a process of framing that consists of distinct stages: frame-building, frame-setting and individual and societal level consequences of framing (d'Angelo, 2002; de Vreese, 2002; Scheufele, 2000).

As Giles (2010) points out that a frame is a combination of various media elements, such as a headline, photograph, text, etc. Every single statement can be put into a particular frame. Such a frame can then be used to influence the audience's attitudes and opinions. According to Giles and Shaw (2009), who offered a complex concept of the media framing analysis, several areas should be carefully observed within the framing process—the story, its characters, its narrative form, the language used, and the way in which the story is interconnected with other stories/topics (i.e. its generalisation). This generalisation forms a media template (Giles & Shaw, 2009). According to Kitzinger (2000), this helps the audience make sense of new information.

There are two types of frames that researchers commonly use to investigate the way media report on a certain issue or event. These major frames are the episodic and thematic frames (Iyengar, 1991). Another type of frames are the five generic frames (conflict, human interest, attribution of responsibility, morality, and economic consequences) identified by Semetko and Valkenburg (2000) which are modified and used in this study.

Humanitarianism and Peacebuilding

To enrich the analysis used in the book, we will also look at another layer that affects the on-ground reality in the MENA region which is not portrayed accurately in European media leading to a skewed notion of the region in the public discourse of the Western imagination.

In 1864, the International Committee of the Red Cross (ICRC) became the world's first official international humanitarian organisation aimed at providing HA to civilian and military victims of conflict. HA today provides relief across an array of contexts but originally it was almost exclusively supplied to conflict areas (Paulmann, 2013). To analyse the history of HA, Barnett (2011) suggests that there are three distinct ages of humanitarianism, "an imperial humanitarianism, from the early nineteenth century through World War II; a neo-humanitarianism from World War II through the end of the Cold War; and a liberal humanitarianism, from the end of the Cold War to the present." As technologies developed during the "imperial humanitarianism" period so did the human costs of conflict; "armed conflict was becoming less and less a chivalrous jousting contest for the few, and more and more a mass slaughter" (Forsythe, 2005). Individuals began imagining new ways to relieve human suffering, through a Eurocentric idea of international community. Before World War I the work of the ICRC was largely a small affair but when the Treaty of

Versailles led to the formation of the League of Nations (later renamed the UN) to protect vulnerable populations and encourage peace, states became increasingly involved in humanitarian action (Barnett, 2011).

A peacebuilding theory and approaches are stressing the importance of Humanitarian Aid to stimulate the general atmosphere during the war and prepare local conditions for the transition to the stage of recovery. However, many questions that have arisen since the beginning of humanitarian aid as a global strategy, which is being offered by many international countries and the international organisations affiliated with the United Nations (Elayah, 2021; Elayah et al., 2021). Some of these questions include—do the mechanisms of delivery of international Humanitarian Aid actually support a fair distribution and access to those who deserve it, or does this Humanitarian Aid, on the contrary, work to aggravate the conflict and is exploited by the conflicted parties? Does international media cover this humanitarianism and the complications of wars, or are most conflicts ignored on the human level and are motivated only by the political side of the peacebuilding processes?

These questions inspire us to research the history and reality of humanitarian aid and understand the most important challenges of distributing it during conflicts and wars. It is also important to understand how they are also covered in the media by rich, democratic, and stable countries, for example, the European media. Increasing an individual's spending capacity enables access to greater options in terms of life priorities, in non-degrading ways, including medical treatment, clothes, housing, and education (Elayah, 2021; Elayah et al., 2021; Mattinen & Ogden, 2006). Reducing negative conditions on a national level, such as food limitations, poverty rates, child labour, and armed group expansion (Lehmann & Masterson, 2014), revives the economy and encourages small businesses. This is an integral step towards a sustainable future (Lehmann & Masterson, 2014; Mattinen & Ogden, 2006) as it aligns the agendas of international humanitarian assistance with the needs of the local people during war and peacebuilding processes. Still, current practices of distributing aid in the form of food have not had the desired effect; conflict has continued, and war economies are thriving as a result. Thus, we are compelled to ask whether cash assistance is a more effective and efficient way of distributing aid in comparison with food-aid. In comparison with food-based aid, cash assistance targets a wider scope of peoples' necessities, in a more efficient and effective delivery approach that can be easily tracked by the EU donors.

The main challenge conflict zones are facing is how to accommodate universalism in a world of diversity, since globalisation clashes with traditional values around the world leading to the development of war economies (Barnett, 2011). In many cases, these war economies have caused governance systems to become weak and have resulted in their collapse, thus leading to long-term issues that result in the recurrence of conflict (Pugh et al., 2005). In Cambodia, natural resources such as timber and rubber have been a large source of funding for armed groups. Afghanistan is also the world's largest opium producer and centre for arms dealing, has a million-dollar trade revenue per year from smuggling these commodities into Pakistan from Dubai (DeLozier, 2019). Furthermore, while HA is desperately needed, international and humanitarian organisations are in danger of being perceived as siding with the West. This was the case in the August 2003 Baghdad bombing, now known as the UN's 9/11, which killed the Undersecretary-General Sergio Viera de Mello and 21 others (Benthall, 2003; Donini, 2004; Hyder, 2007).

The number of people suffering in conflict environments is increasing despite the huge developments and progress within the HA field since the 1990s. The United Nations Office for the Coordination of Humanitarian Affairs (OCHA) estimated that in 2020, 167.6 million people around the world would require HA (~ 1 in 45 people globally) (OCHA, 2020), and Kim (2017) estimates that by 2030, 50% of the global poor will live in areas where conflict and fragility are rife. In Nigeria, South Sudan, Somalia, and Yemen, alone, the number of people suffering from famine reached 20 million in 2018. This figure has increased at such a high rate that the funding gap has risen from around $2.5 billion in 2009 to around $13 billion in 2019 (OCHA, 2020). Thus, the current method of HA application to improve crisis situations has produced much scepticism and cynicism internationally, since humanitarian organisations have often failed to achieve goals and help endangered civilians and aid workers alike (Findley, 2018; Terry, 2011).

In the current climate, it seems that no amount of HA will offset the societal collapse, high food prices and consequently the amount of suffering that the war has produced. The UN claims that the weaponisation of HA highlights a "collective failure and collective responsibility" of all actors involved, since the political unrest has been driven by the efforts of various entities, both governmental and non-governmental, who enable the war economies to thrive (UN, 2019). Thus, it has become vital to seek new approaches to prevent the situation from further deteriorating. The following section will explain the theoretical elements of our proposed solution, cash-aid.

Cash Aid: A Suitable Alternative

Implementing cash transfer projects is underutilised in the NGO sector, as it amounts to only 17.9% of all forms of HA (CaLP, 2020). Nonetheless, it is becoming a more effective alternative in conflict areas and emergency settings and by 2018 the total aid in forms of cash reached 4.7 billion USD (Development Initiatives Report, 2019), a rise from 1.2 billion USD in 2014 (ODI & CGD, 2015). Cash-based interventions are being adopted by various organisations in Yemen including the World Food Programme (WFP) whose previous explicit food-aid mission was altered to include "food assistance." Food assistance programmes offer cash-based aid in different forms including vouchers that can be replaced with what the beneficiaries need at selected stores (Pongracz, 2015). Vouchers are known to be restricted because there is limitation on how and where they can be used. In comparison, cash transfers are unrestricted because they can be spent however the recipient wishes to use them (CaLP, 2020).

A Historical Overview

The first recorded use of HA cash transfers was during the Franco-Prussian War of 1870–1871. The American Red Cross used this method to set up micro-enterprise projects for wounded soldiers recovering from the war. There has been a lot of success since. For example, during the tsunami crisis in 2004, governments decided to use cash-based aid as a replacement for food-aid, enabling people to rebuild, rent and regenerate their livelihoods (Adams & Winahyu, 2006; Harvey, 2007). In 2010, a flood hit Pakistan and the government distributed US 1.7 million in debit cards as aid to help people suffering from the disaster (ODI & CGD, 2015). The same approach is used among some INGOs operating in conflict areas, to permit the vulnerable to decide what to buy based on their individual needs (Mattinen & Ogden, 2006). This form of assistance prevents people from reselling the food-aid supplies to generate an income and buy other necessities "as, for example, 70% of Syrian refugees in Iraq have reportedly done" (Mattinen & Ogden, 2006).

Another form of cash-based relief is vouchers which the World Food Programme employed with the 1 million Syrian refugees they helped in Lebanon (Mattinen & Ogden, 2006; Pongracz, 2015). In essence, the vouchers enable people to purchase items that they need from stores, but they have created another inflation dilemma. For instance, in Lebanon where the World Food Programme offers cash help to one million Syrian refugees in vouchers, due to the vouchers being valid at only certain stores those vendors turned into monopolies. This led to increasing commodity prices every month, resulting in vouchers losing around a million each time the prices increased (Mattinen & Ogden, 2006).

For the NGO sector, cash-based interventions are more efficient and cost-effective compared to distributing food. Studies in Yemen and three other countries concluded that offering cash instead of food will help NGOs give assistance to 18% more beneficiaries at the same operational cost. Another report from Zimbabwe showed the impact of cash interventions on household income, as it stated that every dollar given directly as aid increased the income by $2.59, while food-aid intervention only increased the income by $1.67 (Concern Worldwide, 2011). Operational costs are lower for cash-aid programmes than for delivering food-aid because this method requires less importation, local transport, storage, human resources, and logistics (UN, 2019). INGOs can deliver cash programmes without the need of multiple local NGO involvement, which consequently will decrease the influence of "twilight groups" working with hidden agendas. It lowers the risk of commodity distribution being diverted or resold by these groups on secondary markets to keep funding their own agendas. Furthermore, cash-based interventions offer digital transactions, a less risky method of distribution compared to food-aid and allows equitable access and distribution of HA supplies. According to the UK National Audit Office, 2011 transferring cash and assets to the poor report, cash transfers using electronic methods will increase the safety, cost effectiveness, and reduce fraud risks compared to food distributions (UK National Audit Office, 2011). According to the Overseas Development Institute (ODI) and the Center for Global Development (CGD), this was successfully tested by the World Food Programme in Ethiopia, where the cash-aid project was between 25 and 30% more efficient than existing food-aid projects (2015). Cash-aid has also proven to be effective within unstable countries such as in Somalia, where cash-aid was delivered to one and a half million vulnerable civilians in 2011. Cashless transaction also offers the donors a transparent means to trail the funds until they reach their recipients, to prevent fraud and exploitation, and to reduce the amount of HA being lost to the belligerent actors.

Nonetheless, if cash-aid is not accompanied by accurate monitoring measurements, then it can fall in the corruption trap, and it is likely to be a more attractive commodity than food-aid. Moreover, if the proper research was not done prior to the implementation process the new cash supply injected into the market can negatively affect the economy.

The below table explains the advantages and disadvantages of implementing the cash-aid projects (Table 2.2).

Cash-aid can either be unrestricted, restricted, or conditional. The former allows cash transfer, the second enables vulnerable people to purchase items depending on their needs with vouchers and the latter links the money distributed with performing a certain task. This allows communities to improve and develop and it enables individuals to build their skill sets and have a source of income. This is particularly important for NGOs who are unable to provide the conditions needed to bear their success. The needed people have lost trust in the warring factions, as well as local and international NGOs, due to the lack of effectiveness of current methods of HA distributions due to looting and the risks associated with reaching vulnerable people. Therefore, it has become imperative to restore donor direct HA delivery by providing cash-aid as a superior means of food-aid in many conflicted countries, to ensure the effectiveness of HA and to improve the lives of those who are suffering, in the long-term.

For the aims to explore the food-aid sustainability and practicality in Yemen against, and to identify the challenges and deficiencies facing the aid distribution mechanism in Arab region aligned with the peacebuilding processes spouted by the EU. This comparative Chapter 6 employs the qualitative approach using a purposive sample and secondary data. The primary data was collected through semi-structured interviews, held with Yemeni staff members working at INGOs and NGOs that provide relief through direct implementation of distributing foreign and local aid ($N = 10$). The interviews were conducted in March 2020 and August 2020 among organisations operating or offering aid in Sana'a, Aden, Lahij, Dhale, Shabwah, Hadhramaut, Mahra, Ibb, and Hudaydah governorates in Yemen ($n = 9$). These areas are under the control of the three main political powerhouses in Yemen, Hadi forces, the Houthi movement, and the Southern Transitional Council (STC). To evaluate whether the cash

Table 2.2 Cash as Aid advantages and disadvantages

Cash as Aid

Advantages	Clarification
Maintain people's dignity and increase their basic needs access	Empowering people, to decide on their different basic needs and buy what matters to them based on their situations
Enhance housing conditions	Giving people the chance to rebuild their houses, rent temporary places
Financial Security	People can save up some money, pay back debts, start mini-projects
Better food diet	People can use the money to buy different forms of food
Better living conditions could decrease poverty rates	People who cannot work will have an income, such as elderly and disabled people. However, people with low skills can make an income working for cash projects. This increases their skills and enables them to find other job opportunities
Increases health and education rates	People now will have extra money to spend on health and education. This will give more children the opportunity to go to school
Engages the private sector	High demand together with individuals having cash, provides opportunity for the private sector to supply missing commodities
Decreases the INGOs operational costs	Cash transition programmes need less logistics cost on transportation, storage, etc
Better conditions for children	Family income will decrease the need for children to work. They will have time to study, play, and live a normal life
Digital cash is easier to track and distribute	Decreasing the risk of corruption and supplies being controlled by "twilight groups" and resold into secondary markets, to fund their own agendas
Disadvantages	*Clarification*
Economy stagnation and dependency	People may get used to receive aid money and supplies, and stop looking for different income sources (Mainly with direct cash-aid)

(continued)

Table 2.2 (continued)

Cash as Aid	
Women, children, and elders receive cash HA for others / unintended use of the cash	Due to the high poverty and unemployment rates, men may take advantage of powerless categories, people using the cash only for their needs. Buying redundant commodities like Qat, etc
Safekeep risks/needs more funds towards monitoring and auditing	Cash is a very desirable commodity and thus it needs to be monitored to ensure it doesn't fall into the hands of warring parties or corrupt officials
Prices increase in domestic markets	If prior research was not properly executed, huge cash injections may cause inflation to the economy

Source (Allahi et al. 2019; CaLP, 2020)

transfers approach is suitable for Yemen, the study also included interviews of beneficiaries of the sampled organisations ($n = 10$).

Methodology

The interview guide is relatively straightforward as it corresponds to the main qualitative questions such as: What is your approach to the crisis? How do you reach vulnerable people? Do you see where your aid goes? Do you know how many of your supplies reach the people who need them? Would you say that food has become a weapon of war? Has the blockade on Yemeni ports affected your work and worsened the crisis? Has your NGO made progress in Yemen? What do you think the biggest challenges are in reaching the Yemeni people? Were you active before the conflict? What were you doing before the conflict and how has this been changed by the conflict? Would you say the attempts made by your organisation to alleviate suffering are contrary to the political interests of the Yemeni government? The interview data from NGOs has been handled in a similar way to written sources and we have considered that personal opinions may prevent the research from being completely unbiased. However, it is of utmost importance to be open to all comments made in interviews and to ensure that ideas which one personally doesn't share are not discredited (or attach low weight to). The design of a semi-structured interview guide would not minimise this bias and could perhaps even exacerbate it, as interviewees may be restricted to voicing ideas that solely fit into the frame and questions of this study. Hence, a more open format for interviewing was used (Table 2.3).

Due to the COVID-19 health situation, in-person interviews were not the only method used; phone or Skype interviews were employed heavily. Full information about this study purpose, method, and use were communicated to the participants before the interviews. Confidentiality concerns were thoroughly conversed as participants asked to keep their personal information from being disclosed. The sample includes a diverse number of participants from the chosen 10 NGOs involved in the entire aid process, from submitting the proposal until delivering the aid to its benefiters. The sample included: programme officers managing the entire distribution cycle ($n = 3$), storekeepers responsible for the warehouses and the physical distribution ($n = 4$), staff members working in the administration department from the registering to the verification process ($n = 4$), a field researcher surveying the recipients, an auditor monitoring the process, and two consultants advising NGOs on the procedures.

In fragile and conflict-ridden countries, National Dialogues present a valid way to overcome internal fractions and to rebuild relations between the state and different groups. Over the years, National Dialogues have been considered important in state-building because they are designed for peaceful transformation. Throughout history, many National Dialogues have been supported by the UN, US, and European Union; the recent being in the MENA region, which included Yemen and Syria. The international intervention, in both countries, can be assumed to be the reason behind the increased media attention to wars between the Saudi-led coalition and the Houthi militias in the case of Yemen; and al-Assad forces and the forces of the opposition parties backing the two sides by international military intervention in the case of Syria. These wars have drastically pushed the two countries towards social, economic, and institutional collapse, while the world watches them. The main aim of this book is to examine the peacebuilding processes in Yemen and Syria and analyse how conflict in the middle east is framed in the European media. As such, this book provides an in-depth comparative analyses of selected National Dialogue design processes in fragile settings. However, it is important to understand the on-ground reality first.

As mentioned in the first chapter, the authors present case studies at the regional and international levels and compare them with the Yemeni

Table 2.3 Sample and responses

	NGO focus	Location	On-ground controlling party	Role	Interview situation	Interview date (2020)	Gender
1	Relief work	Sana'a City	Houthi	Officer	Phone	8th June	M
2	Humanitarian assistance	Aden	STC	Storekeeper	Skype	5th April	F
3	Humanitarian assistance	Lahij	Hadi Forces	Storekeeper	Skype	7th April	F
4	Humanitarian assistance	Aden	STC	Beneficiary	In person	2nd July	M
5	Humanitarian assistance	Dhale	Hadi Forces	Storekeeper	Phone	2nd July	F
6	Humanitarian aid	Sana'a	Houthi	Beneficiary	Phone	12th August	M
7	Social work	Sana'a	Houthi	Administration	Phone	16th May	M
8	Relief Work	Sana'a	Houthi	Beneficiary	In person	12th August	F
9	Economic development	Sana'a	Houthi	Beneficiary	In person	12th August	F
10	Humanitarian work	Shabwah	Hadi Forces	Consultant	Phone	21st June	M
11	Humanitarian work	Shabwah	Hadi Forces	Beneficiary	Phone	2nd July	F
12	Social work	Hadhramaut	Hadi	Officer	Skype	28th July	M
13	Social Work	Mahra	Hadi	Administration	Phone	25th May	M
14	Charity	Hudaydah	Hadi Forces	Storekeeper	Phone	27th July	M
15	Charity	Hudaydah	Hadi Forces	Beneficiary	Phone	27th July	M
16	Humanitarian aid	Aden	STC	Beneficiary	In person	2nd July	F
17	Humanitarian aid	Sana'a	Houthi	Beneficiary	Phone	14th June	M
18	Social work	Sana'a	Houthi	Auditor	Phone	22nd July	M

(continued)

Table 2.3 (continued)

NGO focus	Location	On-ground controlling party	Role	Interview situation	Interview date (2020)	Gender
19 Humanitarian development	Aden	STC	Field researcher	Skype	8th August	M
20 Humanitarian aid	Ibb	Houthi	Consultant	Phone	26th July	M
21 Humanitarian assistance	Sana'a	Houthi	Beneficiary	Phone	17th June	M
22 Humanitarian assistance	Sana'a	Houthi	Administration	Phone	13th May	F
23 Humanitarian assistance	Aden	STC	Administration	Phone	28th July	F
24 Humanitarian assistance	Aden	STC	Officer	Skype	8th August	M
25 Humanitarian aid	Aden	STC	Beneficiary	In person	2nd July	F

NDC. Gerring (2007a) distinguishes several types of case study research methods: single case study, comparative, comparative historical, cross-sectional, time series cross-sectional, hierarchical, and hierarchical time series. The type of case study this book is planning to do can be characterised as comparative and more similar case study design, with several cases. We compared the NDC to earlier dialogues in the country as well as with recent National Dialogue experiences elsewhere in the region. Both are based on the literature review as well. In reference to foreign dialogue experiences, we considered the dialogues in Afghanistan (2002), Iraq (2008), Tunisia (2013), and more briefly in Ethiopia (early 1990s):

The following section delineates the techniques for selecting the cases. Gerring (2007b) proposed a rationale for the selection of cases comprising nine categories of techniques for case selection:

- typical
- diverse
- extreme
- deviant
- influential
- crucial

- pathway
- most-similar
- most-different

Our research method can be classified as diverse. For each case, we will test the hypothesis and compare the results of the dependent and independent variables based on the peacebuilding theory model. The diversity has been analysed in categorical values in Table 2.4. Furthermore, we have considered the selection bias. It is possible that a case is selected only because an investigator wants to confirm his/her preliminary findings. It is therefore necessary to be open for contrary findings (Yin, 2009). Finally, the strength of our methodology is that we have selected a variety of cases, which makes it more likely to be representative. We are not able

Table 2.4 Framework for selecting the National Dialogue cases

National Dialogue cases	Relevance	Comments
Afghanistan (2002)	***	• Interest derives from fact that Afghanistan, like Yemen, is characterised by strong tribal organisation • The conflicts in both countries are along ethnic/tribal lines
Ethiopia (1991–1995)	***	• Ethiopia is an interesting international case because it dealt with the issue of federalism, which is significant in Yemen as well
Tunisia (2013)	***	• Interesting because Tunisian dialogue emerged from the Arab Spring, which also rocked Yemen • Tunisia and Yemen are the first two countries among the Arab Spring countries in which National Dialogue Conferences (NDCs) have taken place to break the political deadlock and to solve conflicts peacefully • The NDC in Tunisia is recognised as a successful example in the Arab world, whereas the Yemeni one failed to stop or prevent the war
Iraq (2008)	**	• Recent case, within Arab region • Iraq is culturally similar to Yemen • Related to one main argument, conflicts in both countries have similar ethnic/religion lines

to represent all the cases, such as Sudan, but we are fully able to explain why we have selected these three cases and no other cases.

The main cases that have been selected were chosen based on different considerations and methodological lines in order to ensure the substance of the peacebuilding processes and also the internal conflict dynamics and how the international media outlets cover them:

The tribal line: The Afghanistan (2002) case was considered as Afghanistan shares a similar social setting with Yemen characterised by strong tribal organisation. The conflicts in both countries are along ethnic/tribal lines.

The issue line: Ethiopia has gone through a political crisis that needed comprehensive political dialogue to bring about national consensus, manage, and resolve the conflict among the political parties by also giving a space to other actors in the Ethiopian society. The authors think that the case of Ethiopia is a good lesson to learn from not only among African countries, but it could be for any other country that has a similar political crisis such as Yemen.

The Arab Spring line: Tunisia and Yemen are the first two Arab countries that were engulfed with unrest in 2011, followed by the National Dialogue Conferences (NDCs) that were designed to break the political deadlock and to solve conflicts peacefully. The NDC in Tunisia is recognised as a successful example in the Arab world, whereas the Yemeni one failed to bring the warring parties to a consensus and ended with civil war and regional military intervention.

The ethnic/religion lines: Iraq is culturally similar to Yemen and conflicts in both countries are along similar ethnic/religion lines.

Yin (2009) proposed six sources of evidence: documentation, archival records, interviews, direct observations, participant observation, and physical artefacts. To deal with the first book's inquiry accurately, we used the techniques of documentation, archival records, and interviews. After the hypotheses were formulated, concepts were operationalised, procedures were formulated and criteria for interpreting were described, we collected data. First, we selected all the relevant policy documents. Next, we collected and analysed all the relevant documents. In the final stage, we collected the missing data to accurately answer the main question (Yin,

2009). Also, in this part of the book, the validity and the reliability need to be considered. Yin (2009) distinguished three main principles. First, because we used several methods the data can be compared from one source with another. Using multiple sources and discussing findings with our counterparts and experts increases the validity and reliability of this book (Yin, 2009). We created a database and stored the data systematically; otherwise, it is possible that we lose information. It is not necessary that all the data will be included in the book; however, it is necessary to store it systematically. In addition, the third principle is related to the previous topic, because it is necessary to continuously be aware of the fact that our goal is to answer the main questions. It is possible that during the case studies other pertinent questions came up. Therefore, we were fully aware to link the study questions, protocol, process, database, and report with each other. Consequently, the validity and reliability will be increased to consider the principles seriously (Yin, 2009).

To answer the second part of the book's inquiry, a content analysis was performed on the coverage of military intervention by Saudi-led coalition in Yemen and the Russian military intervention in Syria by four European online news and broadcast. A content analysis is empirical research used to make valid inferences from data in the context of their use (Krippendorff, 2004). According to him there are four primary advantages of content analysis: it is unobtrusive, it accepts unstructured material, it is context sensitive and thereby able to process symbolic forms, and it can deal with large volumes of data. These advantages seem to apply equally to the web and to media such as newspapers and television (Hashim et al., 2007). Therefore, McMillan (2000) identified five primary steps that are involved in the process of conducting analysis research for application to the web. These steps are:

- formulate the research question and/or hypothesis
- select a sample
- define categories
- train the coder to determine reliability
- analyse and interpret the data

However, web content analysis is criticised due to the number of available websites growing explosively, and available directories always incomplete and overlapping, selecting a true random sample may be closer to impossible (Bates & Lu, 1997). Ha and James (1998) also claim that coding a website can be extremely time-consuming and introduce biases based on website size. Nevertheless, the study tried to follow the steps mentioned to ensure a smooth process of conducting content analysis research of the web.

The purpose of selecting the four European media (see Table 2.5) is that the UK and France voiced their support to both military interventions, either by participating in the attacks as in the case of France in Syria or by supplying arms and weapons to the attackers in the case of UK supporting the Saudi war in Yemen. In this regard, for example, an article published in the early stages of launching the military operation in Yemen, the French Foreign Minister Laurent Fabius voiced support for Saudi-led military campaign against Houthis in Yemen by saying Paris is "naturally on the side of its regional partners for the restoration of stability in Yemen" (France24, 12 April 2015).

Additionally, the Netherlands and Switzerland that are amongst the biggest economic and technical aid providers to Yemen and Syria. However, they are considered neutral. In fact, Switzerland's capital city hosted the peace dialogue between Yemeni fractions. Nonetheless, it has very little political influence, not by any means comparable to the categories mentioned above. Therefore, it was a great opportunity to examine the way their media reportage on both cases since they reflect the stances of their European governments. In addition, the EU states have interests in ending the conflict; the failure to act could result in Yemen becoming a new centre for globally oriented terror groups and engulf the whole region into a conflict which could encourage new waves of refugees

Table 2.5 Media outlets & countries

Country	Media outlet	Type	Web address
UK	*The Independent*	Online newspaper	http://www.independent.co.uk/
France	*France24*	Online TV channel	http://www.france24.com/fr/
Switzerland	*SWI Swissinfo.ch*	Online platform	https://www.swissinfo.ch/eng
The Netherlands	*NRC Handelsblad*	Online newspaper	https://www.nrc.nl/

into Europe (Saif, 2015) which has raised social and economic concerns among the EU members.

This book starts out by providing relevant information about the roots of the Yemeni and Syrian conflicts. Next, it presents the literature review and the theoretical framework using media framing theory and then identifies the primary frames that are used in reporting the conflicts in Yemen and Syria, and whether these media outlets differ in their news coverage. It contributes to a better understanding of the nature of wars and National Dialogues based on different regional cases, and it also examines the news frames that were used to present conflicts in MENA by the European media outlets. This book is designed to be a friendly reference guide on the subject, incorporating media analytical lenses, lessons learned, and policy guidelines. The author hopes it will be of good use to those engaged in National Dialogues, media outlets, and policymakers at the national, regional, and international levels. This book examines the news frames used in the coverage of the two cases. The second level of agenda setting is used as a theoretical guide to understand the news frames used to report on both wars. Through analysing the content of non-US media, four European media were selected to answer the following questions:

(1) What is the amount of coverage devoted to the Saudi military intervention in Yemen and the Russian military intervention in Syria by The Independent, France24, NRC Handelsblad, and Swissinfo.ch online news?
(2) How do the four European media outlets frame both conflicts?
(3) Does the online news of the four European media outlets differ in news coverage on Saudi military intervention in Yemen and the Russian military intervention in Syria?

To sum up, firstly, this book gives an overview of the National Dialogue design process in fragile settings at the national, regional, and international levels. It provides a comparative analysis at the international level by examining the 2013 Yemeni NDC with that of Afghanistan and Ethiopia. It then analyses the National Dialogues at the regional level, focusing on Iraq and Tunisia, and compares these to the Yemeni NDC. Then, it goes beyond the traditional exploration of political and social conflicts by adding a rich theoretical layer of analysis of Humanitarian Aid and its contribution to war economies in the Arab region. The situation is examined through an empirical analysis of HA organisations during the war.

Finally, this book takes one step further to integrate a media lens by analysing the extent of media coverage devoted to the Yemeni and Syrian wars by four prestigious European online news publications, The Independent, France24, SWIswissinfo.ch, and NRC Handelsblad.

In the following chapter, we will discuss the on-ground reality of EU's peace interventions in the international setting through a comparative case study of, first Yemen and Afghanistan, and then Yemen and Ethiopia. The chapter will discuss the strengths and weaknesses of both cases, and the consequent lessons learned in terms of the political, social, and geographical aspects.

References

Adams, L., & Winahyu, R. (2006). *Learning from cash based responses to the Tsunami: Case studies*. Overseas Development Institute (ODI).

Aguilar, S. L. C. (2021). Ethnic conflicts and peacekeeping. In *Risks, identity and conflict* (pp. 157–183). Palgrave Macmillan.

Allahi, F., Taheri, S., Kian, R., Sabet, E., De Leeuw, S., Cianci, R., & Revetria, R. (2019). Cash-based interventions to enhance dignity in persistent humanitarian refugee crises: A system dynamics approach. *IEEE Transactions on Engineering Management*.

Arafat, Y., Khan, R. U. A., & Qadri, M. A. (2021). *Framing of international conflict victims: Political proximity vs religious proximity*.

Aryal, A. (2012). *Theories of change in peacebuilding: Learning from the experiences of peacebuilding initiatives in Nepal*. CARE International UK and International Alert. https://www.care.at/images/_care_2013/expert/pdf/COE_Resources/Programming/Theories_of_Change_in_Peacebuilding.pdf

Asim, M. M. (2015). Examining the role of emotion as a dimension of affective agenda setting. *International Journal of Humanities and Management Sciences (IJHMS), 3*, 6.

Autesserre, S. (2017). International peacebuilding and local success: Assumptions and effectiveness. *International Studies Review, 19*(1), 114–132.

Axelrod, A. (2009). *Selling the great war: The making of American propaganda*. Martin's Press.

Ballentine, K., & Nitzschke, H. (2005). *The political economy of civil war and conflict transformation*. Berghof Research Center for Constructive Conflict Management. http://www.berghof-handbook.net

Barash, D. P., & Webel, C. P. (2016). *Peace and conflict studies*. Sage.

Barnett, M. (2011). *Empire of humanity: A history of humanitarianism*. Cornell University Press.
Bar-Siman-Tov, Y. (2004). *From conflict resolution to reconciliation*. Oxford University Press.
Bates, M. J., & Lu, S. (1997). An exploratory profile of personal home pages: Content, design, metaphors. *Online and CD-Rom Review, 21*(6), 331–340.
Bellamy, A. J. (2004). The 'next stage' in peace operations theory? *International Peacekeeping, 11*(1), 17–38.
Benthall, J. (2003). Humanitarianism and Islam after 11 September. *Humanitarian action and the 'global war on terror* (pp. 37–47). HPG.
Bercovitch, J., Jackson, R., & Jackson, R. D. W. (2009). *Conflict resolution in the twenty-first century: Principles, methods, and approaches*. University of Michigan Press.
Boege, V. (2011). Potential and limits of traditional approaches in peacebuilding. In B. Austin, M. Fischer, & H. Giessmann (Eds.), *Berghof handbook II: Advancing conflict transformation* (pp. 431–457). Barbara Budrich publishers.
Boone, C. (2011). Politically allocated land rights and the geography of electoral violence: The case of Kenya in the 1990s. *Comparative Political Studies, 44*(10), 1311–1342.
CaLP. (2020). https://www.calpnetwork.org/wp-content/uploads/2020/07/SOWC2020-Full-Report.pdf
Camaj, L. (2010). Media framing through stages of a political discourse: International news agencies' coverage of Kosovo's status negotiations. *International Communication Gazette, 72*(7), 635–653.
Caparini, M. (2016). Challenges to contemporary peace support operations in Africa. *Journal of Military and Strategic Studies, 17*(2), 19–49.
Cappella, J. N., & Jamieson, K. H. (1997). *Spiral of cynicism. The press and the public good*.
Carter, D. B. (2010). The strategy of territorial conflict. *American Journal of Political Science, 54*(4), 969–987.
Chang, T. K. (1998). All countries not created equal to be news: World system and international communication. *Communication Research, 25*, 528–566.
Chang, T. K., Shoemaker, P., & Brendlinger, N. (1987). Determinants of international news coverage in the US Media. *Communication Research, 14*, 396–414.
Cheng-Hopkins, J. (2010). *UN peacebuilding: An orientation*. United Nations.
Concern Worldwide. (2011). *Hard cash in hard times: Cash transfers versus food aid in rural Zimbabwe*. Brief. Concern Worldwide.
Cunliffe, P. (2018). From peacekeepers to praetorians—How participating in peacekeeping operations may subvert democracy. *International Relations, 32*(2), 218–239.

D'Angelo, P. (2002). News framing as a multi-paradigmatic research program: A response to Entman. *Journal of Communication, 52*, 870–888.
de Vreese, C. H. (2002). *Framing Europe*. Aksant Academic Publishers.
Del Castillo, G. (2008). *Rebuilding war-torn states: The challenge of post-conflict economic reconstruction*. Oxford University Press.
DeLozier, E. (2019). *In Damning report, UN panel details war economy in Yemen* [online]. The Washington Institute. https://www.washingtoninstitute.org/policy-analysis/view/in-damning-report-un-panel-details-war-economy-in-yemen. Accessed 31 March 2020.
Development Initiatives' Report. (2019). http://devinit.org/wp-content/uploads/2019/09/GHA-report-2019.pdf
Dimitrova, D., Kaid, L., Williams, A., & Sweetser, K. (2005). War on the web: The immediate news framing of Gulf War II. *Harvard International Journal of Press-Politics, 10*, 22–44.
Doll, M. E. (2021). *Interpreting peace journalism in East Africa: Individual, organizational, and professional influences* (Doctoral dissertation, University of Washington).
Donini, A. (2004). Western Aid agencies don't have a humanitarian monopoly. *Humanitarian Affairs Review*, 12–15.
Doyle, M., & Sambanis, N. (2000). International peacebuilding: A theoretical and quantitative analysis. *The American Political Science Review, 94*(4), 779–801. https://doi.org/10.2307/2586208
Dudouet, V. (2006). *Transitions from violence to peace: Revisiting analysis and intervention in conflict transformation* (Berghof report, 15). Berghof Research Center for Constructive Conflict Management.
Elayah, M. (2014). *Donors-promoted public sector reform in developing countries and the local knowledge syndrome*. Leiden University and Smart Print.
Elayah, M. (2021). Humanitarian aid and war economies: The case of Yemen. *Economics of Peace and Security Journal, 16*(1), 52–65.
Elayah, M., Al-Daily, W., & Alkubati, M. (2021). The women, peace, and security (wps) agenda between rhetoric and action in the MENA region: A case study of Yemen and Libya. In *Female pioneers from ancient Egypt and the Middle East* (pp. 129–143). Springer.
Elayah, M., Schulpen, L., van Kempen, L., Almaweri, A., AbuOsba, B., & Alzandani, B. (2020). National dialogues as an interruption of civil war–the case of Yemen. *Peacebuilding, 8*(1), 98–117.
Elbadawi, I. (2000). *External interventions and the duration of civil wars*.
Entman, R. M. (1993). Framing: Towards clarification of a fractured paradigm. *McQuail's reader in mass communication theory* (pp. 390–397). Sage.

Fetherston, A. B. (2000). Peacekeeping, conflict resolution and peacebuilding: A reconsideration of theoretical frameworks. *International Peacekeeping, 7*(1), 190–218.
Findley, M. G. (2018). Does foreign aid build peace? *Annual Review of Political Science, 21*, 359–384.
Fischer, M. (2011). *Transitional justice and reconciliation: Theory and practice advancing conflict transformation*. The Berghof Handbook.
Forsythe, D. P. (2005). *The humanitarians: The international committee of the Red Cross*. Cambridge University Press, 16.
Gamson, W. A., & Modigliani, A. (1989). Media discourse and public opinion on nuclear power: A constructionist approach. *American Journal of Sociology, 95*(1), 1–37.
Gerhards, J., & Schäfer, M. S. (2014). International terrorism, domestic coverage? How terrorist attacks are presented in the news of CNN, Al Jazeera, the BBC, and ARD. *International Communication Gazette, 76*(1), 3–26. https://doi.org/10.1177/1748048513504158
Gerring, J. (2007a). *The case study: What it is and what it does*. Oxford University Press.
Gerring, J. (2007b). *Case study research: Principles and practices*. Cambridge University Press.
Gitlin, T. (1980). *The whole world is watching: The mass media in the making and unmaking of the left*. University of California Press.
Goffman, E. (1974). *Frame analysis: An essay on the organization of experience*. Harvard University Press.
Golan, G. (2006). Inter-media agenda setting and global news coverage. *Journalism Studies, 7*(2), 323–333.
Giles, D. (2010). *Psychology of the media*. Palgrave Macmillan.
Giles, D., & Shaw, R. (2009). The psychology of news influence and the development of media framing analysis. *Social and Personality Psychology Compass, 3*(4), 375–393.
Ha, L., & James, L. E. (1998). Interactivity reexamined: A baseline analysis of early business web sites. *Journal of Broadcasting & Electronic Media, 42*(4), 457–474.
Harvey, D. C. (2012). The invisible genocide: An analysis of ABC, CBS, and NBC Television news coverage of the 1994 genocide in Rwanda. *Electronic Thesis and Dissertation Repository*.
Harvey, P. (2007). *Cash based responses in emergencies* (HPG Report 24). Overseas Development Institute (ODI).
Hashim, L., Hasan, H., & Sinnapan, S. (2007). Australian online newspapers: A website content analysis approach to measuring interactivity. In *18th Australasian Conference on Information Systems (ACIS)* (pp. 533–542).

Heathershaw, J. (2008). Unpacking the liberal peace: The dividing and merging of peacebuilding discourses. *Millennium, 36*(3), 597–621.
Heathershaw, J. (2013). Towards better theories of peacebuilding: Beyond the liberal peace debate. *Peacebuilding, 1*(2), 275–282.
Hertog, K. (2010). *The complex reality of religious peacebuilding: Conceptual contributions and critical analysis.* Lexington Books.
Hester, A. (1973). Theoretical considerations in predicting volume and direction of international information flow. *Gazette, 19*(4), 238–247.
Hoelscher, K., Miklian, J., & Nygård, H. M. (2017). Conflict, peacekeeping, and humanitarian security: Understanding violent attacks against aid workers. *International Peacekeeping, 24*(4), 538–565.
Holper, A., & Kirchhoff, L. (2021). Peace mediation as a balancing act between methodology, power and politics. *Peace Mediation in Germany's Foreign Policy: Uniting Method, Power and Politics, 7*, 21.
Houlihan, E. C., & Bisarya, S. (2021). *Practical considerations for public participation in constitution-building what, when, how and why?* (International IDEA Policy Paper No. 24). International Institute for Democracy and Electoral Assistance (International IDEA).
Humphreys, M. (2003). *Economics and violent conflict.* Harvard University Press.
Hyder, M. (2007). Humanitarianism and the Muslim world. *The Journal of Humanitarian Assistance.* www.jha.ac.
Irrera, D. (2021). Non-state actors and conflict management in proxy wars. In *Oxford research encyclopedia of international studies.* https://doi.org/10.1093/acrefore/9780190846626.013.641
Iyengar, S. (1991). *Is anyone responsible?* University of Chicago Press.
Jost, P., & Koehler, C. (2021). Who shapes the news? Analyzing journalists' and organizational interests as competing influences on biased coverage. *Journalism, 22*(2), 484–500.
Jun, H. W., & Reiterer, M. (2021). Preventive diplomacy and crisis management in EU–Korea security relations. In *EU–Korea Security relations* (pp. 98–120). Routledge.
Karlsrud, J. (2017). *The UN at war: Peace operations in a new era.* Springer.
Kenkel, K. M. (2013). Five generations of peace operations: from the "thin blue line" to "painting a country blue". *Revista Brasileira de Política Internacional, 56*(1), 122–143.
Khan, D. (2021). Political economy of uneven state spatiality: Conflict, class, and institutions in the postcolonial state of Pakistan. *Rethinking Marxism, 33*(1), 52–70.
Kim, J. Y. (2017). *Rethinking development finance.* World Bank.
Kinder, D. R. (1998). Communication and opinion. *Annual Review of Political Science, 1*(1), 167–197.

Kitzinger, J. (2000). Media templates: Patterns of association and the (re)construction of meaning over Time. *Media, Culture & Society, 22*(1), 61–84.
Korostelina, K. (2007). *Social identity and conflict: Structures, dynamics, and implications*. Palgrave Macmillan US.
Koser, K. (2007). Addressing internal displacement in peace processes, peace agreements and peace-building. *IDP Newsletter*.
Krippendorff, K. (2004). *Content analysis*. Sage.
Lederach, J. (1997). *Building peace: Sustainable reconciliation in divided societies*. Institute of Peace Press.
Lee, S. T., & Maslog, C. C. (2005). War or peace journalism? Asian newspaper coverage of conflicts. *Journal of Communication, 55*(2), 311–329.
Lehmann, C., & Masterson, D. (2014). *Emergency economies: The impact of cash assistance in Lebanon, an impact evaluation of the 2013–14 winter cash assistance program for Syrian Refugees in Lebanon*. International Rescue Committee.
Lemay-Hébert, N. (2009). Statebuilding without nation-building? Legitimacy, state failure and the limits of the institutionalist approach. *Journal of Intervention and Statebuilding, 3*(1), 21–45.
Li, Z., & Khalaf, T. (2012). Picturing terrorism through Arabic lenses: A comparative analysis of Aljazeera and Al Arabia. *Asian Journal of Communication, 22*(5), 433–348.
Liotta, P. H., & Owen, T. (2006). Why human security. *Whitehead Journal of Diplomacy & International Relations, 7*, 37.
Llewellyn, J. J., & Philpott, D. (2014). *Restorative justice, reconciliation, and peacebuilding*. Oxford University Press.
Masmoudi, M. (1979). The new world information order. *Journal of Communication, 29*(2), 172–179.
Matanock, A. M. (2017). *Electing peace: From civil conflict to political participation*. Cambridge University Press.
Mattinen, H., & Ogden, K. (2006). Cash-based interventions: Lessons from southern Somalia. *Disasters, 30*(3), 297–315.
Maweu, J., & Mare, A. (2021). Introduction. Changing the tide: Re-examining the interplay of media, conflict and peacebuilding in Africa. In *Media, conflict and peacebuilding in Africa* (pp. 1–16). Routledge
McAuliffe, P. (2017). Transitional opportunity? How peace negotiations and power-sharing impede root cause approaches. In *Transformative transitional justice and the malleability of post-conflict states*. Edward Elgar Publishing.
McCandless, E. (2013). Wicked problems in peacebuilding and statebuilding: Making progress in measuring progress through the new deal. *Global Governance, 19*, 227.

Mccombs, M., Llamas, J., López-Escobar, E., & Rey Lennon, F. (1997). Candidate images in Spanish elections: Second-level agenda-setting effects. *Journalism & Mass Communication Quarterly, 74*, 703–717.

Mccombs, M., & Shaw, D. (1972). The agenda-setting function of Mass Media. *Public Opinion Quarterly, 36*, 176–187.

McCombs, M., & Valenzuela, S. (2020). *Setting the agenda: Mass media and public opinion*. Wiley.

McMillan, S. J. (2000). The microscope and the moving target: The challenge of applying content analysis to the world wide web. *Journalism and Mass Communication Quarterly, 77*(1), 80–98.

Mohammadi, A. (1997). *International communication and globalization*. Sage.

Mukhammadsidiqov, M. (2020). The importance of regulating the relationship between the state and religion in ensuring the stability of society. *The Light of Islam, 2020*(2), 12–17.

Murphy, R. (2007). *UN peacekeeping in Lebanon, Somalia and Kosovo: operational and legal issues in practice*. Cambridge University Press.

Mwagiru, N. (2016). *An inquiry into the nature of effective dialogue and discourse and peacebuilding through leadership*.

Nohrstedt, S. A., & Ottosen, R. (2014). *New wars, new media and new war journalism: professional and legal challenges in conflict reporting*. Nordicom.

Nsia-Pepra, K. (2016). *UN robust peacekeeping: Civilian protection in violent civil wars*. Springer.

Odendaal, A. (2011). The role of political dialogue in peacebuilding and statebuilding: An interpretation of current experience. *Working group on political dialogue of the international dialogue on peacebuilding and statebuilding*. http://www.hiwar-watani.org/uploads/1/5/2/3/15238886/a_odendaal_political_dialogue.pdf.

Olaifa, O. (2017). Curbing violent extremism through peace building in Nigeria. *Journal of US-China Public Administration, 14*(4), 221–223.

Overseas Development Institute (ODI) and the Center for Global Development (CGD). (2015). *Doing cash differently: How cash transfers can transform humanitarian aid*.

Özerdem, A., Akgül-Açıkmeşe, S., & Liebenberg, I. (Eds.). (2021). *Routledge handbook of conflict response and leadership in Africa*. Routledge.

Paden, J. N. (2015). *Religion and conflict in Nigeria*. US Institute of Peace.

Paffenholz, T. (2009). Understanding peacebuilding theory: Management, resolution and transformation. *Journal of Peace Research and Action, 14*(2), 4–6.

Paffenholz, T. (2013). International peacebuilding goes local: Analyzing Lederach's conflict transformation theory and its ambivalent encounter with 20 years of practice. *Peacebuilding*. https://doi.org/10.1080/21647259.2013.783257

Paffenholz, T. (2021). Perpetual Peacebuilding: A new paradigm to move beyond the linearity of liberal peacebuilding. *Journal of Intervention and Statebuilding*, 15(3), 367–385.

Paulmann, J. (2013). Conjunctures in the history of international humanitarian aid during the twentieth century. *Humanity: An International Journal of Human Rights, Humanitarianism, and Development*, 4(2), 215–238.

Pavelka, J. (2014). The factors affecting the presentation of events and the media coverage of topics in the mass media. *Procedia-Social and Behavioral Sciences*, 140, 623–629.

Pia, E., & Diez, T. (2007). conflict and human rights: A theoretical framework (SHUR Working Paper Series).

Pondy, L. R. (1967). Organizational conflict: Concepts and models. *Administrative Science Quarterly*, 12(2), 296–320. https://doi.org/10.2307/239 1553

Pongracz, S. (2015). *Value for money of cash transfers in emergencies: Lebanon Case Study*. DFID.

Pruitt, B., & Thomas, P. (2007). *Democratic dialogue: A handbook for practitioners*. International IDEA.

Pugh, M., Cooper, N., & Goodhand, J. (2005). War economies in a regional context: Challenges of transformation. *African Security Review*, 14(4), 128.

QUNO. (2015). Reconciliation—Transforming relationships in divided societies. *UNITAR Workshop on Reconciliation & Peacebuilding*.

Ramsbotham, O., & Woodhouse, T. (2013). *Peacekeeping and conflict resolution*. Routledge.

Rantanen, T. (2004). European news agencies and their sources in the Iraq War coverage. In *Reporting war* (pp. 311–324). Routledge.

Regan, P. M. (2002). *Civil wars and foreign powers: Outside intervention in intrastate conflict*. University of Michigan Press.

Richmond, O. P. (2008). Reclaiming peace in international relations. *Millennium*, 36(3), 439–470.

Richmond, O. P. (2010). A genealogy of peace and conflict theory. In *Palgrave advances in peacebuilding* (pp. 14–38). Palgrave Macmillan.

Richmond, O. P. (2013). The legacy of state formation theory for peacebuilding and statebuilding. *International Peacekeeping*, 20(3), 299–315.

Rosato, S. (2021). *Intentions in great power politics: Uncertainty and the roots of conflict*. Yale University Press.

Rosenthal, C. (2015). Reconsidering agenda setting and intermedia agenda setting from a global perspective: a cross-national comparative agenda setting test. *Londres: Media@ LSE*.

Rozanov, A., Kharlamova, J., & Shirshikov, V. (2021). The role of fake news in conflict escalation: A theoretical overview. *available at SSRN 3857007*.

Ryan, C. (1991). *What's newsworthy? In Prime time activism: Media strategies for grassroots organizing* (pp. 31–52). South End Press.
Saif, A. (2015). *Yemen crisis: what role for the EU*. Accessed on March 13, 2017 from http://www.europarl.europa.eu/RegData/etudes/IDAN/2015/534990/EXPO_IDA(2015)534990_EN.pdf
Sargent, W. M. (2016). *Civilizing peace building: twenty-first century global politics*. Routledge.
Schaefer, C. D. (2010). Local practices and normative frameworks in peacebuilding. *International Peacekeeping, 17*(4), 499–514.
Scheufele, D. A. (2000). Agenda-setting, priming, and framing revisited. Another look at cognitive effects of political communication. *Mass Communication & Society, 3*, 297–316.
Semetko, H. A., & Valkenburg, P. M. (2000). Framing European politics: A content analysis of press and television news. *Journal of Communication, 50*(2), 93–109.
Shoemaker, P. J., Chang, T. K., & Brendlinger, N. (1986). Deviance as a predictor of newsworthiness: Coverage of international events in the U.S. media. In M. L. McLaughlin (Ed.), *Communication Yearbook*, 10. Sage.
Shoemaker, P. J., & Reese, S.D. (1995). *Mediating the message: Theories of influences on mass media content*. Longman.
Smet, S. (2010). Freedom of expression and the right to reputation: Human rights in conflict. *American University of International Law Review, 26*, 183.
Smith, P. M. (1991). *How CNN fought the war*. Birch Lane Press.
Sobel, M. R., & Riffe, D. (2015). US linkages in New York Times coverage of Nigeria, Ethiopia and Botswana (2004–13): Economic and strategic bases for news. *International Communication Research Journal, 50*(1), 3–23.
Spence, R. (2006). *Post-conflict peacebuilding: Who determines the peace? Governance and stability in the Pacific*. University of the Sunshine Coast.
Summers, H. G. (1995). *Persian Gulf War Almanac*. United States: Facts on File.
Terpstra, N., Willems, R., Frerks, G., & Chang Pico, T. (2014). *What the new deal can learn from the human security approach: Scoping study on human security—A multi-level grounded approach towards the new deal*.
Terry, F. (2011). The International Committee of the Red Cross in Afghanistan: Reasserting the neutrality of humanitarian action. *International Review of Red Cross, 93*, 173.
Thomas, K. W. (1992). Conflict and conflict management: Reflections and update. *Journal of Organizational Behavior, 13*(3), 265–274. http://www.jstor.org/stable/2488472
Tschirgi, N. (2015). Bridging the chasm between Domestic and international approaches to peacebuilding: Conceptual and institutional tools. *RCCS*

Annual Review. A Selection from the Portuguese Journal Revista Crítica de Ciências Sociais, (7). https://doi.org/10.4000/rccsar.605

UK National Audit Office. (2011). *Transferring cash and assets to the poor*. Report by the Comptroller and Auditor General. HC 1587, Session 2010–2012.

UN. (2019, July 31). *Implementing a cash transfer project in Yemen*. https://yemen.un.org/en/19047-implementing-cash-transfer-project

United Nations Office for the Coordination of Humanitarian Affairs (OCHA). (2020). Global humanitarian overview 2020. *United Nations-Coordinated support to people affected by disaster and conflict*. (pp. 4–85). OCHA.

Vahabi, M. (2009). A critical review of strategic conflict theory and socio-political instability models. *Revue D'économie Politique, 119*(6), 817–858.

Van Nieuwkerk, A. (2021). Peacekeeping and security through the African Union. In *Conflict resolution and global justice* (pp. 148–167). Routledge.

Van Tongeren, P. (2013). Potential cornerstone of infrastructures for peace? How local peace committees can make a difference. *Peacebuilding, 1*(1), 39–60.

Veneklasen, L. (2006). Last word–how does change happen. *Development, 49*(1), 155–161.

Vicente, P. N. G. (2013). *International News reporting in the multidimensional network: The socio-demographics, professional culture and newswork of foreign correspondents working across Sub-Saharan Africa* (Doctoral dissertation, Universidade NOVA de Lisboa (Portugal).

Whalan, J. (2013). *How peace operations work: Power, legitimacy, and effectiveness*. Oxford University Press.

Wildeman, J., & Swan, E. (2021). What lies ahead? Canada's engagement with the Middle East Peace Process and the Palestinians: An Introduction. *Canadian Foreign Policy Journal, 27*(1), 1–20.

Wolfsfeld, G., & Gadi, W. (1997). *Media and political conflict: News from the Middle East* (Vol. 10). Cambridge University Press.

Wood, E. J. (2003). Review essay: CIvil wars: what we don't know. *Global Governance, 9*(2), 247–260

Yin, R. K. (2009). *Case study research: Design and methods* (4th ed.). Sage.

CHAPTER 3

Wars and EU's Peace Interventions in the International Setting: Yemen Versus Afghanistan and Ethiopia

Moosa Elayah and Bakeel Alzandani

As we move deeper into a wider exploration of National Dialogues, we can keep in mind the theoretical, conceptual, and methodological foundation laid in Chapter 2. We discussed the nature and meaning of the term "conflict" and the other side of the same coin "peacebuilding." While conflict can manifest in different ways and has various motivations, it was established that it is "a struggle or contest between people with opposing needs, ideas, beliefs, values, or goals." Regardless of the cause of the conflict, it is observed that it tends to become a societal threat characterised by insecurity and instability. As touched upon earlier, some of the essential terms we will delineate in this text are peacebuilding, peacemaking, peace enforcement, dialogue, political dialogue, agenda setting, and media framing. Among these, peacebuilding is a well-known, albeit difficult to define concept. However, it does not differ much in theory from the concepts of conflict resolution, National Dialogues, peacemaking, and peacekeeping. Building upon the foundation laid by Johan Galtung, the idea of peacebuilding has undergone great transformation and transmogrification over the years. Although these concepts include a variety of processes and techniques for conflict resolution, it is agreed

© The Author(s), under exclusive license to Springer Nature Switzerland AG 2022
M. Elayah, *Europe and the MENA Region*,
https://doi.org/10.1007/978-3-030-98835-7_3

upon that dialogue is an integral function of any of these processes. While the notion of dialogue entails a wide scope of methods, from high-level negotiations and mediation to community attempts at reconciliation, the main objective is to arrive at practical and peaceful solutions to ongoing clashes and conflicts. At its core, its aim is to address the root of the conflict, in order to build consensus and move forward with a shared vision of the future.

Over the years, the world has witnessed numerous National Dialogues in countries dealing with conflicts and civil wars. Some of these dialogues have changed people's lives socially, politically, and economically; for example, the Tunisian NDC (see Chapter 4) (Murray & Stignant, 2021). Some countries have also suffered from what can be described as "dialogue fatigue" and "dialogue cynicism" (Elayah et al., 2020a). This is a clear indicator of too many "dialogues" that are perceived as having produced little or no change. Some have even "done harm" by undermining the trust in dialogue (Siebert, 2016). Notwithstanding, this chapter addresses this issue by adopting the first (international) multi-level analytical approach. Utilising an international comparative approach, the Yemeni NDC that took place in 2013, is compared to the cases of Afghanistan and Ethiopia. This chapter also highlights the lessons learnt from these dialogues as core elements of state-building in fragile states. Consequently, this chapter contributes to the existing concepts of National Dialogues within peacebuilding literature that have remained under-theorised. In fragile states, dialogues have been defined as efforts by national actors and the international community including the EU to respond to violent conflict in order to build a national vision in fragile contexts (Odendaal, 2011). From an international comparative perspective, this chapter also contributes to understanding the political reconciliation and National Dialogue processes of countries, with different ideological parties and different ethnic backgrounds, such as religious and tribal systems.

We will begin with a comparative case study of the situation in Yemen and Afghanistan, discussing the strength and weak points of each case, and then move onto the important lessons learned from both cases. After that, this chapter will present a comparative case study of Yemen and Ethiopia, with both cases' dynamic and weak points, along with the lessons learnt.

YEMEN-AFGHANISTAN COMPARATIVE CASE STUDY

With the end of the American-EU armed operations in 2000–2001, in collaboration with NATO, which toppled the Taliban regime in Afghanistan, a political dialogue transpired between the different Afghan armed powers, excluding the Taliban which was classified as a terrorist group (Berdal, 2016). The goal was to prevent a future armed conflict between the different ethnic or religious groups, which would ignite chaos (Bird & Marshall, 2011). This was the first step in the national political reconciliation and appeasement in Afghanistan (Berdal, 2019). From a narrow scope, that was "a successful step, where representatives from around Afghanistan came to vote for the Loya Jigra" (ICG, 2002). This was a crucial step in facilitating a dialogue amid different people who support different ideological parties and with different ethnic backgrounds (Papagianni, 2013). Huge obstacles awaited the future of this new country—social, political, ideological, and economic. The presence of religious and tribal leaders further escalated these obstacles, for they were a part of the ongoing warring (Goodson, 2011). Furthermore, they were not fit to lead the new phase due to their low educational levels and their poor political practices and knowledge (Murray, 2007). For drafting a new constitution that would attempt to resolve the country's conflict, build a national army, refresh the moribund economy, collect all deadly arms, and negotiate reconciliation, a professional team was required that had no corrupt past and that embodied trustworthiness (Quie, 2012). The Afghan people had suffered for a long time from external and internal wars and instability. This affected their social life and destroyed the infrastructure of the country and, thus, they needed a qualified committee to formulate solutions for this burdensome inheritance, rather than another conflict to put them back into chaos (Fazilat, 2020).

It became clear that the political reforms in Afghanistan were a thing to move forward with, especially as US and the EU considered them to be a crucial defence mechanism against the war on terrorism (Mihalka, 2017). In itself, this was not an easy step to execute in the absence of the requirements for a smooth democratic transition—this includes the fallen economic state, the lack of effective institutions, and the high percentage of illiteracy (Dandeker, 2020). According to the UNICEF/CSO MICS, "Only 28.7 per cent of Afghans over the age of 15 can read and write. The current primary enrolment ratio is estimated to be about 54.4 per cent, girls' primary school enrolment is still only 40.5 per cent of the total. So not only are the rates of literacy and primary enrolment extremely low, but they are also skewed towards male literacy" (UNDP, 2004).

Education was not the only impediment. International reports indicated that Afghanistan was among the world's least structured countries in most fields—economy, health, roads, electricity, state institutions, and safety. These factors need much discussion, but the focus will be on the National Dialogue that took place after the American invasion of Afghanistan, and how it differs from or is similar to the Yemeni case based on three dimensions—Dynamic Points, Weak Points, and Mutual Lessons—illustrated in different tables in the text (Khan & Rahman, 2020).

Strength Points of the Yemeni and Afghanistan Cases

Afghanistan's dynamic points are embodied in the large support it has received from the west (Dirksen, 2019), which has aimed to present itself as a new model of support for the Islamic world—for countries that have suffered tyranny and injustice (Farhadi, 2020). This was a hopeful step towards motivating other countries in the Middle East to strive towards a democratic transformation (Paragi, 2019). This support from the EU and US was not only political; it impacted the energy field and economy development. It also had a role in the participation of all societal sectors including women, who were represented in the parliament for the first time in the history of Afghanistan—something that was illegal in the past (Banerjee, 2017). Furthermore, the EU and US supported early democratic elections through parliament and drafting a constitution that incorporated all sectors of society—except the Taliban, which was considered a supporter of terrorism (Larson, 2021). The EU and US also drove the political forces in Afghanistan into identifying the hindrances to political reforms so that they could be resolved (Giustozzi & Ibrahimi, 2017). US and the EU tried to strengthen the state's central government through training their armed forces to assure the state's control of all the state's territories, besides encouraging the different armed groups to give up their weaponry in exchange for their participation in the political affairs of Afghanistan (Suhrke, 2007).

Yemen was being monitored by the international community after the upheaval of 2011, when the regime of President Saleh, who had controlled political and economic life in Yemen for over thirty years, was toppled (Fraihat, 2016). The international community encouraged the Yemeni people to take political resolutions and end the confrontations between the different political, revolutionary, and traditional groups (Hill, 2017). This was assisted by the Gulf countries' initiative in Yemen, which came to resolve the prominent internal disagreements via a two-year road map, wherein a two-sided government would be formed, accompanied by a National Dialogue with the involvement of all societal segments including young people and women (Omairan, 2021). Although the Western media reported that the international support was high, it was not sufficient (in comparison to Afghanistan). The countries supporting Yemen only intervened through issuing resolutions, which were not executed even after the capital city, Sana'a, had fallen under the control of the Houthi militia group (Elayah et al., 2020a). This would not have happened were it not for the support of the former Yemeni president, Saleh, who facilitated the way for the Houthis—this very act later became a factor in the failure of the National Dialogue, which almost reached a solution towards the end of 2014 (Elayah et al., 2017). Ultimately, neither the EU and US nor the Gulf countries provided the necessary support for the central state/government.

Despite regional and international support for the National Dialogue in Yemen, it did not live up to that of Afghanistan, essentially because of the role of US, EU, and NATO. US's great aid in Afghanistan might have given it the right to be there after it had invaded the country in 2001 and identified the country as a host for terrorism and Al-Qaida (Elayah et al., 2020b). Thus, the EU and US intervention was effective and continuous. Whereas, there was no real intervention in Yemen; there were only resolutions that had been issued but left unimplemented at the negotiation table Elayah, 2015). There was also no real developmental aid in Yemen or in the political process, which is considered a crucial factor in the success of any dialogue, especially economic development, which is seen as the other face of the political process, as it brings people hope and motivates them to continue (Elayah, 2014; Elayah & Fenttiman, 2021).

The participation of all sectors of society in the National Dialogue is similar to that of Afghanistan (as shown in Table 3.1) and is a dynamic point. Whereas, Afghanistan was able to exclude the terrorising groups, such groups were included in the Yemeni dialogue, as they were one of the reasons behind Yemen's destruction for three decades (Elayah et al., 2020b). Table 3.1 also illustrates how identifying the countries' challenges was a positive factor that pushed the new participating powers

Table 3.1 Strength Points (DP) in the Yemeni and Afghanistan cases

SP	Yemen	Afghanistan
I	The local, regional, and international support for the National Dialogue was extensive	Great international support in various fields, including development, rights, and freedom sectors
II	Promotion of the idea of dialogue as the only way out—as opposed to the option of war	Participation of all political sectors in the transitional phase—even warlords, except the Taliban
III	Diversity in selection of the 565 members of the dialogue conference, including all political spheres, as well as civil society organisations, women's organisations, and young people (except Jihadist groups) Qaeda)	The involvement of civil society and women's organisations for the first time in the history of modern Afghanistan
IV	Drafting a new constitution that guarantees a peaceful transfer of power	Drafting a new constitution where all forces are involved in building a new Afghanistan
V	Inclusion of all issues in the discussions that had been ignored for many years (i.e. South issue, Sa'ada, and marginalised groups)	Strengthening of the central authority to promote peace and security, along with economic development and political reform[b]
VI	Considering issues that are most important and challenging for the future of Yemen, post 2011	Activating the principle of justice and equality as a fundamental value in the National Dialogue

[a]Women entering Parliament and the administrative organ of the state was illegal in the past
[b]The principle of disarmament of all factions and enabling the state to control the whole country

to sit around the table and negotiate. However, it was hard to implement the same in reality because the central government lacked the power (Gaston, 2014). For instance, the restructuring of the army and security armed forces, the incrimination of corrupt people, the withdrawal of weapons, and the resolutions of Sa'ada and South conflicts were complicated processes, facing a lot of resistance to their execution (Feierstein, 2017). Simply, this was due to the fact that the traditional forces that possess the power to change things were not ready to deliver the means to the new agents, who wanted to overturn the inheritance (Zyck, 2014).

WEAK POINTS OF THE YEMENI AND AFGHANISTAN CASES

In the cases of Afghanistan and Yemen, the dynamic points were accompanied by weak points leading to a pullback from the National Dialogues and reconciliations. Table 3.2 shows a comparison of the weak points off the two cases. In Afghanistan, the war did not leave room for any agreements owing to the old regime's interests. And the same happened in Yemen, where the traditional powers fought against any reform process or National Dialogue that would take away their positions and turn them into mere political placeholders that have to follow current politics and not take advantage of the country's resources to reach and obtain unconstitutional goals (Pelham et al., 2021). Also, the regional interventions in both cases were essentially negative because they put their own interests before those of Afghanistan and Yemen (Barnes, 2017). Needless to mention the ideological rivalry in both cases, which led to armed confrontations in both countries. The real challenge in both Afghanistan and Yemen was the absence of a clear and transparent strategy for each phase of the dialogue—to help both the dialogue participants and the general public deal with the current situation (Papagianni, 2013). This

Table 3.2 Weak Points (WP) in the Yemeni and Afghanistan cases

WP	Yemen	Afghanistan
I	The issue of transforming the political system from the simple (central) system to the federal (composite) system	The great influence of the warlords, who constitute a real challenge to political forces in dialogue and the overall reconciliation process
II	The size of the problems versus the outcomes did not meet the ambitions	Some regional intervention forces fed into the process of the struggle between political forces
III	Difficulty of implementing outputs of the dialogue, due to the absence of guarantees	Lack of educational infrastructure in the Afghan society made it hard to recognise events and thus support the right direction
IV	Traditional elites' conflict with the new revolutionary forces on the future of the new state	The impact of the ideological dimension, which had a strong presence in the dialogue
V	South dilemma issue: failed to agree on a common formula	The absence of a clear strategy for the post-Taliban at the national level
VI	Establish a National Dialogue in the light of the almost complete absence of security in Yemen. Also, the weakness of the central government	Financial corruption cases, which involved all sectors of the state including political elites, led to a lack of confidence
VII	Rejection of foreign intervention, which was rejected by some powers	

was especially important in countries where corruption had destructively led to a bankrupt economy.

Afghanistan and Yemen faced difficulties in attaining resolutions as they dealt with many complications. It is true that Afghanistan obtained more support from US and the EU, and thus was able to continue its dialogue more successfully (Benchoff, 2012). However, Yemen fell into the swamp of military conflicts both politically and religiously (Mao & Gady, 2021). These negative factors, according to many writers like Maaß (2006), Stanekzai (2008), Waldman (2015), and Johnson (2010), were weak points, which the international community should be aware of in order to avoid such complications in the future peace dialogues. Although the Afghanistan transition came about rather slowly, it was relatively successful considering the usual difficulties a country of that region undergoes in such a process.

Yemen faced a similar situation with regards to the corruption of the political elite and the influence of religious and tribal groups that were practising a larger role than that of the state, not to mention the fragile economic situation of the two countries, which have been classified among the poorest in the world (Avis, 2020). The two countries have also suffered greatly from the activities of terrorist groups, leading to internal wars that have exhausted the national economy (Feierstein, 2017). Yemen's National Dialogue did not face the same conflicts that Afghanistan encountered on the issues of war on terrorism, internal armed conflicts, and the cohesion of the state institutions (Transfeld, 2016). Nevertheless, social, and religious structures were similar to a large extent because of the influence of those groups in economic and political affairs (Kendall, 2021).

Yemen's National Dialogue brought all the major powers to the dialogue table. It was accepted by all except a few factions from the Southern movement, but these didn't have enough of an impact to thwart the dialogue (Elayah et al., 2020b). The dialogue consisted of 565 delegates representing all the colours of the political spectrum, and some of the forces of civil society as well as young people and women, spread across nine teams, each of which was entrusted with a specific task (Elayah et al., 2020b). Table 3.3 shows the number and duties of the Yemeni national dialogue teams:

The Yemeni dialogue began on 18 March 2013, and it was scheduled to end within one month. Instead, it was delayed for another nine months and ended in January 2014 (Hamidi, 2015). There were many complaints

Table 3.3 The core working groups within the Yemeni NDC 2013

1	2	3	4	5	6	7	8	9
Southern issue team[a]	Team of Sa'ada Issue[b]	National reconciliation and transitional justice team	State-building and constitution team	Good governance team	The independence of the bodies and institutions team	The rights and freedoms team	Comprehensive development team	Re-army and security building team

[a]Members of the Southern movement did not agree to represent themselves as a single bloc, and many analysts considered that it was divided into four factions with each component following a different leadership
[b]Houthi militias

Source National Dialogue Conference Republic of Yemen, Sana'a (info@ndc.ae)

about the length of the dialogue; however, many researchers have indicated that the true reason for the complaints was the withdrawal of the Houthi group and the party of the former president Ali Saleh, and their rejection of some of the dialogue's outcomes (Zyck, 2014). Moreover, the withdrawal of the Southern movement led to a delay in the declaration of the conclusion of the dialogue. Besides, some observers stated that the Yemeni president, Abdurabu Mansoor, moved rather slowly and thus weakened the dialogue (Elayah et al., 2020b). In reality, the National Dialogue needed more time, a strategy, and guarantees from all participants to assure a resolution (Elayah et al., 2020b). From the beginning, there were issues with the technical committee that was assigned to organise the National Dialogue. Many political and academic experts criticised its composition, that it should have consisted of experts rather than members from the different political parties. This committee had a conflict of interest and eventually failed to achieve its ultimate goal, as told to the researchers by the pollsters.

Despite the weak composition of the committee, the dialogue should have been accepted by all, for it was the only way to save the country from the swamp of civil war and to achieve the goals of both the traditional and revolutionary powers (as told to the researchers by the pollsters). The ultimate goal was to guarantee a political future that includes effective participation from all segments. For instance, the revolutionary sectors accepted the dialogue as they knew that its failure would cause the failure of their revolution (as relayed during pollster interviews). They realised that there was a regional and international conspiracy to quash their revolution. Likewise, the traditional sectors realised that the dialogue was the only way to assure a fair political process. Overall, they both knew that the dialogue would form the dynamic factor to help Yemen avoid the ghost of civil war.

Table 3.1 shows some vital dynamic points in Yemen's National Dialogue. One is that the alternative of the dialogue is war. Another is that the variety in the members of the dialogue assured that everyone had a chance to participate in drafting the future of the new Yemen—the dialogue consisted of 565 members from different political sectors, including young people and women, except al-Qaeda as it was classified as a terrorist group. Furthermore, the issues discussed were the most challenging since the protests of 2011. According to experts, another supportive point was the regional and international support, as it was well-received, as told to the researchers by the pollsters. Furthermore, the agenda of the dialogue examined issues which were considered incriminating to talk about before 2011, like the case of Sa'ada and the South. For instance, writer and researcher Sami Noman indicated in his blog that the Yemeni dialogue helped to discuss cases that were unspoken of for a long time. Another writer, Fatima Alaghraby, stated in her blog that the National Dialogue was a true opportunity to build a modern Yemen through its people who come from different sectors and with different ideologies united by the notions of justice, equality, and democratic rule (Elayah et al., 2020b).

These were a number of points that gave hope to the National Dialogue—at least in its early days. From Table 3.1, we can see the commonality between the positive and dynamic factors between the Yemeni and Afghanistan cases. This hope, however, did not last long, because some of the traditional powers felt that its continuation would deprive them of the privileges they had enjoyed for decades. Furthermore, the Houthi group realised that transforming Yemen into a federal state of six regions would reduce the likelihood of them reaching their dream and finding their own state (Williams et al., 2017).

The problematic inheritance that awaited the dialogue had its effects on the dialogue participants, as each party tried to represent their case regardless of the national interest. This attitude led to a division between the political components, and in fact some components began to withdraw from the dialogue. They actually started to declare their rejection of the dialogue under the causes of the Southern case and that of federalization. The Southern case was a challenging one, as some southerners wanted independence for the south and others wanted the success of the dialogue and the promise of a united nation. The idea of federal states came to be seen as a suitable solution, though some considered it to be a way to divide Yemen into city-states (as conveyed by the pollsters). The revolutionary powers demanded a constitution that would serve an equitable community, not to create new political powers that would topple the National Dialogue. Throughout the National Dialogue Conference, "the tension between traditional conservative elites and those seeking change was evident. The former tried to retain the gains they had made over past decades, while the latter tried to curtail these gains and privileges in an effort to guarantee a modern civil democratic state" (ACRPS, 2014a).

The absence of the central state's authority was quite clear in that sensitive stage, which many analysts saw to be in favour of the political powers that declared resistance to the state and its dialogue. The similarity of this weakness in the central government in both Yemen and Afghanistan formed an insecurity in the continuation of the dialogue. Thus, a number of assassinations started to take place among the participating members in the dialogue. Along with this, terrorist acts also began, and they targeted places such as the defence ministry, which symbolised the last point of authority of the country. Also, confrontations arose in the South between the national army and al-Qaeda.

Both the Yemeni and Afghanistan cases have similarities in the ideological and tribal aspects. In Yemen, this was referred to as the traditional powers, whereas in Afghanistan, this was the warlords, who tried to sustain their authority before they lost to the new democratic powers that were aided by internal and international support. The two cases formed a sample of National Dialogue in a region that had been under political tyranny for decades, to the degree where the peoples of these nations had lost hope for any real change.

Lessons Learned

After studying the Dynamic and Weak points of the two cases, Table 3.4 illustrates vital lessons learned. Among the most important lessons for future peace-making in countries that are similar in their geographic, political, and social aspects are as follows. First and foremost is the continuation of the National Dialogue even when it lasts longer than planned. Second, it is crucial to strengthen the central government, as it constitutes a security issue for the country. Third, the dialogue should prioritise internal interests rather than external, international, and regional interests. It is always beneficial to utilise international economic support as it is necessary for a country seeking a successful democratic transformation to be economically strong and stable to satisfy the needs of the citizens; otherwise, chaos can ensue and threaten the political process (Elayah et al., 2020b). Furthermore, respect of human rights and minority groups will create satisfaction among the public and thus encourage them to support the ongoing political reform. Another area of concern is the participation of young people and women, along with minimising the role of traditional groups (warlords) to balance the legal participation of all. This will assure outside supporters to move towards a real transformation, which will give them greater reason to assist in this process (Elayah et al., 2020b).

Table 3.4 Important lessons (IL) from the Yemeni and Afghanistan cases

IL	Yemen	Afghanistan
I	The process of dialogue should not stop even if it reaches a dead end; it may take many years, but an exit must be found	Maintaining benefit from foreign assistance for dialogue stabilises economic dimension
II	Maintaining the central government's power and its institutions is a guarantee for the continuation of dialogues and implementation of their outputs	Building state institutions and respect for human and minority rights are important to pursue a successful dialogue
III	Preserving the National Dialogue at the national level and avoiding regional and/or international tugging assists in a better national consensus	Every country is a unique case, with a distinct culture, ethnicity, language, and religious practice
IV	Improvement of the economic situation goes hand in hand with political reconciliation	Exclusion of warlords from any political peace process in order to achieve its goals
V	Encouraging the participation of young people and women in the political process downsizes the influence of traditional forces of hegemony	The participation of all segments of society in the National Dialogue process equally, without exclusion, leads to its success
VI	The equal participation of all segments of society in the National Dialogue process, without exclusion, leads to its success	Reconciliation is vital to the success of peace even if it takes many years—ultimately, it will serve better than a civil war
VII	The presence of a documented set of regulations agreed upon and followed by all delegates is vital to binding all to abide by those regulations	The setup of coordination between local political forces and the international community supports dialogue
VIII	Community awareness of the importance of National Dialogue must be accompanied by national media, with the focus on training interlocutors in methods of debate	The building of a coherent electoral system which enhances the confidence of the voter in participation
IX	It is rather beneficial to choose specialised people in different areas of debate rather than random selection	Maintenance of international support in the reconciliation process is indispensable in the long-term
X	Maintenance of the principle of transparency in the National Dialogue will heighten credibility	

It should be mentioned that the process of excluding a sphere of around 70% of the society—young people and women—negatively affects any political reforms within a society. Not taking into account those issues would cause the failure of the dialogue, so every sphere of society must be given the opportunity to participate in the process of the dialogue, as shared in an interview with the respondents within the research team of the Conference on Dialogue, 12/07/2015.

Finally, it could be said that the two cases of Yemen and Afghanistan formed an international concern as they are among the countries most affected by terrorism and chaos—Yemen is a source and Afghanistan a host. Therefore, the international community had a real interest to irradiate this for both its safety and the safety of those countries.

YEMEN-ETHIOPIA: A COMPARATIVE CASE STUDY

The events that occurred in Ethiopia were not too different from those that occurred after the collapse of the Soviet Union and the rise of the US as the dominant superpower in the world in the 1990s. In 1990, the National Frontier of Ethiopia appeared under the leadership of Meles Zenawi and stayed in control until 2012 under unfair parliamentary elections, despite international observance of their wrongdoing, in which Zenawi's party tampered with the outcomes of the elections through military force for the favour of his party (Lahra Smith, 2007). In this case, there was a need for civil organisations to mobilise the society towards protesting the status quo. Without this intervention, elections and political mobilisation would have been in vain and would only have served the ruling party through illegal pathways (Lahra Moremi, 2013; Smith, 2007).

The events that Ethiopia witnessed in 2005 resulted in Zenawi's party detaining more opposition under the claim of unconstitutional acts, and more political exiles. After two years of public resentment, Zenawi finally opened the door for a political reconciliation between his party and the opposition in an attempt to solve the deep issues that were taking the country to a civil war, similar to what Somalia went through (Nunzio, 2014). Lahra Smith asked at the time: "How will the ruling party address citizens who, through their voting, demonstrated that they do not support some or all of the EPRDF's policy positions? In the three years remaining before the next election, scheduled for 2010, can citizens be convinced of the ruling party's sincerity in light of its use of extreme force after the 2005 election?" (Lahra Smith, 2007).

From 1991 until 2013, Ethiopia underwent many phases of change through parliamentary elections, which were often described as unfair. In 2010, though, a new phase of elections began, which was the beginning of change in Ethiopia. There were both dynamic and weak points that led to this change.

DYNAMIC POINTS IN THE YEMEN-ETHIOPIA COMPARATIVE CASE STUDY

Table 3.5 shows the main dynamic points in the Ethiopian reconciliation process, and to what extent it was similar to Yemen. For instance, the law of transitional justice and the compensation of war victims were important for the oppositions to enter a National Dialogue. This was not accepted in Yemen because the former president and his party asked for forgiveness for all former political acts before agreeing to any negotiations. In

Table 3.5 Dynamic Points (DP) in Yemen-Ethiopia comparative case study

DP	Yemen	Ethiopia
I	The local, regional, and international support for the National Dialogues was great	Acceptance of the political forces of the transitional justice, prosecution of perpetrators, and compensation of victims
II	Promotion of the idea of dialogue as the only way out—as opposed to the option of war	Call for a national reconciliation conference included all national forces, regardless of ethnic, religious, or regional background
III	Diversity in selection of the 565 members of the dialogue conference, including all political spheres, as well as civil society organisations, women's organisations, and young people (except jihadist groups like al-Qaeda)	Formation of a transitional government in which everyone, without exception, equally participates
IV	Drafting of a new constitution that guarantees peaceful transfer of power	Rejection of the dominance of one authoritarian party
V	Discussion of issues ignored for many years (i.e. South issue, Saada, and marginalised groups)	Acceptance of the adoption of the federal system to allow all factions equal representation of their ethnic, religious, and regional diversity
VI	Foregrounding issues that are most important and challenging for the future of Yemen, post 2011	Exclusion of politicisation of national identity, according to religion, race, or language. Also, recognition of all nationalities equally: culturally, religiously and linguistically, without dominance of any one faction over the other (Fiseha, 2015)

fact, they were forgiven, and this later had a negative effect on the Yemeni dialogue. A common dynamic point in the two cases was the participation of all societal segments in the transitional government, which represented all political powers (Verjee, 2021). Also, the idea of turning Yemen and Ethiopia into federal countries was considered by many scholars a positive move towards a successful transition and peacebuilding (Salisbury, 2015). However, in the case of Yemen, this idea faced many obstacles from the former president and the Houthi militia group. Not politicising the national identity, based on religion, ethnic background, or language, helped shape the recognition of all segments of society as one: "equality, brotherhood, and mutual respect" (Fiseha, 2015). Also, the constitution highlighted that Ethiopia was composed of nations and nationalisms, which assured national rights based on place, ethnicity, language, and the right to self-determination in the future, which was welcomed by Ethiopians:

These dynamic points became a strong motivation for the Ethiopian society, in all its components, towards the building of the country through national reconciliation (Yusuf, 2019). The acceptance of a federal state guaranteed all components of the society participate in the making of the new country (Fiseha, 2015). More than 18 parties and political entities took part in the political transformation of Ethiopia under the slogan of one nation and freedom of expression. The national reconciliation and dialogues in Ethiopia were not an easy task, but the political will of the politicians and the bitter past experiences were a motive to continue the political economic reforms (Elayah et al., 2020b). According to Fiseha (2015), Ethiopia has achieved, in the last two decades, economic growth which surpassed 12%. Also, poverty has decreased from 45% in 1991 to 29% in 2011 (Fiseha, 2015). In the political sphere, the activation of the law of transitional justice, which took warlords to trial through a conventional government, guaranteed social justice. This transformation also transformed the country into 14 regions (later 9 after 5 of them were merged), and this has been considered historic, for it was the only option that presented solutions to conflicts the country had suffered through for decades (Nagar, 2021).

Weak Points in Yemen-Ethiopia Comparative Case Study

Although Ethiopia accomplished great success in political and economic reforms, compared to the neighbouring countries, it also experienced some downfalls, which formed its weak points. Table 3.6 shows the

Table 3.6 Weak Points (WP) in Yemen-Ethiopia comparative case study

WP	Yemen	Ethiopia
I	The issue of transforming the political system from the simple (central) system to the federal (composite) system	The use of military establishment to impose peace by relying solely on force
II	Size of the problems versus the outcomes did not match the ambitions	The elimination of the notion of "People" for the sake of the different ethnicities which threatens the existence of the federal state
III	Difficulty of implementing outputs of the dialogue, due to the absence of guarantees	Failure of government to maintain ability to provide security and the proliferation of weapons around the country
IV	Traditional elites' conflict with the new revolutionary forces on the future of the new state	Minorities that do not rise to the formation of the same in large part under the major threat to the rights of nationalities
V	South dilemma issue: failed to agree on a common formula	Preparing the transition to the federal state was not sufficient according to the opposition because of its weakness and division in the state formation stage
VI	Establish a National Dialogue in the light of the almost complete absence of security in Yemen. Also, the weakness of the central government	Continuation of the ruling party's dominance of the State Administration politically and economically, even if that solved the dilemma as the Federal Constitution was not implemented on ground
VII	Rejection of foreign intervention by some powers	Integrating national identities in one nationality dominated by the issue of the centre, which derived its idea from the former Soviet Union
VIII		Severe shortage of skilled staff and adequate financial resources as a result of the economic decline experienced by the state and the attainment of the public debt of more than $4 billion

common weak factors in Ethiopia and Yemen.

In Ethiopia, national reconciliation was accepted under the condition that there would be free and fair parliamentary elections, inclusive of the ruling party. The transformation faced many obstacles, including the deteriorated economy; in addition, the case of the federalization was protested by the opposition in the beginning because of their weak status at the time (Verjee, 2021). Among the weak factors was the attempt by the ruling party to use its power to exploit the inferior groups, especially in rural areas, with the sole purpose of keeping its policies alive (Kasimbazi & Bamwine, 2021). Furthermore, what made matters worse was the unstable security situation and the spread of weaponry, which gave people the sense of insecurity and danger. In addition, some ethnic groups were concerned about merging all tribal sects under one national identity since they would lose their rights in their distinct ethnicity and would not be able to represent their different sects fairly (Morales al., 2020). Thus, this fear pushed five regions into making one common region.

The Ethiopian case came close to Yemen in the domain of political and civil powers accepting each other for the sake of a national reconciliation aimed at sharing authority and the wealth of the nation. In terms of ethnic divisions, Yemen did not suffer until the Southern movement and Houthi group in Sa'ada felt persecuted and sought a self-governing state (Conveyed in an interview with the respondents within the research team of the Conference on Dialogue, 12/07/2015). A number of politicians believed that the Ethiopian experiment could be applied in the case of Yemen to appease the Southern and Houthi demands. Nevertheless, because Yemen did not suffer from ethnic divisions, it seemed to not assimilate; therefore, other solutions had to be sought for the situation in Yemen. This was analysed by giving the right of participation in the political process to all segments, including women and young people, in order to uphold a transparent approach.

In the case of founding a federal system based on self-ruling regions, there was a discrepancy in the cases of Ethiopia and Yemen. Whereas in Ethiopia there was a common acceptance among all political powers to form a federal state divided into 14 regions, ruled by the new constitution, in Yemen, however, the group of Houthis backed by the former president Ali Saleh, opposed this, justifying their actions by the fact that dividing Yemen into 6 regions would drive constant confrontations and end the country's unity—to the extent that they detained the government and the president, which was described as a coup.

Lessons Learned from Yemen-Ethiopia Comparative Case Study

As shown in Table 3.7, the Ethiopian reconciliation process presents a number of vital lessons to be learned in the field of National Dialogues and reconciliations in similar cases. Primarily, it is crucial to have a timely agenda for the stages of dialogue. This assures people with a sense of transparency and trust on the part of the political representations. This did not happen in Yemen because the Yemeni government took longer than the agreed upon timeframe. This made some powers, namely the Houthi group and the former president's party, rebel against this failure and thus against the dialogue's outcomes. In Ethiopia, the dialogue continued to take place and develop despite differences, whereas in Yemen, the differences brought by Houthi group and the former president's party toppled the dialogue and stopped it from going forward.

The case of Ethiopia presented federalism as a positive mechanism to solve deep-rooted problems that can surface at any given moment (Fiseha, 2015). This cannot be said about Yemen due to the rejection of federalism by some political segments, on the grounds that it would deprive them of their past privileges. Finally, the idea of peaceful coexistence among different ethnic backgrounds proved to be possible in Ethiopia but not in Yemen.

Table 3.7 shows the most important lessons in the Ethiopian case, which should be taken into consideration in achieving successful political and economic reforms, along with enduring peace. The political components in Yemen could have benefitted from the Ethiopian case had they examined its successes. Yemeni politicians failed to realise that the process of transforming into a democratic state is a generational responsibility and not an overnight undertaking. Ethiopia was able to build strong institutions, which paved the way for the historically ignored commoners to move up the ladder to high positions in the government and different state institutions. This was evidenced by the arrival of Mr. Hailemariam Desalegn in the 2013 election to the Presidency of the Ethiopian government, who is from one of the marginalised classes.

Conclusion

From the in-depth comparative case study analyses presented in this chapter, we can discern a number of factors and actors that affected the

Table 3.7 Important lessons (IL) from Yemen-Ethiopia comparative case study

IL	Yemen	Ethiopia
I	The process of dialogue should not stop even if it reaches a dead end; it may take many years, but an exit must be found	Commitment to the transitional period and the specific implementation of its contents creates trust and continues the process of reconciliation
II	Maintaining the central government's power and its institutions is a guarantee for the continuation of dialogues and implementation of their outputs	National approval of dialogue outputs was very important to precede other reforms in spite of all obstacles
III	Preserving the National Dialogue at the national level and avoiding regional and/or international tugging assists in a better national consensus	After more than two decades of practice, the political elites realised that the federal system was a successful option to address the political, economic and ethnic conflicts as an optimal public interest
IV	Improvement of the economic situation goes hand in hand with political reconciliation	The prolonged dominance of some political parties eventually comes to an end as real democracy starts to take shape
V	Encouraging participation of young people and women in the political process downsizes the influence of traditional forces of hegemony	The principle of peaceful coexistence, accepted by all forces, leads to comprehensive economic development in many sectors of the state
VI	The participation of all segments of society in the National Dialogue process equally, without exclusion, leads to its success	
VII	The presence of a documented set of regulations agreed upon and followed by all delegates is vital to ensure all abide by those regulations	
VIII	Community awareness of the importance of National Dialogue must be accompanied by national media, with the focus on training interlocutors in methods of debate	
IX	It is rather beneficial to choose specialised people in different areas of debate rather than random selection	
X	Maintenance of the principle of transparency in the National Dialogue will heighten credibility	

smooth functioning of the dialogue, ranging from time to participation to problematic nature of the dialogue process itself.

In the comparative analysis of Yemen and Afghanistan, it was found that the continuation of the dialogue process is key, even if it overshoots the intended timeframe. It is also important to have a strong central government in place, as it constitutes a crucial security issue for the country. Additionally, the dialogue should go internal over external in terms of its priorities. To achieve a successful democratic evolution, it is important to make use of the international economic aid to be economically sound and ensure the citizens are satisfied, otherwise chaos can impinge on the smooth functioning of the process (Elayah et al., 2020b). Human rights and minority satisfaction also constitute a great part of the process as it encourages various groups to participate and support the reform. Participation and representation of overlooked groups such as young people and women is important for balance and also to diminish the role of traditional groups such as warlords. Overall, these points will ensure a smooth transition, which in turn will present as incentive for support from all groups.

In the comparative study of Yemen and Ethiopia, a timely agenda was a crucial factor in the success of the dialogue. This was not a success in Yemen on part of the Yemeni government taking longer than agreed which made certain powers, such as the Houthi group and the former president's party rebel against the dialogue's outcomes. In Ethiopia, in contrast, the dialogue continued and developed regardless of the differences. In Ethiopia, federalism proved to be a mechanism with positive motivation to solve deep-rooted issues (Fiseha, 2015). However, the same did not stand for Yemen, as some political groups rejected federalism on the ground that they would be deprived of privileges they enjoyed in the past. And the idea of harmonious coexistence of different ethnic background, eventually proved to be successful in Ethiopia but the same was not possible in the case of Yemen.

From this section, we can say that Yemen's NDC had no clear agenda from the beginning, when compared with Afghanistan and Ethiopia. Although it included stakeholders from all segments of Yemeni society, they were confused whether the goals of sitting around a table was for political transformation or to address deep-rooted conflicts. There were some similarities as well as differences between Yemen and the two international cases in this section. However, every dialogue had its own features and approaches, that impacted the implementation process at the end of the dialogue.

References

ACRPS. (2014a). *Outcomes of Yemen's National Dialogue Conference: A step toward conflict resolution and state building*? Arab Center for Research and Policy Studies.

ACRPS. (2014b). *The Comprehensive National Dialogue Conference Draft in Yemen: A step on the way of crisis solving and building state*. Arab Center for Research and Policy Studies.

Avis, W. (2020). International actors' support on inclusive peace processes.

Banerjee, A. (2017). *Violence and female inclusion: Elections and female political participation in Afghanistan*. Georgetown University.

Barnes, C. (2017). Dilemmas of ownership, inclusivity, legitimacy and power. *Towards Transformative National Dialogue Processes, 46*.

Benchoff, P. N. (2012). *Yemen: Preventing the next Afghanistan*. ARMY WAR COLL CARLISLE BARRACKS PA.

Berdal, M. (2016). A mission too far? NATO and Afghanistan, 2001–2014. *Politics, 18*, 3.

Berdal, M. (2019). NATO's landscape of the mind: Stabilisation and state-building in Afghanistan. *Ethnopolitics, 18*(5), 526–543.

Bird, T., & Marshall, A. (2011). *Afghanistan: How the West lost its way*. Yale University Press.

Dandeker, C. (2020). What "Success" means in Afghanistan, Iraq, and Libya. In *How 9/11 changed our ways of war* (pp. 116–148). Stanford University Press.

Dirksen, N. (2019). Afghanistan's altercation: Media influence in Western conflict interventions.

Elayah, M. A. A. (2014). *Donors-promoted public sector reforms in developing countries and the Local Knowledge Syndrome* (Doctoral dissertation, Leiden University).

Elayah, M. A. A. (2015). [Foreign aid effectiveness between the strategic objectives of, and the internal influences within, donor countries] [in Arabic]. *Siyasat Arabiyah* [Arab Policies Journal], *14*.

Elayah, M., & Fenttiman, M. (2021). Humanitarian aid and war economies: The case of Yemen. *Economics of Peace and Security Journal, 16*(1), 52–65.

Elayah, M. A. A., Schulpen, L. W. M., Abu-Osba, B., & Al-Zandani, B. (2017). *Yemen: A forgotten war and an unforgettable country*. Farrar, Straus and Giroux.

Elayah, M., Schulpen, L., van Kempen, L., Almaweri, A., AbuOsba, B., & Alzandani, B. (2020a). National dialogues as an interruption of civil war – The case of Yemen. *Peacebuilding, 8*(1), 98–117.

Elayah, M., van Kempen, L., & Schulpen, L. (2020b). Adding to the controversy? Civil society's evaluation of the national conference dialogue in Yemen. *Journal of Intervention and Statebuilding, 14*(3), 431–458.
Farhadi, A. (2020). *Countering violent extremism by winning hearts and minds*. Springer International Publishing.
Fazilat, S. M. (2020). *Afghanistan civil war and ethnic conflicts: 1992–2018* (Doctoral dissertation).
Feierstein, G. (2017). Is there a path out of the Yemen conflict? Why it matters. *Prism, 7*(1), 16–31.
Fiseha, A. (2015). *Dealing with territorial cleavages in constitutional transitions: Case study of Ethiopia*. Available at: http://www.constitutionnet.org/files/dealing_with_territorial_cleavages_in_constitutional_transitions_-_confer ence_outline_24_september.pdf
Fraihat, I. (2016). *Unfinished revolutions*. Yale University Press.
Gaston, E. (2014). *Process lessons learned in Yemen's national dialogue*. US Institute of Peace.
Giustozzi, A., & Ibrahimi, N. (2017). From new dawn to quicksand: The political economy of statebuilding in Afghanistan. In *Political economy of statebuilding* (pp. 246–262). Routledge.
Goodson, L. P. (2011). *Afghanistan's endless war: State failure, regional politics, and the rise of the Taliban*. University of Washington Press.
Hamidi, H. (2015). A comparative analysis of the post-Arab spring national dialogues in Tunisia and Yemen. *African Journal on Conflict Resolution, 15*(3), 11–35.
Hill, G. (2017). *Yemen endures: Civil war*. Oxford University Press.
International Crisis Group. (2002). *The Loya Jirga: One small step forward?* Available at: http://www.crisisgroup.org/en/regions/asia/south-asia/afghan istan/B017-the-loya-jirga-one-small-step-forward.aspx
Johnson, T. H. (2010). Religious figures, insurgency, and jihad in southern Afghanistan. In *Who speaks for Islam* (pp. 41–65). Stanford University Press.
Kasimbazi, E., & Bamwine, F. (2021). Resolving the grand Ethiopian renaissance dam conflict through the African Union Nexus approach. *Nile and Grand Ethiopian renaissance dam* (pp. 61–78). Springer.
Kendall, E. (2021). Jihadi militancy and Houthi insurgency in Yemen. In *Routledge handbook of US counterterrorism and irregular warfare operations* (pp. 83–94). Routledge.
Khan, H. U., & Rahman, G. (2020). Pakistan's aid to Afghanistan since 2001 and its prospects for state building in Afghanistan. *FWU Journal of Social Sciences, 14*(3), 114–130.
Larson, A. (2021). *Democracy in Afghanistan: Amid and beyond conflict*.
Mao, J., & Gady, A. A. A. (2021). The legitimacy of military intervention in Yemen and its impacts. *Beijing Law Review, 12*(2), 560–592.

Maaß, C. D. (2006). National reconciliation in Afghanistan. Conflict history and the search for an Afghan approach. *Internationales Asienforum*, *37*(1/2), 5.

Mihalka, M. (2017). Conclusion: Values and interests: European support for the intervention in Afghanistan and Iraq. In *Old Europe, New Europe and the US* (pp. 281–304). Routledge.

Morales, A. J. M., Ramírez, A. O. M., Trejo, E. M., González, G. O., López, O. A. R., & Angulo, P. S. (2020). *Progress, death and conflict: An Ethiopian possible future*.

Moremi, P. R. (2013). *Legal dimension of the role of African Union and United Nations in conflict resolution in Africa* (Doctoral dissertation, The Open University of Tanzania).

Murray, T. (2007). Police-building in Afghanistan: A case study of civil security reform. *International Peacekeeping*, *14*(1), 108–126.

Murray, E., & Stigant, S. (2021). *National dialogues in peacebuilding and transitions*.

Nagar, M. F. (2021). The emergence of an Empire and evolution of Federal Democracy in Ethiopia. In *The road to democratic development statehood in Africa* (pp. 97–115). Palgrave Macmillan.

Nunzio, M. D. (2014). 'Do not cross the red line': The 2010 general elections, dissent, and political mobilization in urban Ethiopia. *African Affairs*, *113*(452), 409–430.

Odendaal, A. (2011). *The role of political dialogue in peacebuilding and statebuilding: An interpretation of current experience*. Working Group on Political Dialogue of the International Dialogue on Peacebuilding and State-Building.

Omairan, H. (2021). *Regional and international influence on the Yemen Crisis and the failure of the peace process*.

Papagianni, K. (2013). *National dialogue processes in political transitions* (Civil Society Dialogue Network Discussion Paper, [3]).

Paragi, B. (2019). *Foreign aid in the Middle East*. Bloomsbury Publishing.

Pelham, S., Göth, T., Kamminga, J., Alkadri, H., Ehsan, M., & Tonelli, A. (2021). *'Leading the way': Women driving peace and security in Afghanistan, the Occupied Palestinian Territory and Yemen*.

Quie, M. (2012). Peace-building and democracy promotion in Afghanistan: The Afghanistan Peace and Reintegration Programme and reconciliation with the Taliban. *Democratization*, *19*(3), 553–574.

Salisbury, P. (2015). *Federalism, conflict and fragmentation in Yemen*. Saferworld

Siebert, H. (2016). Beyond mediation: Promoting change and resolving conflict through Authentic National Dialogues. In *Interventions in conflict* (pp. 153–162). Palgrave Macmillan.

Smith, L. (2007). *Political violence and democratic uncertainty in Ethiopia*. United States Institute of Peace.

Stanekzai, M. M. (2008). *Thwarting Afghanistan's Insurgency*. US Institute of Peace.
Suhrke, A. (2007). Reconstruction as modernisation: The 'post-conflict' project in Afghanistan. *Third World Quarterly, 28*(7), 1291–1308.
Transfeld, M. (2016). Political bargaining and violent conflict: Shifting elite alliances as the decisive factor in Yemen's transformation. *Mediterranean Politics, 21*(1), 150–169.
UNDP. (2004). *Security with a human face: Challenges and responsibilities*. Afghanistan National Human Development Report. http://hdr.undp.org/sites/default/files/afghanistan_2004_en.pdf
Verjee, A. (2021). Political transitions in Sudan and Ethiopia: An early comparative analysis. *Global Change, Peace & Security, 33*, 1–18.
Waldman, M. (2015). *Opportunity in crisis navigating Afghanistan's uncertain future*. The Royal Institute of International Affairs.
Williams, P., Sommadossi, T., & Mujais, A. (2017). A legal perspective on Yemen's attempted transition from a Unitary to a Federal System of government. *Utrecht Journal of International and European Law, 33*, 4.
Yusuf, S. (2019). Drivers of ethnic conflict in contemporary Ethiopia. *Institute for Security Studies Monographs, 2019*(202), 46.
Zyck, S. A. (2014). *Mediating transition in Yemen: Achievements and lessons*. International Peace Institute.

CHAPTER 4

Wars and EU's Peace Interventions in the Regional Setting: Yemen Versus Iraq and Tunisia

Moosa Elayah

In the previous chapter, we discussed EU's peace interventions at the international level through a deep and wide comparative analysis of the cases of Yemen and Afghanistan, and Yemen and Ethiopia. We looked at the strengths and weaknesses of both cases, and the lessons learned in terms of the geographical, political, and social aspects of each case. From both cases, we gleaned that each dialogue had its unique approach and features that in turn played a role in the implementation of the larger dialogue process. The previous chapter contributed to the existing theoretical conception of National Dialogues within the ambit of peacebuilding literature that are nascent as of yet. In fragile regions, dialogue entails the efforts of national actors and the international community to respond adequately to conflict and clashes to work towards a shared national vision (Odendaal, 2011). From an international perspective, this chapter contributed to the idea of political reconciliation and National Dialogues in countries that are characterised by a multitude of ideologies and ethnic backgrounds, such as religious and tribal systems.

This chapter aims to analyse the National Dialogues of two countries in the Middle East and North Africa (MENA) region, namely Iraq and Tunisia, and compare them to the Yemeni National Dialogue. This chapter adopts the second (regional) multi-level analytical approach (the other two are: international and local). Although Iraq's National Dialogue is not recent, there are many insightful takeaways from the National Dialogue that was conducted after the invasion and the demise of the former president, Saddam Hussein. Yemen, Iraq, and Tunisia differ in terms of historical experience, socio-economic development, and political structure, but have shared very similar political experiences, having emerged from prolonged dictatorships almost simultaneously by overthrowing their respective dictators through people-powered revolutions, or by military intervention in the case of Iraq, and subsequently initiating National Dialogues to unite their divided societies. The success and failure of these National Dialogues depended on many factors, which will be discussed in this chapter.

Iraq-Yemen: A Comparative Case Study

Iraq is an exceptional case in the Middle East region. It bears similarity to Afghanistan's case since both occurred before the 2011 Arab Spring. The change processes in Afghanistan and Iraq were a consequence of foreign interventions after the military invasion by the US and its EU allies in 2001 and 2003, respectively. Conversely, the changes in Yemen and Ethiopia were due to internal interventions, despite the existence of external intervention to some degree. After the invasion of Iraq, the US and its allies pushed towards political and economic reforms in order to align the country onto a democratic path. This essentially marked the commencement of many dialogue conventions. However, some factions of society protested against this due to the absence of balance of powers. Thus, seeing this to be unjust, some groups espoused violence to resist this situation.

The reconciliation process in Iraq was not smooth despite the enormous support it had received from the international community. According to many researchers, the US blamed the fragmentation within the society as the cause (Morrissey, 2021).

Strength Points of the Iraqi-Yemeni Case Study

There were a number of positive aspects in Iraq's case, similar to Yemen, which are shown in Table 4.1. In both cases, all political and religious groups participated in the national reconciliation. Also, choosing the most

Table 4.1 Strength Points (SP) in Iraqi-Yemeni comparative case study

SP	Yemen	Iraq
I	The local, regional, and international support for the National Dialogues given to the conference was high	Production of the constitution guaranteed everyone the right to a decent life and equal participation
II	Promotion of the idea of dialogue as the only way out—as opposed to the option of war	The participation of all political forces, religious communities, and tribal clans proved its success
III	Diversity in selection of the 565 members of the dialogue conference, including all political spheres, as well as civil society organisations, women's organisations, and young people (except jihadist groups like al-Qaeda)	Support of the national economy in the process of simultaneous political reconciliation
IV	Drafting a new constitution that guarantees a peaceful transfer of power	Agreement of all participants to unite the Iraqi national identity
V	Discussion of issues that had been ignored for many years; for example, South issue, Sa'dah, and marginalised groups	Enhancement of the power of the central authority to facilitate the process of dialogue
VI	Taking issues that are most important and challenging for the future of Yemen, post 2011	The selection of issues important to national reconciliation

important issues to discuss on the table were common in the two cases. In Iraq, all factions agreed on prioritising amending the constitution, distribution of the territories, and distributing the authority and wealth of the nation. In the case of Iraq, the participants did not ignore Kurdistan Iraq's situation, which had represented a historical political dilemma (Sadiq, 2021). Unlike Yemen, Iraq succeeded in partitioning the country into regions: north (Kurds), Sunni, and Shiite. Iraqis also attempted to establish a national identity through this division. This dictated the need to strengthen the central authority in order to make a successful national reconciliation (Hamoudi, 2013).

The Iraqi people were hopeful that these positive steps would help the country overcome the difficult past and enter a new era of freedom, equality, and justice (Connelly, n.d.). As Dai Yamao said, "In the third conference for national reconciliation held in March 2008, the Prime Minister Maliki declared that his regime attempted to accomplish national reconciliation overcoming sectarianism and realizing the equality of all Iraqi peoples" (Dai Yamao, 2011). Also, Sarkin and Sensibaugh, discussing the political powers, mentioned "Instead of causing further divisions in Iraq, it is time for individuals and groups to articulate a strategy that approaches reconciliation on all levels" (2011).

An aspect that had to be addressed in Iraq was the country's economic growth since 1991, which had been lacking for more than 13 years. The American invasion in 2003 further deteriorated the economic status, which led to the spread of corruption and downfall of what was left of the state's institutions. Unemployment reached an unprecedented level of more than 60% (Sassoon, 2016). After the American invasion, Iraq, as one of the world's wealthiest oil-producing countries, suffered from a lack of political stability and primary public services. Also, there was a lack of safety and security. Steele states that "The lack of security and employment, coupled with historic grievances, stereotypes, and growing fears of domination and exclusion, led to an escalation of violence" (Steele, 2008). The consequence of this was reflected in the people's resistance, which translated into violence within the society, particularly in the tribal areas with a Sunni majority and areas of the Kurds who sought to have their own self-governed territory (Gunter, 2013).

WEAK POINTS OF THE IRAQI-YEMENI CASE STUDY

In contrast, Yemen and Iraq shared a number of weak points in their process of reconciliation and National Dialogues. The initiative of a "political will" within the participating parties in the reconciliation processes in both countries created frustration among the public, which aggravated the internal conflicts between the different sects of society (Ghanim, 2011). Table 4.2 shows the significant weak points of both cases. For instance, the uprising of the religious conflict, firstly in Iraq, and then in Yemen was a weakening phenomenon. This was followed by a chain of political revenge acts that left the two societies precarious and unsafe. In turn, this instigated the phenomenon of terrorist groups like al-Qaeda, ISIS, and Iraqi Shiite Coalition. The lack of a transitional social justice law conveyed to the anti-change powers that they still possessed their traditional powers (Gerges, 2017). Furthermore, the policy of regional gravitation affected the role of the state—along with other factors shown in Table 4.2, which later became a big contributor to the failure of the National Dialogue in Yemen.

Religious conflicts were not the only weakening factors of the national reconciliation, although they had a major effect. There was also a conflict among the Iraqi elite groups, alongside a policy of revenge, who were

Table 4.2 Weak Points (WP) of Iraqi-Yemeni case study

WP	Yemen	Iraq
I	The issue of transforming the political system from the simple (central) system to a federal (composite) system	Emergence of sectarian conflict led to a fragmented Iraqi society
II	Size of the problems versus the outcomes did not align with the ambitions	Retaliation policy practised by the Iraqi factions and political forces towards each other led to their own exclusion
III	Difficulty in implementing the outputs of the dialogue, due to the absence of guarantees	Emergence of terrorist organisations that found Iraq a fertile area to exercise their activities (i.e. ISIS, al-Qaeda, Iraqi Shiite Popular-Crowd)
IV	Traditional elites' conflict with the new revolutionary forces over the future of the new state	The absence of transitional justice law
V	South dilemma: failed to agree on a common formula	Regional and international disputes, which were intended to make Iraq a country of external influence
VI	Establishing a National Dialogue considering the absence of security as well as the weak central government	
VII	Rejection of foreign intervention by some powers	

attempting to take control and establish authority—based on *zero-sum* game theory (Wimmer, 2003). The violence and random detention resulting from these conflicts affected the whole society, including women and children. In August 2008, Human Rights Watch reported that 18,000 Iraqis citizens were detained, along with a number of city officials and news reporters (HRW, 2008). This had a great impact on national growth, where the state was unable to respond to people's needs, and the Iraqis, who live in one of the richest oil-producing countries in the world, had to ask for help. "Conflict exists over the distribution of natural resources and the state fails to satisfy basic human needs of the Iraqi people including electricity, clean water, and access to medical facilities" (Sarkin & Sensibaugh, 2011). The state of poverty and social division in Iraq advanced terrorist groups and gave them a chance to recruit and militarise huge numbers of Iraqis; a big percentage of which joined due to financial constraints (Schwartz, 2016).

It is inevitable that when the central authority falls, another authority takes over, and this violates the entire country's internal and foreign sovereignty. The internal conflicts and the emergence of terrorist groups that were rife in Iraq before the Arab Spring, happened again during the Arab Spring in Yemen, Libya, and Syria (Mirkan, 2021). A commonality here was the deterioration of the central government, which gave space for extremist groups to gain control. For instance, in Yemen, extremists became active in different places in the South and North and began to act as the sole authority (Abdulmajid, 2021). Furthermore, international interventions were not always positively effective. Their often prioritised aggravating the extremist groups, while disregarding the country's primary issues such as economic and human development, health, and education. All these issues could have been mitigated or prevented if there was a strong central power in Iraq.

Lessons Learned from Iraqi-Yemeni Case Study

There are a number of important lessons to be learned from the reconciliation and peace dialogues of the Iraqi case, and these are important to consider to avoid future mismanagement of the situation. In Table 4.3, it is clear that safety was an important factor in both Iraq and Yemen, which helped continue the peace process among opposing parties. In both cases, it was believed that negotiation and dialogue were the only ways to reach a resolution—this is needed in any peacebuilding or building state capacity. Another vital lesson was that the most sensitive and complicated issues were put on the dialogue table with transparency, which was described by some observers as a positive step towards the success of the peace talks. Furthermore, the cases of Yemen and Iraq indicate that each case, despite similarities, had their own distinct shape and weight. Therefore, National Dialogues and reconciliations sometimes take different routes in order to reach a final outcome. The policy of avoiding violence and revenge is yet another lesson to be learned from the two cases. Sarkin and Sensibaugh state:

> Unfortunately, achieving reconciliation has been given short shrift in light of the apparent necessity to fight violence using force. While some measure of stability may be achieved by limiting the ability of those wanting to commit violent acts, this approach cannot 'realize a long-term positive result.' (2011)

Table 4.3 Important lessons from Iraqi-Yemeni case study

IL	Yemen	Iraq
I	The process of dialogue should not stop even if it reaches a dead end; it may take many years, but a consensus should be reached	Security and stability are the most important factors influencing positive outcomes in a dialogue
II	Maintaining the central government's power and its institutions can guarantee the continuation of the dialogues and implementation of their outputs	Peaceful dialogue is the only secure way, that leads to a democratic, coherent transition
III	Preserving the National Dialogue at the national level and avoiding regional and/or international tugging assists in a better national consensus	Review all the important issues without discrimination
IV	Economic development goes hand in hand with political reconciliation	Each case has its own specificity and thus cannot be viewed through another's dimension
V	Encouraging participation of youth and women in the political process downsizes the influence of traditional forces of hegemony	Rejecting violence and resorting to open dialogue greatly reduces internal conflicts and contributes to the success of dialogue
VI	The participation of all segments of society in the National Dialogue, equally without exclusion, can ensure its success	Dialogue should lead to a balance of power between the central government and local authorities—distribution is crucial in promoting the overall development and political stability
VII	The presence of a documented set of regulations agreed upon and followed by all delegates is vital for ensuring compliance with the regulations	
VIII	Community awareness of the importance of National Dialogue must be accompanied by national media, focussing on training interlocutors in methods of debating	
IX	It is rather beneficial to choose specialised people in different areas of debating rather than a random selection	
X	Maintenance of the principle of transparency in the national dialogue will gain credibility	

For the aforementioned countries, conducting a National Dialogue and facilitating reconciliation was not an unattainable goal; the only requirement was the will of the political leaders. Many countries around the world have had successful roadmaps for a peaceful and safe transition (Almagro, 2021). Sarkin and Sensibaugh, in this regard, confirm that:

> At the minimum [many countries] have been able to live alongside each other in relative peace. Such examples include South Africa, Namibia, Angola, Mozambique, Northern Ireland, Sierra Leone, Liberia, Nigeria, Cambodia, Chile, Argentina, Honduras, and Guatemala. Extreme violence typified many of these transitions. (2011)

Thus, political powers should realise that the success of National Dialogues and reconciliations depends on the agreement of the parties involved, to coexist under the same national identity, provided that all get an equal share of the national wealth and power, regardless of their backgrounds.

TUNISIA-YEMEN NATIONAL DIALOGUES

National Dialogues greatly differ from one state to another depending on contentious issues, but they all aim at strengthening the agreement among a broad range of actors. In this section, the authors will compare the Tunisia and Yemen National Dialogue experiences by examining certain crucial aspects. The National Dialogue in Tunisia is one of the most recent ones emerging from the Arab Spring wave. An in-depth analysis of the National Dialogues, discussing the strengths, weaknesses and lessons learned from the case of Yemen and Tunisia is conducted based on the following aspects:

1. Credibility of the National Dialogue Sponsor
2. Inclusiveness of the National Dialogue
3. The agenda of the National Dialogue Conference

CREDIBILITY OF THE NATIONAL DIALOGUE SPONSOR

The Quartet Initiative of the National Dialogue in Tunisia was launched after the assassination of the MP Mohammed Brahmi, a member of the National Constituent Assembly (NCA), on 25 July 2013 (Haugbølle et al., 2017). This incident led to a political crisis that caused some of the opposition parties to call for demonstrations that stalled the NCA for a couple of weeks. The public opinion against the Ennahda Movement played an important role in the demonstrations (Mia, 2016). Therefore, the Quartet Organizations Initiative was established, and all the parties agreed, despite their lack of trust in the neutrality of the organisations engaged in the dispute (Ben Salem, 2016). This escalated over the years between Ennahda Movement and the Tunisian General Labour Union, which represents the biggest labour syndicate. The situation caused trust between both parties to deteriorate as the crisis continued (Aljawrash, 2016).

The Quartet Sponsor of the National Dialogue in Tunisia consisted of four major organisations (AMN, 2015). The first was the Tunisian General Labour Union, which was considered one of the most effective unions in the country for decades. This union was established in 1946 as a result of the Tunisian National Movement during the French colonisation, and it still plays an effective role politically and socially (Omri, 2015). This union called for change and was on the frontlines of the demonstrations in December 2010. It has also participated officially in all the events happening in Tunisia since 2010 (Yousfi, 2017). It interfered continually in the National Dialogue leading to political and democratic change. The Tunisian General Labour Union was also a refuge and played an important role in enabling the opposition parties to demand their rights and learn the democratic processes as well (Omri, 2016).

The Tunisian General Labour Union is not only a labour organisation, but also an authority that brings society together, and it is open for all workers—teachers, doctors, manual workers etc. This union unites the middle, lower, and poor classes in Tunisia and boasts one million members in a population of about 10 million people (Yousfi, 2017). The union is considered a link between the government and society, and at the same time it is considered a popular institution that asserted their stance through dialogue rather than violence (Tuğal, 2015).

UTICA (Tunisian Union of Industry, Trade and Handicrafts) was established in 1947. It represents employers in the fields of trade, industry, and handicrafts. This union represents about 150,000 private companies in Tunisia. Apart from its role in the recovery of the Tunisian economy after Zine El Abidine Ben Ali's regime was toppled, it also supported the National Dialogue that led to an agreement to form a National Agreement Government. It is also worth mentioning that it was an important guarantor to facilitate the role of government during the transitional period (Thomassen, 2015).

The Tunisian Body of Lawyers and the Tunisian Human Rights League played an important role before and after the revolution in Tunisia as they resisted for freedom and democracy and many of their affiliates were imprisoned and tortured (Gobe & Salaymeh, 2016). The two organisations also significantly contributed to the demonstrations that condemned repression against political and Islamic figures in Tunisia. The two organisations participated effectively in the success of the National Dialogue and transitional phase in Tunisia (Aleya-Sghaier, 2012).

The Tunisian General Labour Union and UTICA formed a natural effective power against the Troika Government that tried to monopolise the regime (Gobe & Salaymeh, 2016). This league led to an economic crisis that negatively affected workers and employers, but it also averted a disaster and saved the country. The Tunisian General Labour Union and UTICA allied with the lawyers' syndicate that supported the revolution, and the Tunisian Human Rights League, that had been an effective authority since its establishment in 1977. The two unions struck a balance by forcing the Troika Government to a negotiation (Loschi, 2019).

The Quartet Coalition was able to minimise the disputes between the Troika Government and the secular opposition that supported Nidaa Tounes Party, and the national front and other secular parties called National Rescue (Winter, 2016). These organisations proved the importance of civil society in Tunisia, politically, and they made the National Dialogue successful as Tunisian people trusted the Quartet Dialogue (Crowe, 2015).

In Yemen, the National Dialogue was one of the executive mechanisms of the Gulf Initiative signed on 23 November 2011 by the ruling regime represented by the PGC (People's General Congress) and their allies, and the opposition was represented by the Joint Meeting Parties (JMPs) and their partners (Gaston, 2014). This initiative included a detailed timetable delineating the transitive period in Yemen. The 18th article of this initiative stated that at the beginning of the second transitive period, the elected president and the government of the national union called for a national comprehensive dialogue joining all political parties and other entities including young people, the Southern Movement, Houthis, all parties, civil society representatives, and the women's sector (Feierstein, 2017). Women had to be represented in all participating parties (GPC & JMP, 2011).

The Gulf Initiative in Yemen was one of the reasons for the crisis in Yemen and one of the imbalances that accompanied the transitive period (Constitutional Reform Trust Fund, 2012). The Gulf Initiative invalidated the constitution of the country, prolonged the legal period of the parliament, and immobilised the opposition's (JMP) capacity to communicate with the regime. Although the Gulf Initiative was successful in removing Ali Abdullah Saleh from power, it did not make fundamental political reforms to pave the way for final peace (Benomar, 2013). Instead of changing the regime, the initiative merely reformed it. Schematize argued that the Gulf Initiative was important in guaranteeing the interests of the Yemeni elites, the EU, US, and Saudi Arabia, therefore, it did not address the requests of the demonstrators (Hamidi, 2015).

The Gulf Initiative was rolled out in two phases. The first phase was to transfer Ali Saleh's authorities to his deputy (vice president) Abdrabbuh Mansur Hadi. Then, the conflicting parties formed an agreed upon government led by the opposition, dividing the portfolios equally between the last ruling party, PGC, and the JMP. The president appointed a military committee to stop the defection of the military forces, as some of them supported the revolution and others rejected it (Jinping, 2013). The first phase ended with the presidential elections in February 2012 when Vice President Hadi was unanimously elected (Dahlgren & Augustin, 2015).

In the second phase, Hadi and the government were given two years to rehabilitate the military and security forces, to solve the issues of the transitional judiciary, and to commence a comprehensive National Dialogue to review the constitution (Zyck, 2014). Another imbalance was the government of the national union that was formed in accordance with the Gulf Initiative, as it was formed equally between PGC and their leagues and JMPs and their allies (Alwazir, 2012). This government was not successful in winning the trust of the Yemeni people as it failed to make tangible reforms, fulfil the hopes of the people, or to support the people with their needs and necessary services (Elayah et al., 2017). It was questioned three times by the parliament due to its weak performance in solving fuel-related problems and the deteriorating security situations such as organised sabotages for gas lines and electricity towers, security imbalance, and widespread corruption (Al Hammadi, 2014).

The Gulf Initiative was accompanied by some flaws such as the disputes among the political elites. There was a dispute between Saleh and his family, on the one hand, and the Ali Mohsen and Alahmar family on the other. The two parties tried to protect their benefits and eliminate the benefits of their enemies. The economy remained the same since the same families controlled most of the resources, and the country depended on saving interests and patronage (Kestemont, 2018). They also continued controlling the decision-making of the government, military, and political parties. The military forces continued to be divided and the government did not control the remote areas adequately (Qasem, 2013). In north Yemen, Houthis spread their power to control more lands and in the south of Yemen the government still faced some difficulties with the Northern Movement, AQAP, and some militias supported internationally, to create crisis in the country (International Crisis Group [ICG], 2012b).

INCLUSIVENESS OF THE NATIONAL DIALOGUE

The Quartet Dialogue in Tunisia did not exclude any of the political parties vital to the decision-making process. It included all parties that held political, economic, and social influence and could contribute to the success of the dialogue (QAsem, 2013). The Quartet Dialogue that supervised the National Dialogue process specified a list of relevant parties that had direct relation with the dialogue, on the basis of two standards: the Representation Standard, and the Acceptance Standard (Alwazir, 2012).

The Representation Standard in the Constituent National Assembly comprises parties that accepted to sign the Quartet Dialogue initiative text, and these were (Ben Salem, 2016): Afaq Tounes, the National Free Union, the Democratic Alliance Party, Altyar Democratic Party, Tunisian National Front, Republic Party, Magharabi Republic Party, Sha'abi Takhadomi Party, third option, Conference for the Republic, the Social Democratic Path, Mahabah, Ennahdah Movement, Nedaa Tounes, Tunisian Movement for Freedom and Dignity, Republican Movement, Movement of Socialist Democrats, Public Current, Democratic Patriots' Movement, People Movement, Wafa Movement, Alaman Party, Alekla'a for Future Party, Takatoul Democratic Party for Labour and Liberties, Labour Party and Initiative party (Alhaidosi, 2013).

The Acceptance Standard comprised of all parties that signed the text of the Quartet Initiative. The Congress for the Republic and Mahaba Current was excluded despite being representatives in the Constituent National Assembly, due to their refusal to sign the initiative. Both the Democratic Current Party and Wafa'a Movement, also representatives in the Constituent National Assembly, did not participate because they rejected the whole concept of the dialogue (Island Center for Studies, 2014).

Despite the political division between the Islamists and secularists at the beginning of the dialogue, they succeeded in overcoming their differences due to their sense of belonging to their country. Despite the political and ideological differences, particularly regarding the role of religion in society, all of the included parties considered the dialogue as a chance to establish order in the country (Hamidi, 2015).

In Yemen, representation in the National Dialogue Conference was based on the executive mechanism of the Gulf Initiative. The following groups were included in the National Dialogue: GPC and its allies, JMP and its partners, political parties and other political actors, young people's movements, the Southern movement, Houthis, civil society organisations and the women's sector (Zyck, 2014).

One of the Technical Committee's tasks regarding the preparation for the National Dialogue Conference in accordance with Article 4 was to specify the size of the delegations of the groups participating, and to select the members (Day, 2014). In this regard, the Technical Committee held many ad hoc meetings to discuss the issue of representation in the National Dialogue. The Committee assured the following: (1) ensuring the representation of southerners in at least 50% of the total number of members of the Conference, women at least 30%, and young people at least 20%; and (2) achieving balance, which reflects the participation of all components of the Yemeni community in the dialogue. The committee also affirmed that the President's list helped in addressing any imbalance or weakness in any category in society.[1]

The National Dialogue Conference consisted of 565 seats that were distributed as follows: GPC and its allies (112 members), Islah Party (50 members), Yemeni Socialist Party (37 members), Nasserist Unionist People's Organization (30 members), and the five parties in the government (Arab Socialist Baath Party, Unionist Yemeni Congregation, Union of Popular Forces, the National Council for the Peaceful Revolution Forces, and Alhagh Party—4 members each), the Southern Movement

---

[1] Technical report of the Technical Committee of preparing for the Comprehensive National Dialogue Conference, Sana'a, Technical Committee for preparations for the national dialogue Conference, 12 December 2012, p. 14. Arab Socialist Baath party withdrew from the Conference before it began, thus the four seats were transferred to the President's list.

(85 members), Houthis (35 members), young people (40 members), women (40 members), CSOs (40 members), Yemeni Rashad Party (7 members), and the Organization of Justice and Building (7 members). The president's list was made up of 62 members from political and social groups. This list was developed after the agreement about the names on other lists. The president's list contained the following categories: Tribal leaders, scholars, marginalised groups, new political parties, businessmen, artists, exiles, expatriates, the disabled, and others. The purpose of this list was to ensure balance and representation of categories that may not be represented in the lists of groups and other events.[2]

This phase was accompanied by many conditions:

1. The report of the Technical Committee of the NDC preparation pointed out that the selection mechanism was not clear, as the Committee had specified a number of criteria which were not agreed upon. It also indicated that not all actors participated in the NDC and some important groups were ignored despite their demands to be included such as, tribal leaders, Islamic Scholars, religious minorities, new political parties, businessmen, and artists (Al-mikhlafi, 2013).
2. There was a manipulation of representation proportions of the participants in the National Dialogue Conference. Some actors were represented in higher proportions than their actual size, while other actors were minimised in term of inclusion because their proportions did not correspond with their actual size (Al-Akhali, 2014).
3. The exclusion of certain social, tribal, and partisan groups of dialogue.
4. The selection of some representatives of certain actors who were not nominated by their supporters such as the representatives of the South.
5. The emergence of quotas and representatives sharing in the National Dialogue, and inaccurate distribution of seats (Albakeeri, 2013). Women, youth, and independents expected more shares, but their places were taken by the traditional political elites. Another issue was that the representatives of civil society were not independent.

---

[2] Technical Report of the Technical Committee (Responsible for preparation of the Comprehensive National Dialogue Conference), Sana'a, Technical Committee for preparations for the National Dialogue Conference, 12 December 2012, p. 14.

The Committee was selected based on personal relationships, and it is believed that many of the participants and the names included in the NDC were from one family (Seale, 2013).
6. Some actors included in the dialogue were dissatisfied with their terms of reference, including the Houthi group who rejected the Gulf Initiative and its executive mechanism, though they participated in the dialogue. Ironically, some Houthi representatives participated in the dialogue, while other joined the sit-ins in Change Square, though the initiative demanded an end to sit-ins. Consequently, there were no drastic or clear steps in the transition from resolutions to implementation due to lack of transparent procedures. As a result, the powerful elites simply ignored the outcomes of the dialogue (Hamidi, 2015).

NATIONAL DIALOGUE CONFERENCE AGENDA

The agenda of Tunisian National Dialogue Quartet Sponsor set up a roadmap that included the main objectives to evade the crisis. These objectives involved speeding up the accreditation of the constitution. The resignation of Ali Larayedh's government would then be in parallel with the agreement about a new government, which would be technocratic. By speeding up the termination of the democratic transition, accrediting the Independent Supreme Authority members of the election and accrediting the election law, it can be said that the Quartet Sponsor aimed at dialogue to make a compromise pertaining to the main issues of the state among all political parties (Haugbølle et al., 2017). The date of commencement of the dialogue was determined to be within four weeks from 25 October 2013. The roadmap was as follows (Ghannouchi, 2014):

- Neutral or independent Prime Minister to be announced by the end of the first week of the launch of National Dialogue. The Prime Minister would then select his government members.
- Within the second week, the independent national election authority would be formed, selecting all its members as the electoral committee resumed its tasks, accompanied by the return of the withdrawn representatives to the constitutive national council responding to the National Dialogue initiative.

- Initiating the electoral law that would prepare and organize the coming elections.
- Resuming the tasks of the compromises committee with regard to the constitution, which is the core of the constitutive national council, with the return of the withdrawn representatives to the constitutive national council.
- Deciding the issues for argumentation for the final draft of the constitution project.
- Ali Larayedh's government had to officially resign as the technocratic government was formed by the end of the third week of the dialogue.
- Bringing the presidential and legislative elections dates to light by the end of the third week of the dialogue.
- The constitutive national council would accredit and entrust the government by the end of the fourth week of the dialogue, which is the end of the National Dialogue period.
- By the fourth week of the national dialogue, the draft of the Tunisian constitution had to be introduced based on the accreditation of the constitutive council that had been working on it for two years.

In Yemen, the issues of the National Dialogue were divided into nine categories, and each team was assigned to tackle one of the nine issues in the National Dialogue agenda. These main nine issues were as follows: The Southern issue, the Sa'ada issue, national reconciliation, transitional justice, state-building, good governance, fundamentals of structuring the army and security forces and their roles, authority independence that has specialty, rights and freedoms, and long-lasting complete and comprehensive development (Seale, 2013).

The 565 members of the NDC were split into nine teams. 550 members were from the nine teams of the conference and the 15 remaining members were nominated. The presidency of the conference nominated 9 members. The compromise committee nominated 2 members while 4 members were not a part of any team (Jinping, 2013).

This size and diversity were a major success and considered an accomplishment. Some of the teams could have achieved their duties within 6 months (Gaston, 2014). However, many of the issues hit a roadblock and no solutions were found. These were the main reasons for the outbreak of conflict at the end of the National Dialogue. Some of the issues were:

Failure to Implement Trust-Building Procedures

The Technical Committee for preparing and organising the National Dialogue reached a code of solutions on 27 August 2012 that aimed at building trust amongst all political parties as an essential step for the success of the Comprehensive National Dialogue Conference. This step involved accrediting the 20 acts mainly related to the southern issue, particularly after the incident where a couple of southerners had boycotted the National Dialogue Conference. Other acts included the Sa'ada issue, youth revolution, transitional justice, and restructuring the armed and security forces (Alley, 2013).

A month later, the Technical Committee emphasised the need to address what is referred to as 20 acts that tackled certain injustices such as ground property, obtaining state jobs, pensions, freeing political prisoners, apologising for the 1994 war, and reopening prominent Yemeni newspapers, for example, Alayam. The working group on the southern issue in the National Dialogue Conference foregrounded the need to establish more trust-building procedures known as the eleven acts, for instance, withholding the sale of new privileges of gas and oil during the transitional period, and a ban on selling land in the South till the committee finished its tasks.

On 9 July 2013, President Hadi commanded the government to implement the 20 acts admitted by the technical committee towards preparing and organising the NDC. The 11 acts, regarding the procedures and the precautionary measures of trust-building, were also recognised by the Southern issue team in the Comprehensive National Dialogue Conference (Elayah et al., 2020a). Although the government agreed upon the implementation, it delayed it. Therefore, the constituents of the southern movement known as Al-Hiraak boycotted the sessions of the National Dialogue Conference for three weeks, until the government apologised on 21 August 2013 for the summer war in 1994 (Elayah et al., 2020a). Meanwhile, the components of the southern Hiraak welcomed this step and deemed it as positive. Some Hiraak activists had doubts concerning its timing, stressing the continuing demand for secession and restoration of the state (Elayah et al., 2020a). Furthermore, the government agreed on a code of executive procedures for these acts:

- Forming a government committee that would name the cases under political issues. The committee would interrogate and release any detainees due to the protests in the south.
- Preparing a comprehensive amnesty law project pertaining to the leaders and southern personnel without any exceptions.
- Issuing a presidential decree to establish a caring fund for the families of the deceased and the wounded during the civil war that broke out in the south in the summer of 1994.
- The government determined executive procedures to tackle the injustices meted out to the southerners, such as enforced exclusion from state jobs or looting of land and personal property by authoritative people.
- The transitional government agreed to compensate the Alayam newspaper with three million dollars.
- The government cancelled the ceremony due to be held on 7 July (Alhalali, 2013).[3]

Azobah considered the non-implementation of any of the eleven acts, particularly the preparation of the National Dialogue that was agreed upon by the technical committee members—which represented all the components mentioned by the executive mechanism of the Gulf Initiative—as a significant reason for the failure of the National Dialogue.[4]

REPRESENTING THE SOUTHERN HIRAAK[5] AT THE NATIONAL DIALOGUE CONFERENCE

The mission of determining the structure of the state was assigned to the state-building team. Their main mission was to issue fundamentals and principles for the new constitution. Yet this team did not make any decisions regarding this topic. In addition, the team worked on putting the

---

[3] July 7 is the day of commemoration of the victory of North forces against the South forces that is called Separation War.

[4] An interview with Afrah Azobah (Heading one of the NGOs mentioned in the Methodology Chapter), the first vice of the secretary general of the National Dialogue, Amman, Jordan, 25 October 2020 (5 hrs).

[5] Southern Hiraak is a popular movement in the south of Yemen that started with the association of retired military and security who were laid off. The southern Hiraak demands the ruling regime with equity and repositioning the civil and military. The south Hiraak demands southern independence since 7 June. It considered south as a country occupied by North Yemen.

outcomes aside till the southern issue team's conclusions came to light. The issue of state-building appeared to be one of the significant issues before the National Dialogue Conference (Elayah et al., 2016). There was a dispute between several political components that hindered forming a unified leadership and common vision. They had different visions and attitudes that fluctuated between federalism and secession. Consequently, that reflected in the difficulty of determining who actually represented the southerners at the National Dialogue Conference (Haider, 2019).

The technical committee that prepared and organised the comprehensive National Dialogue Conference underlined the necessity of representing southerners with no less than 50% of the National Dialogue members, 565 in total. The southern Hiraak component was represented with 85 seats, meaning 15% of the total, and thus overall, the south representation was limited in the National Dialogue (Elayah et al., 2018).

Only two factions of the southern Hiraak took part in the National Dialogue Conference upon the invitation of President Hadi, despite knowing that they did not represent the southern Hiraak and did not have sufficient on-ground influence. The first faction was the National Congress of the South People, which was announced in December 2012 in the Aden governorate (Elayah et al., 2021). One of its prominent leaders, Mohammad Ali Ahmed, returned to Yemen in March 2012. The president met Ahmed Bin Fared Alsorimi, who had also returned to Yemen after spending 19 years in Oman (Alnoaman, 2013), in an attempt to persuade him to participate in the National Dialogue. The second faction is the Southern Independent led by Abdullah Alasnaj, the former Minister of Foreign Affairs (Qassim et al., 2020).

Meanwhile, the main body of Al-Hiraak which demanded the secession of the south from the north, headed by the former vice president Ali Salem Albeid, refused to participate in the NDC (Al-Akhali, 2014). The same stance was taken by prominent figures affiliated to that body, who called for federalism as a solution to the southern issue, due to the lack of readiness that accompanied the preparation of National Dialogue, which they believed would affect its responsibilities and outcomes (Jinping, 2013). This belief proved to be right later when Mohammad Ali Ahmed and his group withdrew from the NDC. Consequently, Hadi shut them out by claiming other southern figures represented Hiraak, who confirmed the outcomes by the southern issue team and stated that the guarantees in the draft were sufficient to tackle the issue (Farahat, 2014).

However, the different social and political components that made up the southern issue team, consisting of 40 members, offered solutions and guarantees that were fair and comprehensive (Seale, 2013). Based on this vision, a small team was formed on 10 December 2013 out of the south issue team, with 8 members from the south and 8 from the north. It was appointed to hold discussions on the vision offered by the political components, as well as on the solutions and guarantees of the South issue, to reach a consensus (Lackner, 2020).

Although there was a consensus on all the issues in the Comprehensive National Dialogue Conference, the south issue team did not reach a consensus. Thus, a small team of 16 members was formed to devise solutions and guarantees (ACRPS, 2014b). This committee was headed by Mohammad Ali Ahmed, Hadi's ally. He attempted to push for a bordered southern state while holding the same power as the northern regions. The team proposed to form a new federal state with two regions in the south and four in the north. Hadi and the Conference leaders replaced Mohammad Ali Ahmed who led the "8–8" committee with another group of southerners who expressed their readiness to accept the federal state proposal consisting of 6 regions (Al-Dawsari, 2012). Yet, the "8–8" committee could not reach a final recommendation. It overcame its differences, proposing the formation of a technical committee by Hadi, to select between the last two options under consideration: a federal state of two regions (south and north), or 6 regions. However, there was no agreement regarding the number of the regions of the federal state (Foreign Policy, 2014).

Sa'ada Issue

Houthi components (Allah's advocates) participated in the tasks of the National Dialogue Conference. One of the significant issues on the table was the Sa'ada issue. The outcomes that the team reached were firstly to guarantee religious and intellectual freedom, including ritual practices, and prohibiting imposing or banning them forcibly by any authority, and secondly to set principles for schools, by agreeing that the supply of textbooks, and religious and private educational institutions should be under the supervision of the state (Girke, 2015). The state and its apparatuses must be neutral. They must not facilitate or support financially or morally any ideology or school of thought, and prohibit and criminalise the use of armed forces in internal conflicts. The medium and heavy weapons that were confiscated or looted by all sides, parties, groups, and individuals should be exclusively possessed by the state (ACRPS, 2014a).

However, the Houthi fighters kept the heavy weapons they plundered in the former wars,[6] as well as the arms they acquired when they controlled some military camps in 2011. This helped them expand and control territories (ICS, 2014). A war broke out between Houthis and Salafis who settled in the Hadith institution in Damaj, Sa'ada governorate. This was the first test of the agreed outcomes occurring just weeks before the end of the National Dialogue Conference (Kestemont, 2018). That event resulted in moving the Salafis from Damaj through a presidential mediation. The conflict did not stop though; rather, it expanded. The conflict mutated and shifted to the Houthis and the Hashid tribe, which is considered the most influential Yemeni tribe, particularly the Alahmar family. The mediation failed to end this continuing conflict. Moreover, President Hadi and the National Dialogue Conference failed to stop the war (Farahat, 2014).

The Houthis gained a seat at the negotiation table and the national compromises just by taking part in the National Dialogue Conference. They expressed views that are popularly advocated, including the establishment of the federal state based on democratic principles, political pluralism, religious freedom, and balance between powers. As a result, this group gained a reputation as being neutral (Hamidi, 2015). In other words, they were against the conflicting powers during Saleh's rule and the transitional government that is not popularly supported. The Houthis group gained further support even with their stronghold in the north, which has a Zaidi majority—one of the Shia sects closest in terms of theology to Hanafi Sunni Islam. Consequently, there was a fluctuating coalition for competing religious, tribal, and even liberal entities. They cooperated under the umbrella of animosity towards the state institutions. This coalition had not been formed yet. But this group could have

---

[6] Battles waged between the Ali Abdullah Saleh government and Houthis (the advocates of Allah) known as Armed Zaidi Houthi. The war started on July 2004 when the Yemeni authority arrested Hussain Al Houthi, accusing him of establishing an armed organisation inside the country. Most of the fighting was in Sa'dah governorate and moved recently to the governorates of Aljof, Hajah, and Amran. Ali Abdullah Saleh's Government accused the Houthi movement of restoring the Zaidi Imamate and overthrowing the Republic of Yemen, while the Houthi movement accused the government of discrimination and supporting the Salaffi forces to crackdown on the Zaidi ideology.

become a party, social movement or armed militia, or a mixture of all (Esfandiary & Tabatabai, 2016).

Despite the participation of the Houthi group in the NDC from the preparation and organisation period until the conference, they refused to sign the national dialogue draft due to their withdrawal from the concluding session of the NDC, upon the assassination of one of their members a few hours before the end of the conference. Second, they refused to sign the final report of the federal regions because they thought that the draft was not a solution to the south issue, but a division based on political fundamentals.

Transitional Justice (TJ)

There was a considerable disagreement between the Yemeni political forces on the issue of transitional justice measures. Since the signing of the GCC initiative and its implementation mechanism on 23 November 2011, a widespread controversy began in Yemen about a number of laws that had to be approved according to this mechanism since it was a part of the political solution, and the legal means to enforce national reconciliation and the transitional justice process (Lewis, 2015). Therefore, Law No. 1 for 2012 on immunity was passed, which precludes the legal prosecution of former president Ali Abdullah Saleh and his associates, protecting them from criminal accountability for breaches of international law.

The second law included a clause, also approved by the GCC initiative, related to transitional justice and national reconciliation. The argument between the political parties was regarding the time period. The Joint Meeting Parties (JMP) proposed legislation and plans of transitional justice that looked into abuse going back to the 1990s, while President Abdrabbuh Mansur Hadi proposed a different plan on the law that did not go beyond 2011, which is consistent with the perception of the General People's Congress on the subject of transitional justice (Palik, 2017). The Office of the President justified that any investigation would have to take place under the transitional justice law and would be subjected to the law of immunity passed in 2012. It is clear in both cases that the time period was employed politically to protect the violation records of each party (Issaev & Zakharov, 2021). Note that they both denied the victims of the 60s and 70s, in the north and south, that stretched to the Yemen uprising in 2011 (Almzehagi, 2016).

In the same vein, dozens of human rights activists and relatives of a number of the missing people held continuous protests against the draft law of transitional justice adopted by the government. They argued that the proposed projects of transitional justice laws in reality concealed the gruesome past violations in Yemen, committed by most of the political parties that signed the Gulf Initiative and were part of the governing regime at different periods of the shared history of north and south Yemen. The protesters also believed these proposals intended to discriminate against the victims and deny their rights to justice which is not in compliance with international standards of human rights and transitional justice (Almzehagi, 2016).

Political Support for the National Dialogue

The impact of international forces on the political transition process in Tunisia was obvious, in particular France (given its historic role in Tunisia) and the US (as the first actor in international relations since the end of the Cold War in 1991). But there is greater and wider freedom of movement for the national parties in Tunisia away from the pressures and influence of international forces (Abdel Shafi, 2014). Conversely in Yemen, there is the influence of regional powers—Saudi Arabia, the Gulf Cooperation Council and Iran—but only to satisfy their own interests, and this eventually led to a regional war in the Yemeni arena (Mancini & Vericat, 2016).

Therefore, it can be said that the impact of international and regional powers was direct on the Yemeni case and the fluctuations of the internal political conditions had direct external influences. In any case, the decisions regarding the Yemeni case were not made internally, but there were external rooms from which the decisions were exported to Yemen in the framework that served the policies of the exterior, which increased the fragility and hostility in Yemen and ruptured the fabric of society (de Jongh & Kitzen, 2021). From an external perspective, international actors are governed by the principle of national interests. Therefore, Yemeni people must fully understand that they are alone in this journey and others who are externally in control are far away and in safety (de Jongh & Kitzen, 2021).

LESSONS LEARNED FROM TUNISIA-YEMENI CASE STUDY

After reviewing the experiences of the National Dialogue Conferences in Tunisia and Yemen, we believe that successful dialogues are those that can bring about specific results and ensure the implementation of the outcomes. Accordingly, we have reached the following conclusions: It is likely that National Dialogues will remain a prevalent tool in the coming years and therefore worthy of further study and research. The historical experience of the countries that managed to build strong democratic systems has shown that the basic condition for the establishment and continuity of such systems is the ability of the diverse political parties to organise dialogues in order to different kinds of consensus. In the space of dialogues and negotiation mechanisms, there are no losers or winners. The process entails open and transparent discussions among all political parties, keeping aside preconceived notions. There needs to be compatibility between multiple points of view, which requires mutual compromise on equal grounds, without adhering to a singular goal, or putting preconditions, or threatening, and adopting flexibility in dealing with the objectives as well as the methods used.

The process of National Dialogue in both Tunisia and Yemen illustrates the importance of designing the practical aspects of the dialogue effectively. In Yemen, the National Dialogue focused on the dialogue process, but it did not focus on how to resolve the problems. The NDC in Yemen was more comprehensive than the one in Tunisia (Kurze, 2015). It highlighted a lot of issues and broadcasted all the National Dialogue sessions in the press and television with transparency. The conference concluded with 1800 recommendations and plans to continue the transition process. This was approved by the majority of the stakeholders, but the dialogue in Yemen did not aim to solve the kind of problems faced by Tunisia. It was not a dialogue between those who would implement the dialogue agreements as it was in Tunisia (Lamont, 2015). There were no serious and concise steps in the transition from the decision phase to the implementation phase because of the lack of clear decision-making procedures, which allowed the powerful elites to simply ignore the dialogue outputs (Murray, 2014).

The biggest disadvantage of the National Dialogues in both Tunisia and Yemen was the failure to address economic issues. While the National Dialogue in Yemen resulted in an agreement and a vision to build Yemen, the economy deteriorated significantly over the same period, because of the drop in oil production, resulting in poor security conditions. Tunisia avoided that by calling for economic dialogue to help bring the country out of its economic crisis (Paffenholz & Ross, 2016).

Gomanah Farahat believes that after the completion of the comprehensive National Dialogue Conference, instead of establishing a new phase to meet at least part of Yemenis' aspirations, the conference ended with a new war in the North and continuing injustice in the South, due to a failure to meet the impartial causes and core issues that were raised and agreed upon in the conference (Feierstein, 2017). It seemed that the dialogue's objective was limited to the re-distribution of power between the traditional centres of power after having President Hadi added to them, and ensuring anything that might threaten their interests in the future was not adopted. However, it is clear to see that the dialogue has taken advantage of the low impact of youth participation in the dialogue and the poor preparation for the dialogue doomed it to fail from the beginning (Farahat, 2014).

Providing one recommendation to conclude this chapter, the Yemenis have to recognise that the success of the National Dialogue should be an internal affair and not external. The interventions of third parties do not serve the national interest (Elayah et al., 2016). External parties are working to dismantle the social fabric in Yemen, and all parties must be aware of the dangers of such tactics that will not end before reducing Yemen to a non-state phase. It seems that Yemenis have not learned the lessons from the numerous dialogues throughout the history of the country (Elayah et al., 2020b). To help the readers better understand the Yemen and the history of external interventions, the following chapter will look at the relationship of conflict with Humanitarian Aid, an important factor that determines the media coverage and the imagination of Yemen in public discourse in the West. While it is assumed that HA is overall an unproblematic support, it is important to explore the on-ground reality and its subsequent influence on media coverage of the Middle East region. Chapter 5 compares the cash transfer or cash aid and food-based humanitarian assistance in conflict situations. It examines the cash distribution projects in the Arab region, specifically Yemen, a country with a quasi-total state failure facing multiple humanitarian crises. To fully understand the challenged facing the HA processes, this chapter employs primary research using a purposive sample to augment the study with empirical data. It takes into account the on-ground practices of INGOs and NGOs and discusses how HA can contribute to the war economy dynamic by being exploited by certain groups, consequently increasing the disparity in reality.

REFERENCES

Abdel Shafi, E. (2014). *Egypt and Tunisia: Unfair comparison.* Centre Island for Studies.

Abdulmajid, A. (2021). *Extremism in the digital era: The media discourse of terrorist groups in the Middle East.* Springer Nature.

ACRPS. (2014a). *Outcomes of Yemen's National Dialogue Conference: A step toward conflict resolution and state building?* Arab Center for Research and Policy Studies.

ACRPS. (2014b). *The Comprehensive National Dialogue Conference Draft in Yemen: A step on the way of crisis solving and building state.* Arab Center for Research and Policy Studies.

Al-Akhali, R. (2014). *The challenge of federalism in Yemen.* Universitäts-und Landesbibliothek Sachsen-Anhalt.

Albakeeri, N. (2013). *Success and failure indicators of the national dialogue in Yemen.* www.aljazeera.net//knowledgdgate/opinions/14l2l2013

Al-Dawsari, N. (2012). *Tribal governance and stability in Yemen* (Vol. 24). Carnegie Endowment for International Peace.

Aleya-Sghaier, A. (2012). The Tunisian revolution: The revolution of dignity. *The Journal of the Middle East and Africa, 3*(1), 18–45.

Alhaidosi, A. (2013). *A list of the parties concerned to participate in the national dialogue.* www.hakaeonline.com/?p=38865

Alhalali, A. (2013). The government recognizes urgent action to win back southerners. *Marib Press.* www.marebpress.net/mobile/news_details.php?sid=59290

Al Hammadi, K. (2014). Yemen: Yemen's consensus government faces some threats of withdrawing trust and the parliament giving more days to pass the insuperable conditions. *Al-Quds-Al-Arabi.* www.alquds.co.uk/?p=171982

Aljawrash, S. A. (2016). National dialogue in Tunisia. *SWI swissinfo.ch.* www.swissinfo.ch/ara/37576704

Alley, A. L. (2013). Tracking the "Arab Spring": Yemen changes everything… and nothing. *Journal of Democracy, 24*(4), 74–85.

Almagro, M. M. (2021). Indicators and success stories: The UN sustaining peace agenda, bureaucratic power, and knowledge production in post-war settings. *International Studies Quarterly, 65*(3), 699–711.

Al-mikhlafi, A. (2013). *Report of the technical committee for the preparations for the national dialogue.*

Almzehagi, M. (2016). *Laws of transitional justice in Yemen: Manipulating the truth and muting the voices of the victims.* www.legal-agenda.com/print.php?id=261&folder=articles&lang=ar

Alnoaman, M. (2013). *The southern Hirak forces rejected the Yemeni dialog: It demands the retake of the south state.* The Global Center of Rapprochement between Islamic Sects. www.taghrib.org/pages/content.php?tid=174

Alwazir, A. Z. (2012). *Youth inclusion in Yemen: A necessary element for success of political transition* (Arab Reform Brief, 64). Arab Reform Initiative.
Arabic Media Network. (2015). Who is the quartet sponsor of the dialogue. www.moheet.com/2015/10/09/2326163
Benomar, J. (2013). Is Yemen a new model? *Journal of International Affairs, 67*(1), 197–203.
Ben Salem, M. (2016). The national dialogue, collusive transactions and government legitimacy in Tunisia. *The International Spectator, 51*(1), 99–112.
Connelly, A. (n.d.). The iraqi constitutional process. *The Michigan Journal of Public Affairs*.
Constitutional Reform Trust Fund. (2012). *The Yemen National Dialogue and Constitutional Reform Trust Fund (YNDCRTF)*.
Crowe, M. (2015). Tunisia's historic step towards democracy. Carnegie Center for Peace. http://carnegie-mec.org/2015/01/14/
Dahlgren, S., & Augustin, A. L. A. (2015). The multiple wars in Yemen. *Middle East Research and Information Project, 18*.
Day, S. W. (2014). The 'non-conclusion' of Yemen's national dialogue. *Foreign Policy, 27*.
de Jongh, S., & Kitzen, M. (2021). The conduct of lawfare: The case of the Houthi insurgency in the Yemeni civil war. In *The conduct of war in the 21st century* (pp. 249–264). Routledge.
Elayah, M. A. A., van Kempen, L. A. C. M., & Schulpen, L. W. M. (2016). *Civil society's diagnosis of the 2013 National Dialogue Conference (NDC) in Yemen: (Why) did it fail?* (Policy Brief).
Elayah, M. A. A., Schulpen, L. W. M., Abu-Osba, B., & Al-Zandani, B. (2017). *Yemen: A forgotten war and an unforgettable country*.
Elayah, M., Schulpen, L., van Kempen, L., & Aglan, M. M. (2018). *The role of the United Nations and its special envoys in the current Yemeni War: Floundering in a tragic reality*.
Elayah, M., Schulpen, L., van Kempen, L., Almaweri, A., AbuOsba, B., & Alzandani, B. (2020a). National dialogues as an interruption of civil war—The case of Yemen. *Peacebuilding, 8*(1), 98–117.
Elayah, M., van Kempen, L., & Schulpen, L. (2020b). Adding to the controversy? Civil society's evaluation of the national conference dialogue in Yemen. *Journal of Intervention and Statebuilding, 14*(3), 431–458.
Elayah, M., Al-Daily, W., & Alkubati, M. (2021). The women, peace, and security (WPS) agenda between rhetoric and action in the MENA Region: A case study of Yemen and Libya. In *Female pioneers from ancient Egypt and the Middle East* (pp. 129–143). Springer.
Esfandiary, D., & Tabatabai, A. (2016). Yemen: An opportunity for Iran-Saudi dialogue? *The Washington Quarterly, 39*(2), 155–174.

Farahat, G. (2014). The end of the national dialog on Yemen.... Start of wars. *Bydayat Magazine*, 7. www.bidayatmag.com/node/145

Feierstein, G. (2017). Is there a path out of the Yemen conflict? Why it matters. *Prism: A Journal of the Center for Complex Operations*, 7(1).

Gaston, E. (2014). *Process lessons learned in Yemen's national dialogue*. US Institute of Peace.

Gerges, F. A. (2017). *ISIS: A history*. Princeton University Press.

Ghanim, D. (2011). *Iraq's dysfunctional democracy*. ABC-CLIO.

Ghannouchi, R. (2014). The Tunisian experience. *The Cairo Review of Global Affairs*, 13, 98.

Girke, N. C. (2015). A matter of balance: The European Union as a mediator in Yemen. *European Security*, 24(4), 509–524.

Gobe, E., & Salaymeh, L. (2016). Tunisia's "revolutionary" lawyers: From professional autonomy to political mobilization. *Law & Social Inquiry*, 41(2), 311–345.

Gulf initiative between GPC and its allies and JMP partners signed on 23 November. (2011). www.almotamar.net/news/95152.htm

Gunter, F. R. (2013). *The political economy of Iraq: Restoring balance in a post-conflict society*. Edward Elgar.

Haider, H. (2019). *National dialogues: Lessons learned and success factors*. Institute of Development Studies.

Hamidi, H. (2015). A comparative analysis of the post-Arab spring national dialogues in Tunisia and Yemen. *African Journal on Conflict Resolution*, 15(3), 11–35.

Hamoudi, H. A. (2013). *Negotiating in civil conflict: Constitutional construction and imperfect bargaining in Iraq*. University of Chicago Press.

Haugbølle, R. H., Ghali, A., Yousfi, H., Limam, M., & Mollerup, N. G. (2017). Tunisia's 2013 National Dialogue. *Berghof Foundation Report, Şubat*.

Human Rights Watch. (2008). *Iraq Events of 2008*. https://www.hrw.org/world-report/2009/country-chapters/iraq

ICG. (2012a). *The persistence of conflicts and threats to the transition process* (Middle East Report, 125). International Crisis Group. http://www.crisisgroup.org/~/media/Files/Middle%20East%20North%20Africa/Iran%20Gulf/Yemen/Arabic%20translations/125-yemen-enduring-conflicts-threatening-transition-arabic.pdf

ICG. (2012b). *Yemen: Conflict continuity and threats to the transition process*. International Crisis Group.

Island Center for Studies. (2014). *Mechanisms and Prospects*. www.studies.aljazeera.net/ar/files/discussionstrategytosolvearabworldconflict/2014/02/201426105920985479

Issaev, L., & Zakharov, A. (2021). The Chaotic Federalism: Yemen. *Federalism in the Middle East* (pp. 71–93). Springer.

Jinping, Z. (2013). *National Dialogue Conference and political transition in Yemen*. West Asia and Africa.

Kestemont, E. (2018). *What role(s) for the European Union in national dialogues? Lessons learned from Yemen* (EU Diplomacy Paper 05/2018).

Kurze, A. (2015). *Tunisian National Dialogue Quartet wins Nobel peace prize.*

Lackner, H. (2020). The role of the United Nations in the Yemen crisis. *Global, regional, and local dynamics in the Yemen crisis* (pp. 15–32). Palgrave Macmillan.

Lamont, C. (2015). *The Tunisian National Dialogue Quartet: A model for Asia?*

Lewis, A. (2015). Divide and rule: Understanding insecurity in Yemen. *Security, clans and tribes: Unstable governance in Somaliland, Yemen and the Gulf of Aden* (pp. 65–91). Palgrave Pivot.

Loschi, C. (2019). Local mobilisations and the formation of environmental networks in a democratizing Tunisia. *Social Movement Studies, 18*(1), 93–112.

Mancini, F., & Vericat, J. (2016, November). *Lost in transition: UN mediation in Libya, Syria, and Yemen.* International Peace Institute.

Mia, M. (2016). National Dialogue Quartet in Democratic transition of Tunisia: An analysis. *Asian Studies, 35*, 125–134.

Mirkan, H. H. (2021). Potential challenges and opportunities in Iraq's future. In *From territorial defeat to global ISIS: Lessons learned* (pp. 24–40). IOS Press.

Morrissey, A. (2021). *Iraqi militias, state management, and security* (Doctoral dissertation).

Murray, C. (2014). National Dialogues in 2013. In *Constitution building: A global review* (pp. 11–15). IDEA.

Odendaal, A. (2011). *The role of political dialogue in peacebuilding and state-building: An interpretation of current experience* (Working Group on Political Dialogue of the International Dialogue on Peacebuilding and State-Building).

Omri, M. S. (2015). No ordinary union: UGTT and the Tunisian path to revolution and transition. *Workers of the World, 1*(7), 14–29.

Omri, M. (2016). *Confluency (tarafud) between trade unionism, culture and revolution in Tunisia*. Tunisian General Labour Union.

Paffenholz, T., & Ross, N. (2016). Inclusive political settlements: New insights from Yemen's national dialogue. *Prism, 6*(1), 198–210.

Palik, J. (2017). "Dancing on the heads of snakes": The emergence of the Houthi movement and the role of securitizing subjectivity in Yemen's civil war. *Corvinus Journal of International Affairs, 2*(2–3), 42–56.

QAsem, A. (2013). Five barriers to youth engagement, decision-making, and leadership in Yemen's political parties. *Resonate Yemen and Saferworld, 5*, 5.

Qassim, A., Amin, L., Transfeld, M., & Strzelecka, E. (2020). *The role of civil society in peacebuilding in Yemen.*

Sadiq, I. (2021). *Origins of the Kurdish genocide: Nation building and genocide as civilizing and de-civilizing processes.* Rowman & Littlefield.

Sarkin, J., & Sensibaugh, H. (2011). Why achieving reconciliation in Iraq is possible: Suggestions for mechanisms and processes including a truth and reconciliation commission. *The Fletcher Journal of Human Security, 23* (2008).
Sassoon, J. (2016). Iraq's political economy post 2003: From transition to corruption. *International Journal of Contemporary Iraqi Studies, 10*(1–2), 17–33.
Schwartz, M. (2016). *War without end: the Iraq war in context*. Haymarket Books.
Seale, P. (2013). Yemen seeks to talk its way out of chaos. *Washington Report on Middle East Affairs, 32*(2), 24.
Steele, D. (2008). *Reconciliation strategies in Iraq*. Institute of Peace. http://www.usip.org/sites/default/files/sr213.pdf
Thomassen, A. (2015). *How do trade unions contribute to democratisation?* (Master's thesis). The University of Bergen.
Tuğal, C. (2015). Elusive revolt: The contradictory rise of middle-class politics. *Thesis Eleven, 130*(1), 74–95.
Wimmer, A. (2003). Democracy and ethno-religious conflict in Iraq. *Survival, 45*(4), 111–134.
Winter, B. (2016). Women's human rights and Tunisian upheavals: Is 'democracy' enough? *Global Discourse, 6*(3), 513–529.
Yamao, D. (2011). *National reconciliation as a tool of political struggles: An inquiry into nation building in post-war Iraq*. Third Global International Studies Conference. http://www.wiscnetwork.org/porto2011/papers/WISC_2011-500.pdf
Yousfi, H. (2017). *Trade unions and Arab revolutions: The Tunisian case of UGTT*. Routledge.
Zyck, S. A. (2014). *Mediating transition in Yemen: Achievements and lessons*. International Peace Institute.

CHAPTER 5

EU's Peace Interventions in the Regional Setting (MENA) and the Effectiveness of Humanitarian Aid in Arab Region

Moosa Elayah and Qais Jaber

In Chapter 4, we looked at a comparative analysis of two countries in the Middle East and North Africa (MENA) region, Iraq, and Tunisia, compared to the Yemeni National Dialogue. The chapter adopted second (regional) multilevel analytical approach (the other two are: international and local). The three countries, Yemen, Iraq, and Tunisia are different in terms of historical context, socio-economic status, and political framework but they shared certain political experiences and subsequently engaging in National Dialogues to unite their divided societies. Chapter 4 looks the important takeaways from each case. In both Yemen and Iraq, negotiation and dialogue were needed to reach a resolution as safety was a common issue in both countries. Dialogues warrant transparency as it ensures a successful peace process.

To enrich the in-depth analysis of the chosen case studies in this text, we will look at another important aspect of the conflict resolution process, Humanitarian Aid. This will add another layer to the argument about the abstract media coverage of the region by international media outlets, which are not entirely rooted in the on-ground reality. The portrayal of the humanitarian crisis is often different from the reality and actual nuances of the crisis and conflict owing to the narrative gaze adopted by the West when looking at the MENA region.

Despite considerable development and progress within the arena of Humanitarian Aid (HA) since the 1990s, the number of people suffering in conflict-torn regions continues to increase exponentially. The United Nations Office for the Coordination of Humanitarian Affairs (OCHA) estimated that in 2020, 167.6 million people around the world would require HA, that is, 1 in 45 people globally (Global Humanitarian Overview, 2020). Kim (2017) estimated that by 2030, 50% of the global poor will live in areas where conflict and fragility are rife. In Nigeria, South Sudan, Somalia, and Yemen, alone, the number of people suffering from famine reached 20 million in 2018. This figure has increased at such a high rate that the funding gap has risen from around $2.5 billion in 2009 to around $13 billion in 2019 (Global Humanitarian Overview, 2020). Thus, the current method of HA application to improve crisis situations has triggered much scepticism and cynicism internationally, since humanitarian organisations have often failed to achieve goals and help endangered civilians and aid workers alike (Findley, 2018; Terry, 2011).

HUMANITARIAN CRISIS AND THE ARAB REGION

Generally, in the Arab region and specifically, since the start of the Yemeni conflict in 2015, the humanitarian situation has been deteriorating. Yemen is facing the biggest humanitarian crisis in the world since World War II. Around three million people have fled their homes, whilst two million are still internally displaced, and one million houses have been destroyed (Global Humanitarian Overview, 2020). More than twenty-two million people, ten million of which are children, are in dire need of humanitarian assistance. Furthermore, about eight million Yemenis have lost their livelihoods (Global Humanitarian Overview, 2020). A huge percentage of Yemeni people used to work for the public sector but due to economic deterioration, more than one million government employees have stopped receiving wages (Bandsom, 2018; UN, 2019). The economy has been continually declining since the start of the war, Gross Domestic Product (GDP) has decreased by 40% and the Yemeni Riyal has lost more than 75% of its value, consequentially increasing the prices of imported goods exponentially (UN, 2019; World Bank, 2018a). According to a World Bank report, the private sector in Yemen has been successful in maintaining the supply of goods, but the negligible demand

and purchasing power incapacity have been major obstacles and these factors are driving Yemen towards a famine (World Bank, 2018a).

Non-governmental Organisations (NGOs) play a major role in the development of societies as they are the actors entrusted by donors to deliver aid programmes to the beneficiaries. NGOs are tasked with the design and implementation of efficient and effective projects, that align with the respected communities' needs and growth objectives, to further social and political goals. In conflict-torn countries such as in the Arab Region, aid programmes have shifted towards relief work, offering emergency humanitarian assistance by distributing everyday commodities, mainly food. Yet offering food-aid has proved inadequate in similar situations (Barrett & Maxwell, 2005; Clay, 2005). In recent years, delivering those supplies in Arab Region has become less effective due to ubiquitous corruption, ununified aid policies, de facto-state influence (Governing bodies not officially recognised), and the fragility of public institutions (Elayah, 2016). This was accompanied by an increased number of financial and non-financial public corruption scandals in the foreign aid industry, including the global NGO sector (Gibelman & Gelman, 2001; Hoelman, 2009; Kiley et al., 2019). Food-aid may not be suitable all the time and it has proven to be less efficient and effective than cash-based assistance (Castillo, 2021; Doocy, 2017; Vogel et al., 2021). Consequentially, International Non-governmental Organisations (INGOs) recognised that they had to innovate and diversify the delivery mechanisms of aid in conflict areas. INGOs started to provide aid to people in emergencies in the form of cash; either conditional (cash for work), unrestricted (direct cash transfer), or restricted (through vouchers). Moreover, the cash transfer is aimed to empower people to independently make the best decisions for their basic needs, as well as making it easier for them to access. Existing literature on cash-based assistance presents positive results, but the impact is still unrecognised in countries of conflict because organisations have been hesitant to implement this system (Harvey, 2005).

This chapter aims to compare the impact of cash transfer and food humanitarian assistance during emergency and conflict situations. It examines cash distribution projects implemented in the Arab Region, especially Yemen, a country with a quasi-total state failure facing multiple humanitarian crises. The chapter discusses cash intervention utilisation, impact, and limitations, in contrast to food-aid. In order to understand the challenges and inadequacies fronting the aid distribution process in

Arab Region, especially Yemen, this chapter explores primary research, using a purposive sample to enrich this study with empirical data. Discussing the challenges facing NGOs' aid distribution in Yemen and various reasons behind food-aid diversion, the findings attempt to explain how cash-based interventions can overcome the limitations of the current used aid mechanism, and the way in which this solution should be implemented.

THE HUMANITARIANISM RATIONALE

To begin our intrinsic exploration of the scope of Humanitarian Aid, let us first look at its underpinning rationale. In the "humanitarianism" period following World War II, the number of intergovernmental humanitarian agencies grew rapidly. In the four years succeeding the war over 200 new NGOs were formed globally and the UN grew in both size and significance (Rysaback-Smith, 2016). The UN's progress led to the ratification of the Universal Declaration of Human Rights in 1948, designed to enable international intervention during both civil and international conflict, and the formation of many organisations under the auspices of the UN such as the WHO (1948), UNICEF (1946), and UNHCR (1950) (Paulmann, 2013). Randolph Kent argued that this was a turning point for HA as "it was only in the midst of World War II that governments began to fully appreciate the need for greater international intervention in the plight of disaster-stricken people" (1987). The relief effort became increasingly international due to advancements in technology, transport, and communication and this resulted in a shift of focus from Europe to less developed countries, thus laying the foundation for the international HA network we have today.

More recently, Barnett (2011) coined the third age "liberal humanitarianism" due to the global efforts to create a liberal peace. The proliferation of NGOs in the 1980s resulted in an increase in public awareness through increased media coverage and advertising campaigns. The 1984 televised video footage of starving children in Korem, Ethiopia and the 1985 Live Aid concert, the first big, televised concert to raise money for HA, highlighted the problems of poverty globally (Westley, 1991). However, the modern concept and system of HA—characterised by humanity, neutrality, impartiality, and independence—have only become commonplace since the 1990s when these basic principles were established by the UN General Assembly in 1991 (Elayah, 2021; Rysaback-Smith, 2016).

Over the past three decades, there have been radical advancements in medicine, delivery systems, and logistical capacities enabling humanitarian action to become more efficient. However, the new global environment has also created many dangers and challenges. Following the 9/11 attacks there was major concern with the dangers that failed states posed to themselves and others, and saving them became a matter of international human security.

To sum up, the main challenge conflict zones are facing is how to accommodate universalism in a world of diversity, since globalisation is clashing with traditional values around the world leading to the development of war economies (Barnett, 2011). In many cases, these war economies have caused governance systems to become weak and have resulted in their collapse, thus leading to long-term issues that result in the recurrence of conflict (Pugh et al., 2005). In Cambodia, natural resources such as timber and rubber have been a large source of funding for armed groups. Afghanistan, the world's largest opium producer and centre for arms dealing, has a million-dollar trade revenue per year from smuggling these commodities into Pakistan from Dubai (DeLozier, 2019). Furthermore, whilst HA is desperately needed, international and humanitarian organisations are in danger of being perceived as siding with the West. This was the case in the August 2003 Baghdad bombing, now known as the UN's 9/11, which killed the Undersecretary-General, Sergio Viera de Mello, and 21 others (Benthall, 2003; Donini, 2004; Hyder, 2007). From this section, we can glean the rationale of Humanitarian Aid and its multiple dimensions and effects in a conflict zone.

HUMANITARIAN AID AND WAR ECONOMY IN ARAB WORLD

HA organisations have been particularly active in the Arab World since the Arab Spring. The Tunisian government was overthrown on 14 January 2011, sparking protests in Egypt, Morocco, Syria, Yemen, and Oman, calling for a replacement of the repressive regimes. However, these protests were met with extreme violence from state forces and, as a result, these conflicts have led to deteriorating humanitarian situations (Amiri, 2011). The situation became particularly bad in Yemen, the poorest country in the Arab world, as malnourishment levels rose with increasing food insecurity (Global Humanitarian Overview, 2020). The situation in Libya worsened due to economic collapse, a lack of food supplies and internal and cross-border displacement, and the uprisings to rid Muammar Gaddafi of his presidency soon progressed into a Civil War. The violence continued and the Gulf Cooperation Council (GCC) took a political stance and challenged Gaddafi's dictatorship after the regime's violent response to protestors was condemned internationally and the League of Arab States (LAS) supported both UN and NATO-led military operations in Libya, with active participation from Qatar forces. In August, during the Battle of Tripoli the government of Gaddafi was overthrown; rebel troops then captured and assassinated Gaddafi in October, bringing an end to the Libyan Civil War. Meanwhile, the conflict in Syria led to a similar humanitarian crisis and in May 2012, the conflict between protestors and police was evident after the massacre of 108 people in Houla (Amiri, 2011). Given the severity of the situation in Syria, 3.7 million people have fled to Turkey, as legislation there provides people in need with international protection and a range of rights. As a result, Turkey hosts the largest number of refugees in the world. Furthermore, economies in the Arab world were undermined, basic services were hit with reductions in funding and foreign investment dropped, leading to millions of people struggling for survival.

Since this period and its unrest, there has been a proliferation of NGOs, and HA organisations have been very outspoken, condemning the extreme levels of force and other human rights violations that have been committed by both states and the rebel groups. However, access restrictions have been a high cause for concern; social unrest has led to high involvement from the state, which has reduced the number of operational areas and blocked the usual entry points for HA workers. A successful humanitarian response is "built on independently assessing needs, responding to them in accordance with humanitarian principles and upholding International Humanitarian Law (IHL) and human rights law," but humanitarian organisations haven't had accurate needs assessments and IHL cannot always be invoked in times of civil unrest. (Amiri, 2011) For this reason, humanitarian organisations have had to use human rights advocacy to gain access, except in Libya where IHL applies (Amiri, 2011). A multitude of problems have continued in the Arab world, including continued corruption and the formation of war economies and, thus, crises have continued to thrive. The Arab Spring was driven by the strong desire of people for a peaceful political change, but this desire did not become a reality, despite the political changes that occurred. Instead, it resulted in large-scale violence in Yemen, Syria, and Libya and autocratic consolidation in Egypt and Bahrain (Elayah & Verkoren, 2020).

The economy of the war in Syria is based on international and domestic mechanisms, Iran and Russia, who saved the Assad regime financially. Between 2011 and 2013, the sum of Iranian aid to Syria reached around $10 billion, whilst Russian aid is unknown and unlimited. Russia also provided a set of facilities for the Syrian regime in the form of trade-offs and oil exchanges, opening accounts in Russian banks and transferring Syrian assets in their pursuit of Western sanctions imposed on the Syrian regime. There are local sources of financing for the Assad government, including raising tariff rates at times, in addition to the support provided by networks of businessmen associated with the political system. Regarding the economy of opposition groups' war, the most prominent sources of income are international aid, looting, kidnappings, and smuggling. In addition, they seized both oil wells that were under the control of the Syrian regime and treasures of the central bank branch in some cities that have been taken over by fighting groups, such as the Al-Nusra Front (Anderson, 2019).

In the case of Libya, it went through comprehensive chaos and provided various opportunities for armed groups to rise and prosper, especially with the country's rich natural resources and geographical location. These groups were able to seize and smuggle natural resources as well as seize cash. In addition, armed groups have also relied on ransoms from the government, and black markets have played their role, particularly in the issue of currency exchange differences, manipulation, and the extortion of the financial sector. The conflicting parties also relied on new means and sources, most notably human smuggling, and the accompanying emergence of new organised criminal networks (Eaton, 2018).

From this historical and political context of the Arab region, we can get a better idea of the complicated relationship between conflict and Humanitarian Aid. The following will discuss the context of the worst affected region—Yemen.

The warring parties impede the delivery of HA in Yemen as part of a larger plan to gain power and control in the conflict, whilst making money from looting and selling HA on the black market and providing preferential treatment to the communities supporting them (Elayah & Fenttiman, 2021). The war economy began from the loyalist militias for all fighting parties dealt with the country's capabilities and stockpiled the HA, which it harnessed to finance its wars and enrich its loyalists. For example, the Houthi group used oil revenues, extortion, and levies imposed on citizens and merchants, even at the level of kidnappers and their families. Their control begins at the ports, which facilitate their imposition of levies and taxes on shipments, as well as enabling them to seize the HA coming into the country (Elayah & Fenttiman, 2021). This has resulted in Yemen turning into a black hole for HA, where supplies do not go to those who need it but on the contrary, it travels through the lobbies of warlords who play the most important role in prolonging and sustaining a war, by financing it (Elayah & Verkoren, 2020).

The Yemeni Humanitarian Aid Projects and INGOs

In the early nineteenth century, Yemen comprised an array of sheikhdoms and sultanates. In 1839, British forces moved in to occupy the southern city of Aden and then expanded in the 1920s to seize the sheikhdoms surrounding Aden. The British established the Federation of Arab Emirates of the South in 1959, which brought western and eastern Aden Protectorates together under British ruling (Halliday, 2013). This sparked a Civil War in 1962 when Yemenis in the North revolted against the monarchy, resulting in a new entity known as the Yemen Arab Republic (YAR). This revolution inspired Southern Yemenis in their resistance against the British and consequently, in 1963, the National Liberation Front (NLF) was formed. Following a four-year armed struggle, the British withdrew their troops in 1967 and handed over their power to the NLF who immediately established the People's Republic of South Yemen (PRSY), later renamed the People's Democratic Republic of Yemen (PDRY) in 1970. In the following decade, there were attempts to unify the US-backed north and South causing much conflict, but after a second PDRY-YAR war, a unity agreement was signed in 1979. In 1990, the PRDY and the YAR finally unified into the Republic of Yemen (ROY) with a Northern President, Ali Abdullah Saleh, and a Southern Vice President. However, in the same year, Iraq invaded Kuwait and Yemen was the only state at the United Nations Security Council to vote against the use of force towards Iraq due to Saleh's close ties with Saddam Hussein. This resulted in the US cutting off $70 million in aid to Yemen and the expulsion of 800,000 Yemeni people from nearby GCC states such as Saudi Arabia. This had an extremely damaging effect on the economy and led to high levels of unemployment and dissatisfaction. The reduction in remittances, which were previously used to fund community level investments, coincided with the discovery of oil and this exacerbated the crisis by further weakening the economic power of individuals and communities and strengthening the state (Lackner, 2019). In 1994, a civil war broke out between the north and the south of Yemen, which lasted till July, and, with the support of the US, Saleh's forces entered Aden and victory was theirs, resulting in a constitutional change to give Saleh more power. Saleh continued to rule over Yemen until 2011, favouring northerners and dismissing thousands of southerners from both military and civilian jobs, intensifying the humanitarian crisis (Elayah & Verkoren, 2020).

HA organisations have been active in Yemen since the early 1920s when the British colony seized Aden. The following decades saw more involvement from humanitarian organisations in response to increasing conflict, but it was only in the 1990s that the number of humanitarian organisations boomed due to the "newly pluralist political climate" (Elayah & Verkoren, 2020). HA organisations were operating due to new laws which allowed the access and registration of new establishments, meaning assistance from various humanitarian actors became a possibility. The increased political freedom also enabled existing organisations to expand their reach. However, corruption and nepotism were ubiquitous, and the Yemeni ruling elite was weakening the power of the people through "a mixture of repression, co-optation and divide-and-conquer tactics," worsening the humanitarian crisis (Elayah & Verkoren, 2020).

The Arab Spring brought about a new era with protests occurring all around the country condemning the poverty and corruption that had spread throughout the nation. The protests started in early 2011 with several dozen activists and students outside of Sana'a University, triggered by the protests in Tunisia. The protesters tended to be young, pro-democracy activists who did not identify with a particular political group (Lackner, 2019). The protests continued to grow across the country, especially following the resignation of President Mubarak in Egypt, with the protesters demanding the same in Yemen. This movement led to the formation of the Civil Coalition of Revolutionary Youth, which incorporated the four main youth associations, and had the goal "to lay the ground for a civic, modern and democratic state which can interact with the realities of the modern world on the basis of equal citizenship, human rights, social justice, a plural political system, and the freedom of expression and opinion" (Nevens, 2011). The Houthi movement in the north and Al-Hirak (now known by the southern transitional council STC) in the south, as well as various anti-government parties, joined together on the streets in support of these protests. The security forces responded to these uprisings with violence. On 18 March, over fifty protestors were shot by snipers in a massacre known as "Friday of Dignity" (Lackner, 2019). The violence continued, on 3 June many were killed in an attack during Friday prayers at a mosque and President Saleh was wounded and taken to Saudi Arabia for treatment. The Yemeni Spring lasted until February 2012 when Hadi took over from Saleh as president for a two-year transitional period. However, the problems in Yemen did not subside as there were still high levels of corruption, unemployment, food insecurity as policies were purposefully implemented to "constrain" the Houthi economy. Violence has continued to thrive amongst jihadists, Saleh's security personnel, and the separatist movement forming in the South (DeLozier, 2019).

The Houthi movement, which is comprised mainly of Yemen's Shia Muslim minority, took over the Saada province and the surrounding areas. Many Sunnis supported the Houthis as the rebels seized the capital, Sana'a. The Houthis have since been able to launch missile and drone attacks on Saudi Arabia, maintain their presence in Sana'a and siege Taiz. Forces from al-Qaeda in the Arab Peninsula (AQAP) and the Islamic State Group (IS) took control of territory in the south and carried out lethal attacks in Aden (Lackner, 2019). The violence has continued and many humanitarian organisations have established themselves in Yemen to provide HA to vulnerable people as the situation is now catastrophic due to the lengthy duration of this conflict (OCHA, 2017). The country is suffering an economic crisis, public sector salaries have not been paid, with funds diverted to the Alessi Group whose owner advises president Hadi, and the private sector has faced a huge decline (DeLozier, 2019). Starvation is rampant due to an increase in food prices, and together with the economic crisis and the loss of livelihoods, buying food is not within the means of the majority of the population. HA aims to alleviate this suffering but despite the efforts there is still an inordinate number of people needing help (OCHA, 2017).

In response to the ongoing Yemeni humanitarian catastrophe, the World Bank formed the Emergency Crisis Response Project (ECRP) in 2016. The first phase collected US$50 million, to offer temporary jobs and basic commodities. The second phase garnered US$250 million, to tackle starvation amongst children (World Bank, 2018b). In 2017, the third phase of the World Bank programme raised US$ 200 million, targeting an additional 1.5 million families (World Bank, 2018a). Due to its success, the World Bank approved the fourth phase of funds, US$140 million, to keep the programme functional in 2018 (World Bank, 2018a). In total, the World Bank fund was US$640 million, divided into two main cash programmes. Firstly, the cash for emergency programme amounted to US$340 million and has been employed by the United Nations Children's Fund (UNICEF) and secondly, the cash-for-work programme totalled US$300 million and has been employed under the (UNDP) United Nations Development Program (World Bank, 2018a).

Using the above assigned funds, INGO's executed multiple cash projects in Yemen, with a variety of goals, targeting different groups of people. Some were designed to provide immediate and unconditional help to people who cannot work and were listed in the Yemeni national social protection programme (1.5 million cases). Others were conditional programmes, formed to create job opportunities for low skill workers by contracting with them to build, maintain and renovate vital and historical infrastructure assets. Moreover, this encouraged small handmade business to create stable income projects (Kimball & Jumaan, 2020). The following section will highlight some of those projects and explain their impact on the Yemeni community through the categories of unrestricted and restricted cash projects.

The Emergency Cash Transfer Project (ECT project): An unrestricted cash project and UNICEF's biggest cash-based project, started its implementation in 2017, targeting at meeting people's basic needs. It was designed to help the neediest individuals, those in vulnerable positions (women/children), and those who cannot work (sick and elderly) (UNICEF, 2019). The cash distribution is unconditional, empowering people with the choice to buy what they want with "dignity" (UNICEF, 2019). The programme targeted the pre-conflict recipients of the Yemeni Social Welfare Fund, then it expanded to help those classified with "high-risk and volatile livelihood." To collect the funds, beneficiaries can go to the closest payment sites out of the thousands of designated places spread all over Yemen, including banks and local shops, and on-ground teams assist those who cannot access those sites (UNICEF, 2019). Moreover, the project introduced a messaging platform to communicate with beneficiaries. To ensure the project's transparency, an independent organisation is responsible for the monitoring and compliance during the project's life cycle (UNICEF, 2019). According to UNICEF, the project helped 1.4

million beneficiaries "indirectly impacting nearly 9 million people – about one-third of the country's population" (2019).

The other type of cash projects adopted in Yemen is a conditional one; cash-for-work projects differ from digital cash distribution projects, as they link the money distributed with performing a certain task. This allows communities to improve and develop and it enables individuals to build and enhance their skill sets and have a source of income to meet their basic needs. The project was designed to offer temporary jobs to people with low skills and no sustainable salary, especially in distant areas. It also sought to employ the local human resources to build or maintain the surrounding assets. The project helped multiple sectors, farmers were employed to protect the soil from erosion, improve and restore agricultural lands to maintain the Yemeni agricultural productivity. Others also helped in building wells, roads, and other assets. The cash-for-work projects have been implemented in Yemen by multiple NGOs targeting different sectors.

The Emergency Solid Waste Management Project: During the cholera crisis in Yemen and especially in Hodeidah. The UNDP funded a programme, implemented by the Sustainable Development Foundation (SDF) to use paid low skill labour to help collect solid municipal waste around the city (UNDP, 2019). Throughout the project's life cycle in 2019, the total participants were around 2800, receiving YR 3270 (roughly US$6.50) per day for 15–48 working days (UNDP, 2019). The project targeted 25,828 households who directly and indirectly benefited from the cash and cleaner environment. "The UNDP so far created 7.1 million employment workdays, reaching 290,000 participants in cash-for-work programs (indirectly benefiting over two million)" (UNDP, 2019).

Promoting Livelihood Opportunities for Urban Youth in Yemen: The UNESCO and the European Union adopted the cash-for-work approach, to firstly, push the Yemeni youth to become actors in the protection and restoration of the heritage sites, especially in Sana'a, Shibam, Zabid and Aden. The second aim of the project was to "retain traditional skills" and increase cultural public involvement (UNESCO, 2019). Other organisations, such as the USAID, adopted similar approaches, the USAID helped 10,700 people through a one-year rehabilitation cash-for-work infrastructure project in Amran and Hajjah governorates (USAID, 2018).

The Yemeni Cash-for-Work (CFW) project according to the UNDP was spent as follows:

1. Nine out of ten used the money to buy food commodities
2. One in four used the cash for treatment
3. One in five paid back debts

The shift towards cash projects (food assistance) as a substitute or a collaborator with food-aid, is not custom-made towards Yemen. The World Food Programme (WFP), the world's foremost humanitarian agency, has realised the shortcoming of abundantly depending on food-aid projects. According to the (WFP) "food-aid is a tried and tested model, proudly woven into WFP history, it sprang from a largely unidirectional, top-down vision: people were hungry; we fed them." Food assistance, by contrast, "involves a more complex understanding of people's long-term nutritional needs and of the diverse approaches required to meet them" (Diouf, n.d). This transformation towards cash interventions in Yemen goes beyond food-aid deficiencies, as they try to tread over generic operational and political issues facing aid providers in Yemen.

Challenges Facing Food-Aid Distributors in Yemen

Food-aid distributors face many administrative, social, and economic hurdles in Yemen. INGOs regularly contract with local NGOs to help deliver their food-aid, giving local NGOs the reign to choose the beneficiaries and the methods of distribution, which in conflict areas divert the aid to align with the "local NGO's" dogmatic allegiances. In the article *Civil Society During War: the case of Yemen*, Elayah discusses how Yemeni local NGOs do not operate as unbiased but quite the opposite—they are the palms of factions in the war (Elayah & Verkoren, 2020). In 2014, the estimated number of Yemeni NGOs was 9,996, almost doubling in numbers by 2018 to 18,650. Unfortunately, many of those organisations were established by different partisan actors for their own political interests, varying from, "Hadi forces, the Southern movement and the Houthis" (Elayah & Verkoren, 2020) where the different fighting parties use some of those organisations to establish their presence as a "legitimate" party and collect foreign aid through legal channels (Elayah & Verkoren, 2020). Consequently, food-aid programmes fell in the corruption trap as the World Food Program announced that 12,00,000 kilogrammes of food never reached their destination (Kiley et al., 2019). Also, it was discovered that the food that was supposed to help people in need was being sold by different groups in the secondary market and standardised food packs were being sold with the INGOs' logos on them. This was even documented with a video that went viral showing the food supplies being misused in Sarwah, an area controlled by the Houthis in Northern Yemen (Kiley et al., 2019). Consequently, the UN suspended a part of its food-aid programme to Yemen, as donors pushed to cut UN programmes food-aid funds towards Yemen (Barrington, 2020; BBC, 2019). In an article, Barrington mentions, "The U.N. humanitarian coordinator in Yemen, Lise Grande, told Reuters that 31 of the United Nation's 41 major programmes in Yemen will be reduced or cut in April 2020 without more funding" (Barrington, 2020). This was due to donors being afraid that maintaining food-aid support with no guarantees to reach its targeted beneficiaries will lengthen the duration of the war, which was the case in the South Sudan war when commodities that aimed to reach people who were suffering were hijacked by different parties, further aggravating the war (Kiley et al., 2019). However, discontinuing the funds towards Yemen because of the misuse of food-aid could be catastrophic, especially with the COVID-19 health dilemma. Hence, it became essential for the NGOs to find another mode to distribute aid to people in dire need—to increase the number of HA operations and limit the amount of aid diverted to the warring parties.

Apart from the administrative problems facing food-aid operators in Yemen, there are some social and economic fundamental shortcomings attached with food-aid. Distributing food commodities humiliates people as it neglects their own priorities such as housing and health; it does not change the beneficiary's situation as "they are only used as a set of passe-partout standard responses in emergencies" (Levine & Chastre, 2004). Food-aid being under local prices, whether it is free or subsidised, also negatively affects the local food and agricultural market. This consequentially increases the amount of people in need of humanitarian assistance, as farmers and others working the same production cycle lose their sources of income due to the huge flood of imported food commodities, decreasing the prices and demand for local grown products (Singer, 1988). Some activists have highlighted that developed countries use food-aid programmes to spread their "market dominance" with the excess products providing a profit for donor countries (ActionAid, 2003). It has been discovered that some countries keep local grain prices steady, and remove the extra supply from their market by dumping it as aid. This striving towards market dominance can be observed in the example of US food-aid under the 1954 Public Law 480, which was historically initiated as the "surplus disposal programme," was changed to the more likeable and politically correct name "Food for Peace" (Arestis & Sawyer, 2001). Another common criticism of food-aid is that it may encourage recipient developing countries to stop working on evolving their national food sector, as they may attain "food dependency" on foreign funds. Furthermore, many emerging nations historically have shown "urban bias" towards deserting crop and cattle production (Arestis & Sawyer, 2001).

Cash as an Aid Alternative in Yemen

To further explore the complexities and hindrances of aid in Yemen, a sample was selected and interviewed. The interviews with the selected sample highlighted multiple issues with the food-aid distribution process, from both the workers and the beneficiaries' perspectives. The initial findings from the Yemeni food-aid mechanism case study are divided into two sections—the organisational distribution issues by the various different NGOs and the complaints raised by the recipients to the sample organisations regarding the lack of diversification and low quality of food products.

The primary research showed that the diversion and misuse of food-aid typically happen during the verification and distribution processes. Usually, the initial recipients list prepared by the organisations is accurate and includes the names of people in dire need of help, as members of the donor organisations regularly supervise the procedure. However, because of the de facto-governmental pressure and the logistical obstacles such as the change/delay in delivery timings, transportation costs, or individual's health cotions, recipients are hindered from attending the distribution process and food-aid gets averted. According to the interviewees, the diversion of aid occurs due to political pressure or security threats targeted at the NGO staff members. Aid workers are pushed by warring parties to divert the food baskets to certain members affiliated with the de facto parties, who use it for their economic or political gain. The interviews have shown that mostly organisations working in the Houthi controlled areas complained about the political pressure influencing their aid operations. From a logistical perspective, when a recipient fails to attend during the distribution process, the names on the beneficiaries list get modified with different recipients by NGO members responsible for registering and verification process. However, many interviewees stated that people are being added without checking if they are in need for the food supplies and sometimes, they add people from within their close circle, such as family members or friends, who will resell it for personal gain. Food supplies used to be distributed on certain dates, and once a recipient has not turned up, they remove their name from the list and put someone they know instead, even if they do not meet the criteria of individuals who deserve the food baskets supply. Another issue is that once the distribution cycle ends and extra food bags are available, they try to discard them by any means "sometimes even to random people on the street." This happens to make sure that they get another full batch from the donor organisation and to avoid the expiration of certain products. One more observation, another staff member added, is that there will be a truck next to the distribution warehouse buying the supplies from the recipients once they collect their share; he added that they do this in front of the staff members and that the only commodity beneficiaries keep is the cooking oil. Moreover, they add that local shop owners have complained that they cannot sell their products anymore as food-aid goods have been flooding the market, pushing them to use their shops to resell food-aid products because, although they are of lower quality, they are below the average market prices. This has led to the abolishment of local food manufacturers and market share, contributing to the already catastrophic economy dilemma. From the interviews, we noticed that when the donors are local, the diversion of food items tends to be less than the usual as they closely supervise the distribution process and have fewer predetermined beneficiaries compared to the international donors.

The aid recipients mostly complained about the quality of the products as the grains were usually in below average conditions and the products were always repetitive. This has led them to frequently store extra quantities of products they have an abundance of and are not going to use; so, they end up selling or exchanging them for other products. Furthermore, recipients continuously complained about the transport costs as they cannot use local transportation to take home their products; car rental prices have been high and were for some beneficiaries around 50% of the price of resold aid supplies. This humiliates people as sometimes they cannot sell the food items and even if they do, they are under-priced. The beneficiaries stated that they are inclined to resell their assigned food-aid products as soon as possible, to fulfil other crucial needs such as paying for medical bills, rent, etc.

In contrast, the greatest advantage of cash-aids is that it empowers people to independently decide their priorities and increase their purchasing power, to have a healthier diet, housing, medical bills, education, pay back debts, and in some cases save up to start small business (ODI and CGD, 2015). The restricted and unrestricted cash projects have helped improve people's dignity as they have enabled higher access to more essential products. However, the primary research showed that in some underprivileged cases, the modest amounts of money offered were not enough to meet the basic living conditions required and, by default, has not enhanced their dignity. Thus, cash aid has not worked as intended; hence, more research is needed to understand and decide the correct amounts that will significantly improve people's livelihoods, in a respectable manner.

Nevertheless, the major concern that all participants share was the fear of donor organisations stopping or minimising the amount of aid towards Yemen. Donors have lost their trust in the HA distribution process and halted funds due to the project's deficiencies and misappropriation. With this, NGOs working in Yemen desperately need to avoid new scandals by offering a secure and effective method to support the Yemeni population, whilst maintaining the flow of humanitarian funds. Cash-based projects as an aid alternative, accompanied with a digital trackable method, offer a swift way to overcome the diversion of aid by the war parties. It has become essential, to gain back the trust of UN donor members to remobilise the funds towards Yemen. The distribution of cash-aid through rigorous and various digital payments offers a fast, flexible, secure, and discrete aid distributing channels with beneficiaries (ODI and CGD, 2015). It allows for better control, by reducing the ability of NGOs to modify the primary recipients lists, reducing and eliminating the risk of third-party assistance confiscation, by minimising the physical circulation of aid. It also offers beneficiaries a simpler and cheaper way to receive the aid by removing the transportation costs they had to bear every distribution cycle. Moreover, conditional cash projects funds, being tied with individuals preforming certain tasks, enable local residents to build essential infrastructural projects that can be used by the surrounding community. Cash-for-work projects also tackle the assumption that people capable of work will get lazy and dependent once they start getting cash as aid, leading to high levels of unemployment. NGOs would still need to monitor spending patterns, inform people about digital payments, and reach those who do not have the technology or access.

Allocating funds towards cash-aid as opposed to food-aid also has an economic advantage due to the lower logistical costs. Saving up on the operational costs by physical cash exchange or digital transfers should accordingly increase the impact of the cash-based projects to reach more people than the food-aid projects. This was the case in Somalia, where only 35% of the actual food-aid funds reached the beneficiaries, compared to 85% that reached the cash-aid recipients (Hedlund, 2013; ODI and CGD, 2015). Moreover, cash-based aid has a higher percentage of impact on the society, as shown by the UNICEF project, which was directed at 1.4 million recipients and another 9 million lives were positively affected, whilst the scale of impact of food-aid projects is limited to the targeted population. Increasing the amount of cash supply in the market will help decrease the economy stagnation, through growing people's purchasing power. This will consequently increase the market demand and supply of different products, pushing the private sector to be involved in providing enough supplies of necessities and increasing the local production cycle, creating jobs and investments, and indirectly benefiting a larger scale of people. However, it is important to note that it could also cause inflation because as incomes rise so does the cost of living, unless measures are put in place to control this increase.

Although all the participants agreed on the superiority and effectiveness of cash-aid over food-aid projects, cash-aid projects are still small scale compared to the large-scale food-aid projects in Yemen. The staff members claimed that local NGOs prefer to work with food-aid, as they have a higher funding approval rate, being a tested model that they have experience with and is easier to justify during the proposals phase than cash projects. A staff member added that the NGOs' "supply and demand mentality" has pushed many of them to shift their purpose and activities towards food-aid distribution programmes. This is especially the case given that almost all aid funds offered by the donors nowadays are fixated towards emergency humanitarian projects in the form of food-aid. However, due to the adversities NGOs face with the misappropriations of food-aid supplies, Yemen is now fronting the danger of donors cutting the funds greatly needed by the Yemeni population, especially with the current COVID-19 health situation. Hence, cash projects should no longer be the anomaly in Yemen, the international community needs to start considering cash-aid instead of food-aid, as it has been proved that it can be an efficacious method in conflict-torn countries. Adopting more cash projects in Yemen would also decrease local NGOs' role in direct aid distribution, encouraging them to focus on sustainable development projects, education, women rights, and other pressuring matters.

Conclusion

The Yemeni population is facing the worst humanitarian crisis in the world. The massive food-aid programmes in Yemen have marginally helped decrease the severity of the hunger situation, but they have created a bigger dilemma with donors threatening to stop the flow of funds, due to the diversion of food-aid by the de facto parties resulting in food-aid becoming a weapon of war (Barrington, 2020). Thus, it has become essential to gain back the donors' trust and maintain the flow of funds, offering cash-aid as a superior method to food-aid in Yemen, capable of decreasing the deviation of aid. Adopting more cash-aid programmes does not imply eliminating food-aid projects. As both cash and food-aid cannot omit all the risks involved during the distribution of aid. But cash aid offers a way to mitigate the aid distribution risks in Yemen. Especially due to the war ongoing since 2014, calling for long-term options instead of the widely used short-term HA methods. Cash-based intervention effects are long-term when compared with food-aid, as they aim to "alleviate hunger here and now with the broader objective of ending hunger once and for all," aligning with the UN's first and second sustainable development goals (SDGs) to eliminate poverty and hunger (Diouf, n.d).

Cash-aid has proved to be more efficient than food interventions in conflict-torn countries such as "Somalia where 2.5 more of aid budgets went directly to beneficiaries with cash than with food-aid" (ODI and CGD, 2015). However, for them to work in Yemen as Somalia, cash-aid projects need to be integrated within a trackable electronic cash transfer system, that can be implemented through customised NGO systems such as "The Electronic Cash Transfer Learning Action Network, convened by Mercy Corps" or by collaborating with the private sector (ODI and CGD, 2015). Cash-aid will aim to either mobilise the existing various currency transfer platforms in Yemen offered by money transfer companies and banks or create a new platform with the support of the mobile network companies. Adopting the digital payment methods during humanitarian crises in a war-torn country has already proved its success in the case of Somalia, where it reached more than a million recipients (ODI and CGD, 2015). In addition, the digital distribution of cash-aid, if implemented correctly, could be the solution for the global lack of data concerning the real amount of aid reaching its destined recipients. Although, this information would help donors to more efficiently "monitor, evaluate and communicate the aid projects results with both the affected populations and the tax-paying public in donor countries," (ODI and CGD, 2015) the data protection risks increase so NGOs need to make sure to employ a secure "closed loop system" that must be "collected, managed, stored and shared in line with good data management practices" (Burton, 2020). Moreover, using digital platforms is not the only feasible way to distribute cash aid as creating functional, secure electronic system for the HA in Yemen will take time. Multiple methods to distribute cash can be employed at the same time where this was done by the ICRS in the Democratic Republic of the Congo. The ICRS uses three methods: "cash payments directly to people, digital payments via mobile money, and digital payments via personal accounts held with cooperatives" (Burton, 2020).

Nevertheless, for the cash-aid projects to be successful in helping the 8 million who lost their sources of income and the 2 million internally displaced Yemenis, once implemented, unrestricted cash-aid packages should not be standardised. They should take into consideration the number of family members, the health of individuals, housing, and other economic and social factors. Conditional cash programmes should include skill training for its participants and offer them a way to earn a decent income after the projects end, such as carpentry, plumbing etc., and grants to allow the local people to set up small businesses. The list of recipients should be audited regularly by either the donor organisation or a third party, or secure digitalised verifications should be used, such as fingerprint or face ID methods that can only be accessed by the designated person. Lastly, NGOs need to track spending patterns to prevent socially destructive habits and protect marginalised beneficiary groups from being exploited by offering them a variety of aid delivery methods. It will also help track the spending patterns to assess whether different projects have met their objectives.

After discussing the challenges facing NGOs in conflict areas, examining empirical information about cash transfers as an alternative aid mechanism, and drawing on the experience from different countries with complex circumstances against the food-aid programme in Yemen, this chapter concludes that cash-based interventions during emergencies offer a great alternative as an aid mechanism. This method targets a wider scope of peoples' necessities in a more efficient and effective delivery approach that can be easily tracked by the donors. Hence, a significant proportion of the huge funds allocated for food-aid in Yemen should be redirected towards cash-aid when NGOs are able to provide the required conditions to ensure significant success and impact.

Now that we have covered the analysis of the on-ground reality in the Arab region, specifically, Yemen and its ongoing humanitarian crisis, we can move onto a deeper analysis of the amount of coverage devoted to the conflicts in Yemen and Syria to understand the difference in both the analysis and the reality along with its abstract portrayal in European media. The following chapter will also look at media frames used in reportage to understand if there the various media outlets differ in their coverage of the two cases.

To help the readers grasp the history of the Yemeni NDCs, in contrast with other National Dialogues, along with the added rich context of the Humanitarian Aid aspect, the following chapter will be bolstered by this analysis to provide a unique perspective of the Yemeni crisis which has not been attempted before this study.

REFERENCES

ActionAid. (2003). *Human Security Policy Briefing Note 1 Food Aid: An ActionAid Briefing Paper*. http://www.actionaid.org.uk/doc_lib/food_aid_background_briefing_paper.pdf

Amiri, A. (2011). The humanitarian challenge in the Middle East. *Humanitarian Practice Network (HPN), 51*, 2–9. https://odihpn.org/wp-content/uploads/2011/09/humanitarianexchange051.pdf. Accessed 1 June 2020.

Anderson, P. (2019). Beyond Syria's war economy: Trade, migration and state formation across Eurasia. *Journal of Eurasian Studies, 10*(1), 75–84.

Arestis, P., & Sawyer, M. C. (Eds.). (2001). *A biographical dictionary of dissenting economists*. Edward Elgar Publishing.

Bandsom, K. (2018). *Fighting Hunger with Cash*. https://www.welthungerhilfe.org/our-work/countries/yemen/fighting-hunger-with-cash/

Barnett, M. (2011). *Empire of humanity: A history of humanitarianism* (1st ed., pp. 29–32). Cornell University.

Barrett, C., & Maxwell, D. (2005). *Food aid after fifty years. Recasting its role*. Routledge.

Barrington, L. (2020, April 9). *WFP to halve food aid in Houthi Yemen as funding drops*. https://www.reuters.com/article/yemen-security-aid/wfp-to-halve-food-aid-in-houthi-yemen-as-funding-drops-idUSL5N2BX4YH

BBC. (2019, June 21). *Yemen crisis: UN partially suspends food aid*. https://www.bbc.com/news/world-middle-east-48716258

Benthall, J. (2003). Humanitarianism and Islam after 11 September. *Humanitarian Action and the 'Global War on Terror*, 37–47.

Burton, J. (2020). "Doing no harm" in the digital age: What the digitalization of cash means for humanitarian action. *International Review of the Red Cross, 102*(913), 43–73.

Castillo, J. G. (2021). Deciding between cash-based and in-kind distributions during humanitarian emergencies. *Journal of Humanitarian Logistics and Supply Chain Management, 11*(2), 272–295.

Cash for Work: Promoting Livelihood Opportunities for Urban Youth in Yemen. (2020, March 3). https://en.unesco.org/news/cash-work-promoting-livelihood-opportunities-urban-youth-yemen

Clay, E. (2005). *The development effectiveness of food aid—Does tying matter?* Organisation for Economic Co-operation and Development.

DeLozier, E. (2019). *In Damning Report, UN Panel Details War Economy in Yemen*. [online] The Washington Institute. https://www.washingtoninstitute.org/policy-analysis/view/in-damning-report-un-panel-details-war-economy-in-yemen. Accessed 31 March 2020.

Diouf, S. P. (n.d.). *Food assistance: Cash and in-kind*. Retrieved July 10, 2020, from https://www.wfp.org/food-assistance

Donini, A. (2004). Western Aid agencies don't have a humanitarian monopoly. *Humanitarian Affairs Review*, 12–15

Doocy, S. (2017). The effectiveness and value for money of cash-based humanitarian assistance: A systematic review. *Journal of Development Effectiveness, 10*(1), 121–144.

Elayah, M. (2016). Lack of foreign aid effectiveness in developing countries between a hammer and an anvil. *Contemporary Arab Affairs, 9*(1), 82–99.

Elayah, M. (2021). Women, Peace and Security (WPS) agenda between rhetoric and action in the MENA Region: A case study of Yemen and Libya. In A. A. Karim, R. Khalil, & A. Moustafa (Eds.), *Female pioneers from ancient Egypt and the Middle East: On the influence of history on gender psychology* (pp. 101–119). Springer.

Elayah, M., & Fenttiman, M. (2021). Humanitarian aid and war economies: The case of Yemen. *The Economics of Peace and Security Journal, 16*(1).

Elayah, M., & Verkoren, W. (2020). Civil society during war: The case of Yemen. *Peacebuilding, 8*(4), 476–498.

Eaton, T. (2018). *Libya's War Economy. Predation, Profiteering and State Weakness* (Chatham House Research Paper). https://www.chathamhouse.org/sites/files/chathamhouse/publications/research/2018-04-12-libyas-war-economy-eaton-final.pdf

Findley, M. G. (2018). Does foreign aid build peace? *Annual Review of Political Science, 21*, 359–384.
Gibelman, M., & Gelman, S. R. (2001). Very public scandals: Nongovernmental organizations in trouble. *Nonprofit and Voluntary Sector Quarterly, 12*(1), 49–66.
Halliday, F. (2013). *Arabia without sultans*. Saqi.
Harvey, P. (2005, February). *Cash and vouchers in emergencies* (Discussion Paper). Humanitarian Policy Group, Overseas Development Institute. http://www.odi.org.uk/hpg/papers/cash_discussion_paper.pdf.
Hedlund, K., Majid, N., Maxwell, D., & Nicholson, N. (2013). *Final evaluation of the unconditional cash and voucher response to the crisis 2011–12 in southern and central Somalia* (Executive Summary). Humanitarian Outcomes and United Nations Children's Fund, Somalia, UNICEF.
Hoelman, M. (2009). *Social Audit in Development Sector*. https://www.changemakers.com/
Hyder, M. (2007). Humanitarianism and the Muslim world. *The Journal of Humanitarian Assistance*, 1–19.
Kent, R. C. (1987). *Anatomy of disaster relief: The international network in action* (pp. 137–138). Pinter.
Kiley, S., Sirgany, S. E., & Lainé, B. (2019, May 20). *CNN exposes systematic abuse of aid in Yemen*. https://edition.cnn.com/2019/05/20/middleeast/yemen-houthi-aid-investigation-kiley/index.html
Kim, J. Y. (2017). *Rethinking development finance*. World Bank.
Kimball, A. M., & Jumaan, A. (2020). Yemen: The challenge of delivering aid in an active conflict zone. *Global Security: Health, Science and Policy, 5*(1), 65–67.
Lackner, H. (2019). *Yemen in crisis: Road to war*. Verso Books.
Levine, S., & Chastre, C. (2004, July). *Missing the Point: An Analysis of Food Security Interventions in the Great Lakes* (Network Paper 47). Humanitarian Practice Network, Overseas Development Institute. http://www.odihpn.org/documents/networkpaper047.pdf
Nevens, K. (2011). Yemen's youth revolution. *The Arab Spring: Implications for British Policy*, 24–27.
OCHA. (2017). *Humanitarian Needs Overview: Yemen*. https://www.unocha.org/sites/dms/Yemen/YEMEN%202017%20HNO_Final.pdf
Overseas Development Institute (ODI) and the Center for Global Development (CGD). (2015). *Doing cash differently: How cash transfers can transform humanitarian aid*.
Paulmann, J. (2013). Conjunctures in the history of international humanitarian aid during the twentieth century. *Humanity: An International Journal of Human Rights, Humanitarianism, and Development, 4*(2), 215–238.

Pugh, M., Cooper, N., & Goodhand, J. (2005). War Economies in a Regional Context: Challenges of Transformation. *African Security Review, 14*(4), 128.

Rysaback-Smith, H. (2016). History and principles of humanitarian action. *Turkish Journal of Emergency Medicine, 15*(1), 5–7.

Singer, H. W. (1988). Food aid: Pros and cons. *Intereconomics, 23*(2), 79–83.

Terry, F. (2011). The International Committee of the Red Cross in Afghanistan: Reasserting the neutrality of humanitarian action. *International Review of the Red Cross, 93*, 173.

UN. (2019, July 31). *Implementing a cash transfer project in Yemen.* https://yemen.un.org/en/19047-implementing-cash-transfer-project

UNDP. (2019, December 22). *Supported cash-for-work initiative helps deal with mounting solid waste crisis in Hodeidah: UNDP in Yemen.* https://www.ye.undp.org/content/yemen/en/home/stories/undp-supported-cash-for-work-initiative-helps-deal-with-mounting.html

UNESCO. (2019, November 12). *Yemen: Cash for Work.* https://en.unesco.org/news/yemen-cash-work

UNICEF. (2019). *Emergency Cash Transfer Project.* https://www.unicef.org/yemen/emergency-cash-transfer-project

United Nations Office for the Coordination of Humanitarian Affairs (OCHA) 2020. Global Humanitarian Overview. (2020). *United Nations-coordinated support to people affected by disaster and conflict* (pp. 4–85). OCHA.

USAID. (2018, January). *Success Stories report.*

Westley, F. (1991). Bob Geldof and live aid: The affective side of global social innovation. *Human Relations, 44*(10), 1011–1036.

World Bank. (2018a). *The World Bank Yemen Emergency Crisis Response Project—Third Additional Financing Report 2018.* The World Bank.

World Bank. (2018b, May 29). *Yemen food imports: A focus on critical challenges and priority interventions.* https://www.worldbank.org/en/country/yemen/publication/securing-imports-of-essential-food-commodities-to-yemen

Vogel, B., Tschunkert, K., & Schläpfer, I. (2021). The social meaning of money: Multidimensional implications of humanitarian cash and voucher assistance. *Disasters.*

CHAPTER 6

Framing Conflict in the Middle East: Yemen and Syria in European Media

Moosa Elayah and Fatima Al Majdhoub

One of the most powerful assets or commodities in this day and age is information, and information begets and grants power. Media, known as the fourth pillar of democracy, can wield this power of information and often influences perception. A free media can represent a multitude of opinions in a society whereas media that is controlled by a few can descend into practices of censorship, propaganda, inciting hatred, and ultimately aggravating, if not inciting conflict. In times of war and conflict, Tony Brenton said, "truth is the first casualty." When it comes to journalism, certain ideals and ethics take precedent, however, the case is different when considering factors allyship, monetary funding etc. in a conflict situation. How media houses present conflict and deal with misinformation is highly significant when it comes to reporting on war, violence, and identity-based tension in regions that are usually underreported in the news.

In the case of the conflict between Russia and Ukraine, there are several levels and dimensions to the media reporting. Local media outlets in Russia were prone to propaganda and spreading harmful rumours about the conflict. An information war was essentially waged which helped Russia meet its ultimate agenda. Several state-owned Russia media outlets replaced Ukrainian ones. While Western media houses criticised Russia's actions, Russian outlets presented the same as Russophobia and a humanitarian crisis. Quoting Peter Pomerantsev and Michael Weiss, Ben Nimmo calls this "weaponization of information." As in, Russia "uses a network of officials, journalists, sympathetic commentators, and internet trolls to create an alternative reality in which all truth is relative, and no information can be trusted." He goes to discuss the four tactics predominantly used by the Russian propaganda machine: "dismiss the critic, distort the facts, distract from the main issue and dismay the audience." The narrative that once claimed that Ukraine "is 'our brother nation', now it has become Russia's deepest enemy." Using these unethical means to twist the narrative of the war is one of the downfalls of the media reporting.

Effective media reporting needs to be driven by context and bolstered by background. Often reportage of violent conflicts, countries ridden with strife and terror, is driven by a superficial outline, a caricature, of the situation on ground. To combat this dangerous tactic, the concept of peace journalism is a useful touchstone. It is described as

> Peace Journalism is an established academic field that offers a remedy to the propaganda-driven mainstream media. It has infused journalism practices with the lessons of Peace & Conflict studies and provides journalists the tools to combat us vs. them, zero-sum game reporting by giving voice to the often-ignored peacebuilders in society and thereby offering nonviolent solutions to conflict.

However, it is important to note that these concepts and theoretical solutions are not always effective on ground especially in the case of identity-based clashes. Often, the violence of these conflicts is reported to evoke emotions and sympathy, but it should also be noted that they are often underpinned by a certain narrative gaze that the West holds over regions that are underreported or ignored. The case picked for the purpose of analysis in this book are among those. For example, the conflict in Yemen is often portrayed in the context of sectarian clashes. Since European media outlets almost always focus on the gore of the violence, the conflict and by extension the entire geographical region is viewed through the similar lens, making difficult it difficult to actually heal the social fabric and combat the humanitarian crisis. National Dialogues are immensely useful in debunking the muddled nature of the conflict, ideological or otherwise.

Since the Arab uprising until now when this chapter is being written, Yemen and Syria have been devastated by wars. In the case of Yemen, the conflict is between forces led by Saudi Arabia which are loyal to the internationally recognized government of President Abdrabbuh Mansur Hadi and those allied to the Houthi rebel movement. Since March 2015, over 7,640 civilians have been killed and 50,237 injured—the majority in air strikes by a Saudi-led multinational coalition that backs the president. The conflict and blockade imposed by the coalition triggered a humanitarian disaster. Of the total Yemen population of 27.5 million, 22.2 million are those in need of Humanitarian Aid, including nearly 10 million children. 10.6 million people suffer from severe lack of food security, which includes around 2 million suffering from deep starvation. At least 2 million children are suffering from malnutrition and 3 million + 1.1 million have very severe malnutrition (OCHA Yemen, 2017).

In the case of Syria, as the conflict between Assad's regime and their allies, and the opposition and rebel groups, enters its seventh year since 2011, more than 465,000 Syrians have lost their lives in the fighting, more than a million injured and over 12 million Syrians, which is half the country's pre-war population, displaced from their homes. On September 30, 2015, Russia launched a bombing campaign against what are claimed to be terrorist groups in Syria that included ISIL as well as rebel groups backed by Western states. Russia also deployed military advisers to back up Assad's defenses.

In today's globalised world, technology advancement in media and the way people communicate from around the globe at high speeds has been conducive for debates on issues that concern the international community (Harvey, 1989 cited in Tomlinson, 1997). The role of media in democratic governance has always been to provide space and platform for people's views and to initiate and bolster public dialogue and discourse. The role of the media is not limited to reporting and keeping the public abreast of worldly issues. It also includes raising issues and shaping and initiating positive or negative changes. Considering that the media determines and guides opinion on global issues, it has a crucial role to play in shaping the opinion of the society on certain conflicts or crises. This chapter compares the media coverage devoted to the wars in Yemen and Syria by selected European media outlets. This chapter explores and examines the reportage and online news broadcast of leading newspapers (The Independent, United Kingdom; NRC Handelsblad, the

Netherlands) and the international broadcast news (France24, France, and Swissinfo.ch, Switzerland).

In the case of Yemen, it is noticed that there is little empirical data and only a few studies available on the media coverage of the Saudi Arabian-led intervention in Yemen war that was launched in March 2015 and it is assumed that the Yemeni war is underreported as compared to the case of Syria. This chapter comprises empirical observations that allow explorative assumptions as a starting point for future research. It examines and compares the amount of news coverage devoted to the Saudi-led coalition military intervention in Yemen and Russian military intervention in Syria by European media over a period of one year. The analysis initiates research into the nature of news coverage by the European media of both Saudi-Yemen war and Syrian war. As a result, the researchers are able to prove that the Saudi-Yemen war is underreported or receives little attention by the media and international agenda especially in Europe as it is one of serious crises that engulfed the Middle East similar to Syria. The chapter also examines the news frames were used to present both conflicts. By comparing the news coverage, the researchers are able to achieve the following objectives:

1. Identifying the amount of online coverage of Yemen and Syrian conflicts by The Independent, NRC Handelsblad, France24 and Swissinfo.ch.
2. Positing the primary frames used in reporting the Yemen and Syria conflicts by the four European media outlets.
3. Determining whether these media outlets differ in their news coverage on both conflicts.

To analyse the content of non-US media, four European media outlets were selected to answer the following questions:

1. What is the amount of coverage devoted to the Saudi military intervention in Yemen and the Russian military intervention in Syria by The Independent France24, NRC Handelsblad, and Swissinfo.ch online news?
2. How do The Independent, France24, NRC Handelsblad, and Swissinfo.ch frame both conflicts?

3. Do The Independent, NRC Handelsblad, France24, and Swiss-info.ch online news differ in their news coverage on Saudi military intervention in Yemen and the Russian military intervention in Syria?

MEDIA AND INTERNATIONAL PEACE INTERVENTION

The media in critical times play a key role in relaying, analysing and portraying events to reflect the reality and for the public to understand current affairs. The proliferation of content by the media has the ability to influence the relevance of topics regarding public agenda and policymakers. In other words, if a news item is covered frequently and prominently, the public will regard the issue as more important (Scheufele, 2000). The main objective is to influence people in terms of either shaping or changing the public opinion and attitudes toward a certain issue and then trigger action. Thus, the media is the main source of information for the public to know what is happening in the world and to learn about their government's approach towards international conflicts (Baum & Zhukov, 2016).

The international media has the ability to attract a worldwide attention to conflicts or crisis, no matter where they are in the world. However, the coverage of conflict or crisis depends on a complex set of factors which include the relationship of the reporting country with the actors involved in the conflict, the independence the media has, and the power holders in society (Puddepphatt, 2006). Throughout history, several conflicts have attracted serious concern from the international community, and those that have, have had a significant impact.

The imbalance approaches to media reporting of conflicts around the world could be seen as the only explanation for the lack of media coverage. On the one hand, there is no doubt that the importance and the political dimensions of some conflicts affect the response of powerful world leaders and definitely affect the media's coverage of conflict and the way it is reported. On the other hand, it is the extent to which the media agenda of covering one conflict over another in turn shapes the response of the international community. In some studies, as mentioned by Puddepphatt, Rosendale, and Longcore, the main factor is that the media pays great deal of attention to public concerns. This is evidenced in the case of the European population who need deep clarification about the conflicts to attract their attention and involvement. Consequently, some conflicts received great international attention through media exposure while some failed to get this attention and some cases were neglected. Through the analysis of online news articles of four major news sites in Europe, this chapter compares the media coverage of the wars that occurred during the same period of time in Yemen and Syria.

CONTENT ANALYSIS

This study has used content analysis to collect the data and also used the deductive approach to investigate frames that are defined and operationalized prior to investigation. Content analysis is the analysis of written content of any type of communication material such as textbook, newspapers, magazines, novels, political speeches, or pictures (Frankel & Wallen, 2009). Weber (1990) defines content analysis as "… a research method that uses as set of procedures to make valid inferences from text." While Krippendorff (2013) defines it by emphasizing reliability and validity. He states that content analysis is a research technique for making replicative and valid inferences from data to their context. In this study, the researchers conduct content analysis of four Western media (non-US media) by selecting a purposive sample of online English news outlets that are prestigious and have widespread readership and a large circulation in Europe. Vreese (2004) pointed at the majority of studies investigating media framing focus on print media due to the availability of the material over time. But in this study, due to the difficulty in accessing print newspapers and traditional broadcasting channels, the researchers selected and analysed the content of four European online English news outlets on the Saudi-Yemen war and Syria to meet the objectives of the study.

PROCEDURE

To create the context of this study, we only took online articles that deal with wars in Yemen and Syria. In the case of Yemen, the articles were selected from the time period of 26 March 2015, until 26 March 2017. While the articles about Syria were chosen from 30 September 2015, until 30 September 2017. The reasons for choosing the time frame of two years include firstly, the severity of the events in both countries. The second reason is that we noticed that there was no coverage in the early months of the war in Yemen. Same articles were repeated later from time to time and there was no new news. In other words, there was not enough data and the sample would not be enough for examination. Therefore, we decided to extend the time period to two years to have enough data and to get a clear picture of the coverage of some incidents that happened over two years in both cases.

The researchers captured the online articles by going into each website's archive and choosing the advanced search option. The following keywords were used to narrow down the search result: such as Saudi war, Syrian war, Yemen war, al- Assad, Houthis, Saudi-led coalition etc. In one instance, the displayed results listed about 341 articles (All) for "Saudi-Yemen war" and 1255 articles for Syrian civil war in the archive of *SWI swissinfo.ch*; however, the researchers noticed that the source option showed articles from previous years as well. Therefore, articles had to be eliminated and selected according to the time frame of the study. A similar procedure was done for the *France24* and *The Independent*.

As for NRC, since the newspaper is circulated in Dutch, the website keeps whole versions of the newspaper in PDF form. The co-author and the second coder of this paper are from Radboud University Nijmegen and, thus, helped in translating the content of the relevant articles from NRC into English. Generally, for all online news articles, the researchers read through the articles one by one to decide which one would be relevant for this study.

In the next step, the researchers identified the most common frames used and modified them for the purposes of this study. These frames are:

- Conflict
- Attribution of Responsibility
- Consequences
- Human Interest
- Morality.

Then the researchers performed the inter-rater reliability by randomly selecting 60 articles out of 605 and test the level of agreement. Cohen's kappa is used for summarizing nominal variables as the ideal binary reliability was originally proposed as a measure of agreement between two raters or two observers who independently rate each of the same samples of objects (Warrens, 2012). In this study, the researchers used Cohen's kappa test to examine the level of agreement between them, and since reliability measure for Kappa ranges from 0 to 1.0, it was found that the inter-coder reliability for news frame was 0.83 with $P<0.001$, The rule of thumb for kappa is accepting at least the value of 0.6 for the level of agreement between coders (Landis & Koch, 1977), therefore, the level of agreement between the two coders this study considers good is the value 0.83 which is above 0.6.

OPERATIONALISATION OF NEWS FRAMES

The following definitions of the five frames were developed by Semetko and Valkenburg (2000) and modified by the researchers to meet the objectives of the study. According to the operationalization of these frames, the researchers were able to identify which content of the article matches the frame category:

1. **Conflict**: News that emphasises conflict between the conflicted parties or groups; news that reflects the disagreement between the warring parties; labels the good and bad; news items that refer to two or more sides of the war; news items refer to winners or losers; dispute over the actions; news item reports clashes, tensions, shelling, bombardment or violence; construct antagonism between opposing opinion or stances.
2. **Consequences**: News items that report the impact of the conflict on individuals, or its consequences at the national level; reportage about damages, casualties, or losses; reportage about the steps taken to resolve an issue/ problem; report warnings given by individuals, groups, parties, institutions or country over an action; reportage about the arrests of individuals; reports the steps taken by government or any external body; reports on economic hardships; report on starvation/ famine/ humanitarian crisis; reportage about external interference to facilitate national, regional or international dialogue among the warring parties.
3. **Attribution of responsibility**: News that attributes responsibility for the war or solutions or attacks to governments, parties, or groups; reports that carry suggestions that certain events require urgent reaction.
4. **Morality**: News items that situate conflicts/war in the context of morality and social prescriptions or action; emphasising Humanitarian Aids, peace talk, and negotiation.

5. **Human interest**: News that humanise or add an emotional angle to the presentation of events; refer to the efforts to personalise, dramatise, or emotionalise the news in order to capture and retain audience interest; employs adjectives or personal vignettes that generate feelings of outrage, empathy, concern, sympathy, or compassion; emphasise how individuals and groups are affected by the events; news items that go into the private or personal lives of the actors.
6. **Other**: Any content that could not fit in the above categories but is along the same lines when it comes to reporting the issue in hand.

Results

An analysis of two years was undertaken covering the media coverage of the Saudi-led coalition military intervention and the Russian military intervention. The media outlets selected for this study have online news archives which make it easy for the researchers to access the subject in hand. This study collected 605 online articles from the four media outlets. Then, they used and modified the five frames adapted from Semetko and Valkenburg (2000). The analysis is shown in Table 6.1.

Based on the content analysis of four different European online media outlets, Table 6.2 indicates the number of articles based on the European

Table 6.1 The amount of coverage on the Yemeni and Syrian crises by European media outlets

	The Independent UK	*France24 France*	*SWI Swissinfo.Ch Switzerland*	*NRC Netherlands*	*Total and Valid Percentage*	*Time Frame of the Coverage*
Yemen crisis	160 26.45%	141 23.31%	210 34.71%	94 15.53%	605 100%	26 March 2015–26 March 2017
Syria crisis	312 24.86%	408 32.51%	13 1.04%	522 41.59%	1255 100%	30 September 2015–30 September 2017

countries selected and the amount of news reportage on the military intervention by Saudi-led coalition in Yemen and Russian military intervention in Syria for a year. It was found that *SWI Swissinfo.ch*, based in Switzerland, devoted the greatest amount of coverage (210 articles), followed by *The Independent*, UK (160 articles), *France24*, France (141 articles), and *NRC*, Netherland (94 articles).

Table 6.2 The amount of coverage of Yemeni and Syrian crises by European countries

	The Independent (%) N = 160	France24 (%) N = 141	SWI Swissinfo.ch (%) N = 210	NRC (%) N = 94
Conflict (%)	43.13	46.81	38.09	40.43
Consequences (%)	45	33.33	38.09	41.48
Attribution of responsibility (%)	5	7.80	15.24	10.60
Morality (%)	0.00	0.71	2.86	4.20
Human interest (%)	6.25	0.71	1.91	2.12
Others (%)	0.62	10.64	3.81	1.06

Table 6.3 News frame used for the coverage of Saudi-Yemen war by European countries

	The Independent (%) N = 160	France24 (%) N = 141	SWI Swissinfo (%) N = 210	NRC (%) N = 94
Conflict (%)	43.13	46.81	38.09	40.43
Consequences (%)	45	33.33	38.09	41.48
Attribution of responsibility (%)	5	7.80	15.24	10.06
Morality (%)	0.00	0.71	2.86	4.20
Human interest (%)	6.25	0.71	1.91	2.12
Others (%)	0 0.62	10.64	3.81	1.06

Table 6.4 News frames used for the coverage of Syrian Civil war by European countries

	The Independent N = 312	France24 N = 408	SWI Swissinfo N = 13	NRC N = 522
Conflict	47.43%	49.10%	38.46%	47.89%
Consequences	36.85%	34.31%	23.07%	19.15%
Attribution of responsibility	8.97%	7.84%	0.15%	18.19%
Morality	0.64%	2.20%	0	2.10%
Human interest	6.08	6.61%	23.07%	12.63%
Others	0	0.00%	0.00%	0.00%

(a) **News frame**

Table 6.3 and Table 6.4 show that the Conflict frame scored the highest across the four media outlets in both cases followed by the Consequences, Attribution of Responsibility, Human Interest, and Morality frames. In the case of Yemen, *France24* (46.81%) devoted the highest percentage to the Conflict frame, followed by *The Independent* (43.13%), *NRC* (40.43%) and *the SWI swissinfo* (38.09%). The Consequences frame again is found to be the highest across the four outlets. *The Independent* scored 45%, followed by *NRC* 41.48%, *SWI swissinfo* 38.09%, and France24 33.33%. The Attribution of Responsiblity frame is the highest for *SWI swissinfo* (15.24%) followed by *NRC* (10.06%), *France24* (7.80%), and *The Independent* (5%). The Human Interest frame scores the highest for *The Independent* (6.25%) followed by *NRC* (2.12%), *SWI swissinfo* (1.91%), and *France24* (0.71%). With regard to reporting in the Morality frame *NRC* scored the highest (4.2%), followed by *SWI swissinfo* (2.86%), and *France24* (0.71%) while there were no articles that met the definition of morality in *The Independent* (0.00%). The "Others" category was the highest for *France24* (10.64%), followed by *SWI swissinfo* (3.81%), *NRC* (1.06%), and *The Independent* (0 0.62%).

Table 6.4 shows the most frequent news frames used in the coverage of the four media outlets in the case of the Syrian civil war. The Conflict frame scored close in percentage across the three outlets: *France24* (49.1%), followed by *NRC* (47.89%), *The Independent* (47.43%), and finally *SWI swissinfo* (38.46%). The Consequences frame had the highest percentage for *The Independent* (36.85%) followed by

France24 (34.31%), *SWI swissinfo* (23.07%), and, lastly, NRC (19.15%). Regarding the Attribution of Responsibility frame, *NRC* scored the highest (18.19%), *The Independent* (8.97%), *France24* (7.84%), and *SWI swissinfo* (0.15%). The Morality frame scored the lowest among all the frames with *France24* at 2.20%, followed by *NRC* at 2.10% and *The Independent* at 0.64%.

Conflict

Based on Tables 6.3 and 6.4 it was found that the most prominent frame across the four European media, covering both cases, was Conflict. By using the Conflict frame, most of the articles relied on here-now news, such as clashes, exchange bombardments, and air strikes by the warring parties. For instance, the disagreement between Houthis and Haid relating to peace talks and criticism of violating the ceasefire to allow Humanitarian Aids by both parties. Focusing on Saudi Arabia and the reason behind military intervention, it was reported that the Saudis could not allow the Houthis to take control of Yemen as that would threaten national security (*France24*, March 26, 2015).

Most of the articles by the four European media outlets reported on clashes, shelling, bombardment, and attacks involving the Houthi and its allies, the Saudi-led coalition and Russian air force and the opponents of al-Assad regime. Most of the articles also reported on the violence by the air strikes that have caused loss of civilian lives, most of them being children and women, who died when bombs were dropped in crowded areas (*The Independent*, April 11, 2015; October 13, 2016). Many articles on the Yemeni case criticised the delay in peace talks by the warring sides and for not respecting the announced ceasefire. A senior official in Saleh's part said, "There's no point in going to Kuwait if there's no respect for the ceasefire." A Houthi spokesman also said, "it has been the movement's demand from the start that dialogue took place in an atmosphere of peace and stability." Unfortunately, "aggression" did not stop and air strikes continued in different areas. Regarding the peace processes in Syria, articles pointed at the UN's efforts to mediate the conflict in Syria. Four UN envoys tried to bring the warring parties to engage in a National Dialogue but they failed. *France24* reported that the UN envoys accused the Syrian government of not seeking true dialogue with the opposition and missing the golden opportunity for peace (*France24*, December 15, 2017).

Within the Conflict frame, some articles also mentioned that UN's mediator failed his mission in Yemen and a new mediator was appointed. In this regard, it was reported that the warring sides failed to reach an agreement and were accused of preventing vital aid from reaching the civilian population. According to an article in *France24*, Houthis were stopping convoys of trucks from reaching Aden, the capital of southern Yemen, while Saudi-led coalition navies were searching ships for weapons and holding up food deliveries by sea. (*France24*, April 27, 2015).

In many articles, *The Independent* highlighted the standpoint of some UK opposition parties and their condemnation of the role of the UK in supporting Saudi-led coalition war in Yemen, but displaying double standards when it comes to human rights violations by Saudi's policies and actions. In this regard, using sardonic language, an opinion article published by a writer accusing the UK government of being blind to the actions of its close ally (Saudi) in Yemen, and being involved in the war in Yemen since UK supplied the Saudis with 72 fighter jets—some of which were used to bomb Red Cross and MSF hospitals in Yemen. It was reported that the activists and pressure groups who, on World Humanitarian Day, called for PM May to vote against Saudi Arabia retaining its membership of the UN Human Rights Council were met with ignorance (Hennessy, 2016). Some articles published by *The Independent* reported on deadly gas attacks in Syria by Russia and the Western-led effort at condemnations in the UN. The UN requested Russia and its Syrian allies to cooperate with the international inquiries into these attacks.

Interestingly, an article in *NRC* titled "the drama in Yemen with the blessing of the west" has raised the matter of Yemen receiving negligible attention in general. It has been pointed out that Yemen has been lost among the ongoing wars in the Middle East. The NRC also accused some Western countries, such as the UK, for fuelling the war. *NRC* reported the condemnation by human rights organisations strongly criticising the United Nations' decision to remove Saudi Arabia from a blacklist of countries violating the rights of children. The Saudi bombings in Yemen were responsible for about 60% of the deceased children as a result of the conflict.

Consequences

By applying the frame of Consequences to both cases, a majority of the articles published by the four media outlets focused mainly on the damage to hospitals, schools, factories, and losses of civilian lives, which were predominantly children and women. In addition, the humanitarian and economic situation caused by the wars were reported. The headline of an article mentioned, "The world has forgotten the Yemen war" in which a senior UN humanitarian official warns that the world is ignoring the worsening humanitarian crisis in war-torn Yemen. The official highlighted that the country was suffering from food insecurity before the war and after the war began, a famine forced people to eat from rubbish. Over 10,000 people have been killed and nearly 37,000 wounded; more than 30,000 refugees fled to Djibouti during the conflict putting a strain on the country's scarce resources as well as posing a security threat (*The Independent*, December 7, 2016; *France24*, April 12, 2015).

Highlighting the Syrian case, almost all the articles across the four media outlets reported on the civilian causalities caught in the crossfire of the warring parties. The heavy shelling of residential areas including hospitals in Syria caused thousands of civilian casualties. The government in most of the news reports warned the militants that the patience is running out and if they don't stop targeting civilians, they would pay a high price (*France24*, May 3, 2016).

The Consequence frame also highlights the steps taken and warnings issued by some other parties to douse the situation if it continues progressing in Yemen. There were many attempts at initiating peace talks between the warring sides in Oman, Kuwait, and Switzerland backed by the UN. These attempts aimed at finding ways to resolve the conflict between Yemen's internationally recognised government, which is backed by a Saudi-led military coalition, and the Houthis and their allies, which include forces loyal to former long-time Yemeni President, Ali Abdullah Saleh (*France24*, April 22, 2016). It was also reported that the UK and US vowed to increase diplomatic pressure on their ally, Saudi Arabia, to ensure protection of civilians and reducing the targeting of crowded areas. This step was taken following the bombing of a packed funeral hall in Sana'a that killed more than 140 people and injured as many as 600 more, in one of the deadliest massacres of the country's civil war (*The Independent*, October 9, 2016; *NRC*, August 8, 2015). The year 2016 was described by the UNICEF as the worst year for child deaths in the Syrian war as at least 652 children were killed and 1.7 million students were out of school (*France24*, March 13, 2016).

Attribution of Responsibility

Administering the Attribution of Responsibility frame, the four media firms mentioned, from time to time, that the warring sides agreed to ceasefire to allow Humanitarian Aids and initiate peace talks to find a solution for the conflict in Yemen. *France24* reported that through a sense of shared responsibility, the warring sides pledged to honour the UN-brokered ceasefire given the other side does not violate it. UN Special Envoy, Ismail Ould Cheikh Ahmed, invoked the warring sides to be more responsible and respect the ceasefire; he said, "I ask all the parties and the international community to remain steadfast in support for this cessation of hostilities to be a first step in Yemen's return to peace"; "This is critical, urgent and much needed. Yemen cannot afford the loss of more lives." (*France24*, April 11, 2016; *SWI*, July 27, 2016). It was also reported that he urged both sides to demonstrate "good intentions" and "make concessions." He told the delegates that only they can bring stability back to Yemen and that they needed to "turn the page" for the country's future (*France24*, August 8, 2015).

The urgent solution for the conflict and the only way to end the civil war was to adopt and accept the drafted roadmap for peace talks proposed by the UN. It is reported that the US was concerned and urged Yemeni factions to accept the UN plan after they rejected it. Department spokesman Mark Toner said, "We call on the Yemeni government to accept the roadmap ... We recognize that the roadmap does contain difficult choices and underscore that compromises and concessions by all parties will be necessary to reach a durable political settlement." (*SWI*, December 7, 2016). Furthermore, it was reported that US Secretary of State John Kerry also presented proposals for ending Yemen's conflict and resuming peace talks in meetings with Saudi leaders and other Gulf countries. The meeting about Yemen was for sharing ideas and initiatives to resume the political discussions, to devise a political solution, and address the delivery of aid (*SWI*, August 24, 2016). *The Independent* reported that the Saudi-led coalition was accused for committing genocide in Yemen killing 140 people and injuring hundreds; it also blamed the UN and the wider international community for being silent bystanders during a humanitarian emergency (*The Independent*, October 9, 2016). UN experts, who investigated the incident, accused the Saudi-led coalition of violating international humanitarian law by attacking civilians, the wounded, and medical personnel (*The Independent*, October 21, 2016).

NRC reported that the double air attack on the funeral hall in Yemen by the Saudi-led coalition was intentional. They were reported as violating the obligations of international laws (*NRC*, October 21, 2015).

A majority of the news reports within the Attribution of Responsibility frame focused on urging the international community to take action to end the war on civilians in Syria and Yemen. The reports attributed the rise of the conflict and atrocities in the Middle East to arms and weapons deals that break the war rule and must be controlled. In an article, the Swiss foreign ministry urged the warring parties to be responsible and abide by international humanitarian law, which forbids attacks on medical facilities, and to properly protect civilian populations (*SWI swissinfo*, October 29, 2015).

HUMAN INTEREST

The Human Interest frame manifested by bringing an emotional angle into the presentation of the news which was usually supported by visual accompaniments. It was reported dramatically how individuals, especially women and children, have been affected by the war in both countries. *SWI swissinfo.ch* published images of an 18-year-old Yemeni girl's emaciated body shocking the readers and turning a spotlight on the worsening humanitarian crisis across war-torn Yemen. Even after the girl was admitted in specialist hospital care, she barely spoke and found it difficult to eat; at least she could smile. Nearly two years of war between a Saudi-led Arab coalition and the Iran-allied Houthi movement deepened the unfortunate and unjust plight of the girl's family and millions of other Yemenis. In her parched village on the Red Sea coast, impoverished residents have long struggled to put food on the table (*SWI*, December 6, 2016). In an article titled "Which child should we save?" *The Independent* presented an emotionally charged report on the painful choice that the family of two-year-old, Osama Hassan, faced

> ... as his tiny body wasted away. Should they use the little money they had, in a time of war, to take him to a hospital? Or should they buy food to feed their other children? His family chose food ... grimly observed his frail grandson, who was lying on a wooden cot and staring blankly at the gray sky. His hair was sparse, his teeth decayed, his arms sticklike. He could no longer walk on his spindly legs. With every raspy breath, Osama's ribs

protruded through his dry skin. "There's nothing we can do for him," Sadek said. "I know he's going to die."

Most of the articles reported the tragedy of Syrian toddler, Alan Kurdi, who was found lifeless and lying face down on the shore of Turkey, illustrating the magnitude of human suffering in Syria (*France24*, February 11, 2016). "They all had a name" was the title of the poignant and evocative article written by Jan Egeland pinpointing that over 4,100 drowned after Alan Kurdi's death and how politicians, overcome with emotion, promised to support the Syrian refugees (*NRC*, August 30, 2016). *The Independent* also published an article with a photograph of Alan Kurdi smiling with his brother, narrating their life story until the day he was found at the Turkish shore (Withnall, 2015).

Morality

Within the morality frame, there were only a few articles in both cases. *NRC* and *France24* devoted almost a similar number of articles within the framework of the morality covering the Yemeni and Syria wars respectively. *NRC*'s news coverage within the morality frame emphasised peace talks and providing Humanitarian Aid. It was reported that the former president, Saleh, called all Yemeni factions to return to political dialogue and end the devastating war. According to *France24* Saleh said he is ready to reconcile with all parties that have opposed him since 2011: "I will reconcile with all (parties) for the interest of the nation." (*France24*, April 25, 2015). It was stated that UAE announced its war is over after troops had been engaged in Yemen for almost a year. Then Minister of State for Foreign affairs, Anwar Gargash, was quoted from Crown Prince Mohammed bin Zayed's official twitter account, saying in a closed-door speech, "We are looking at political arrangements and our political role now is to empower the Yemenis in the liberated areas" (*SWI*, June 16, 2016).

The morality frame in the case of Syria focused more on easing the suffering of refugees and expressing empathy and support for the public. The Swiss public, for instance, established a charity campaign to help Syrian victims and those from war-torn countries. This campaign called for public solidarity for war victims and managed to raise $20.5 million, most of it directed towards projects that aim to ease the conditions of the Syrian refugees and called also the members of the UN to hold regular meetings aimed at expediting international Humanitarian Aid (*SWI*, September 30).

OTHERS

This category was developed for the content of the articles that do not fit the operationalization of the aforementioned news frames but aim to convey and disseminate similar information. Surprisingly, there were only articles published under this category in the case of the Yemeni conflict and for the Syrian war. Reading through the articles, it was found that they portrayed the events in Yemen as a sectarian conflict between Shia and Sunni groups. In the articles that did not meet the definitions of the news frames for this study, they either mention the Saudi-Yemen war as Shia versus Sunni or Iran versus Saudi or the proxy war in Yemen describing that Iran supports Houthis as well as other Shia groups in the region. An article titled "Yemen - The Escalation: Could Sunni-Shiite divide engulf the region" promulgated by *France24*, reported that Shia allies and Sunni allies in the region are at war. The report also stated that the Arab reaction is a clear message to Iran, which enjoyed a free hand in the region by using and exploiting the Shia communities in Arab countries, and mobilised them against their governments and to destabilise the states (*France24*, March 27, 2015). In another article by *SWI* reported Britain's Foreign Secretary, Boris Johnson, said that Iran is engaging in proxy wars across the Middle East and the absence of real leadership in the Middle East had allowed people to use religion as subterfuge and engage in proxy wars (*SWI*, December 7, 2016).

A study conducted on MENA's online newspapers reporting on the same issue using the same theory with a different approach found that the regional newspapers did not rely on the sectarian frames to invoke the emotions of their audiences. Instead, they rely more on blame shifting and the humanitarian crisis that transpired due to the actions of the opposition party. This way, defaming each other fanned an already existed inter-sectarian understanding. In other words, where the hatred and understanding against other sects are so deep-rooted, there is no need to remind people about the archness of the opposite sects. In contrast, the Western media (US and UK) portrayed this conflict as a sectarian issue, since people in the West are neither pro-Sunni or pro-Shia, nor do they have strong sentiments toward any side (Asim, 2015).

CONCLUSION

This chapter deeply explored and performed an intrinsic analysis of the amount of coverage devoted to the deadliest conflicts in Yemen and Syria spanning over two years by four prestigious European media outlets. It also examined the media frames used in reportage concerning the two cases, and whether the chosen media outlets significantly differ in their news coverage. Table 6.1 above indicates the relevant countries, the media outlets, and the websites from where the articles were extracted. Table 6.2 summarises the amount of coverage on both cases by each media outlet. A total of 605 articles were gathered from the four media outlets on the war in Yemen while 1255 articles were collected on the war in Syria. In Table 6.3, *SWI swissinfo.ch* scored the highest number of articles on the Yemen war over two years from March 2015 to 26 March 2017. It is found there was a great difference between the numbers of articles published by the four channels. *SWI swissinfo.ch* published 210 articles, while the lowest number of articles were published by *NRC* at only 94 articles, and this has caused the difference of 116 articles between the two.

Table 6.4 indicated that *NRC* devoted more articles to the Syrian war from 2015 to 2017. It published 522 articles as compared to the other media platforms, with *SWI* at only 13 articles. There is a significant difference in the coverage across the four selected platforms which resulted in a difference of 590 and a total of 650 articles between the coverage of Yemen and Syria wars by the four European media outlets in favour for the Syrian war.

Conflict was the most salient frame across the four platforms in both cases followed by the Consequence, Attribution of Responsibility, Human Interest frames with the Morality frame scoring the lowest. The four media outlets relied on hard news (as first-hand reportage) or what is called here and now news, "breaking news and currently happening" according to Rosendale and Longcore (2015), to report the Saudi-Yemen war. That is, the issue that entails armed conflict, violence, disagreement and exchange accusation between warring parties attracts the most amount of media attention (Carlman & Svedlund, 2013). Surprisingly, none of the four European media outlets reported on why the conflict or the war transpired between Saudi and Yemen. Based on our observation, the four media channels failed to analyse or explain the background or context of the war to help the readers (European population) understand the military campaign and form their opinions towards countries' alliances. In most of the articles only the Houthi group was described as a rebel, accused of halting the peace talks, and blocking the Humanitarian Aid which made the media outlets seem biased in their coverage.

Unsurprisingly, *The Independent* as it is well known for being neutral, in many reports, severely criticised and accused the UK government of supporting Saudi with arms and weaponry that have been used to kill people in Yemen, and for their blatant double standards over Saudi's violation of international law in Yemen. Within the Consequences frame, the four media outlets focused on reporting civilian deaths and injuries due to air bombings and violence, especially children and women, as well as the devastating economic situation that resulted in a humanitarian crisis, warning that the county is on the brink of famine.

In conclusion, from our observation, the war in Yemen had a lack of coverage in the early months of the military campaign led by Saudi, and some of tragic incidents that were described as war crimes committed by Saudi-led coalition reported by human rights organisations such as UNICEF were underreported or entirely ignored. Compared to that, the coverage of Syria war from day one was adequately detailed. This study also concluded that despite the difference in the amount of coverage, the way the four European media outlets report on Yemen and Syria wars appeared to be similar. That is, through focusing on the Conflict frame given the nature of the events.

The results indicate that the four media houses portrayed the conflict in Yemen as a sectarian conflict between Shia and Sunni groups in Yemen. The researchers believe atrocities have been committed against innocent Yemeni people on a scale as serious as the conflict in Syria, yet the conflict in Yemen does not get much media attention. The researchers believe that the lack of media coverage of the war in Yemen war compared to the Syrian war, which has the lion's share of reports, is due to the involvement of international actors or major players such as Iran, Turkey, US, Hezbollah, and Russia backing the Syrian regime.

From our analysis in Chapters 3 and 4 wherein we covered the conflicts in Yemen, Afghanistan, Ethiopia, Tunisia, and Iraq through various social, political, economic, and geographic dimensions, along with the added layer of the empirical analysis of Humanitarian Aid and its effectiveness in Chapter 5, it is clear that the data presented in Chapter 6 works against the on-ground reality presented in the preceding chapters. In Chapter 6, we learn that European media outlets belie the truth of the challenges, demise, and unparalleled suffering in the Arab region. They fail to convey a holistic idea of the conflicts facing the region, especially Yemen, as we can see from the nominal news coverage devoted to the conflict in Yemen as compared to the Syrian conflict.

It is noticed that there is a little or almost no sentiment from the European nations towards the humanitarian crisis in Yemen. This is because the media that people rely on did not provide enough information that might have helped the public and various groups to assume the appropriate stance and pressurise their governments, such as in the UK or France that support Saudi. One point worth mentioning is that the source of most news was other news agencies, such as Reuters. This means that the media enterprises of some European countries are influenced by the agendas of other media giants.

A recommendation for future research would be conducting a comprising study to understand the difference in the amount of coverage Western media devoted to Yemen and other conflicts in the Middle East, such as Syria, and the factors that influenced Western media to situate Syria in their daily news headlines and for a wider international audience, but not the case of Yemen. Through an analysis of media coverage, this chapter has unveiled where the conflict in Yemen stands in the world's agenda and whether the country matters to the international community especially in European countries. It is noticed from the findings of this research that the war in Yemen has been almost forgotten in the media agenda of the countries in the study over the course of two years of conflict. The fact is that, by ignoring the violence, genocide, and humanitarian crisis in Yemen, the scenario of the Syrian civil war will repeat and the world will soon have to grapple with the next major refugee crisis, which has already begun.

References

Al Batati, S. (2015, March 29). Who are the Houthis in Yemen. *Al Jazeera*. https://www.aljazeera.com/news/middleeast/2014/08/yemen-houthis-hadi-protests-201482132719818986.html

Al Majdhoub, F. (2016). Framing the ISIL: Acontent analysis of the news coverage by CNN and Aljazeera. *Malaysian Journal of Communication., 32*, 335–364.

Asim, M. M. (2015). Examining the role of emotion as a dimension of affective agenda setting. *International Journal of Humanities and Management Sciences (IJHMS), 3*, 6.

Bates, M. J., & Lu, S. (1997). An exploratory profile of Personal Home Pages: Content, Design. *Metaphors. Online and CD-Rom Review, 21*(6), 331–340.

Baum, M., & Zhukov, Y. M. (2016). *Media ownership and news coverage of international conflict*. Retrieved on April 14, 2017 from https://www.hks.harvard.edu/fs/mbaum/documents/BaumZhukov_MediaOwnershipAndWar-WORKINGDRAFT.pdf.

BBC (2017, March, 28). *Yemen Crisis: Who is fighting whom?*. Retrieved on April 10, 2017 from http://www.bbc.com/news/world-middle-east-29319423

Boone, L. (2011). *How the media missed Rwandan genocide?* Retrieved on 29 April 2017 from http://www.1stcasualty.com/?p=609.

Carlman, A., & Svedlund, A. I. (2013). *Peace journalism, How media reporting affects wars and conflicts*. The Kvinna till Kvinna Foundation.

Cappella, J. N., & Jamieson, K. H. (1997). *Spiral of cynicism. The press and the public good*. Aksant Academic Publishers.

Chang, T. K., Shoemaker, P., & Brendlinger, N. (1987). Determinants of international news coverage in the US media. *Communication Research, 14*, 396–414.

Chang, T. K. (1998). All countries not created equal to be news: World system and international communication. *Communication Research, 25*, 528–566.

D'Angelo, P. (2002). News framing as a multiparadigmatic research program: A response to Entman. *Journal of Communication, 52*, 870–888.

Durac, V. (2012). Yemen's Arab Spring—Democratic opening or regime maintenance? *Mediterranean Politics, 17*(2), 161–178.

Entman, R. M. (1993). Framing: Towards clarification of a fractured paradigm. In *McQuail's reader in mass communication theory* (pp. 390–397).

Egeland, J. (2016, August 30). *They all had a name*. Retrieved from https://www.nrc.no/perspectives/2016/they-all-had-a-name/

France24. (2015, March 26). *Saudi could not allow Houthis to take control of Yemen*. Retrieved on April 22, 2017 from http://www.france24.com/en/20150326-saudi-arabia-coalition-military-intervention-yemen-houthi-rebels.

France24. (2015, April 12). *France voices support for Saudi campaign in Yemen*. Retrieved on April 22, 2017 from http://www.france24.com/en/20150412-france-fabius-support-saudi-campaign-yemen-houthis.

France24. (2015, April 25). *Former Yemen president calls for dialogue to end war*. Retrieved from http://www.france24.com/en/20150425-yemen-saleh-dialogue-talks-houthi-saudi.

France24. (2015, April 27). *Saudis pound Houthi targets as UN picks new mediator*. Retrieved on March 30, 2017 from http://www.france24.com/en/20150427-saudis-pound-houthi-targets-un-mediator-yemen.

France24. (2015, August 8). *UN official warns of 'deliberate starvation' in Yemen*. Retrieved from http://www.france24.com/en/20150812-un-official-warns-deliberate-starvation-yemen.

France24. (2016, February 11). *Human smugglers on trial over Syrian toddler Aylan Kurdi's death*. Retrieved from https://www.france24.com/en/201 60211-turkey-syria-aylan-kurdi-toddler-human-traffickers-trial-refugees-death

France24. (2016, May 3). *Shelling by rebels in Syria's Aleppo kills more than a dozen people*. Retrieved from https://www.france24.com/en/20160503-She lling-rebels-Syrias-Aleppo-kill-more-dozen-people.

France24. (2016, March 13). *Worst year yet for child deaths in Syria war, says UNICEF 3)*. https://www.france24.com/en/20170313-worst-year-yet-child-deaths-syria-war-says-unicef

France24. (2016, April 11). *Warring sides pledge to respect Yemen ceasefire*. Retrieved fromw.france24.com/en/20160411-yemen-warring-sides-pledge-respect-ceasefire-un.

France24. (2016, April 22). *UN-backed Yemen peace talks begin in Kuwait*. Retrieved from http://www.france24.com/en/20160422-un-backed-yemen-peace-talks-begin-kuwait.

France24. (2017, December 15). *Three UN envoys who tried and failed in quest for Syria peace*. Retrieved from https://www.france24.com/en/20190115-three-un-envoys-who-tried-failed-quest-syria-peace

Frankel, J.R., & Wallen, N. E. (2009). *How to design and evaluate research in education* (7th ed.). McGraw-Hill.

Gamson, W. A., & Modigliani, A. (1989). Media discourse and public opinion on nuclear power: A constructionist approach. *American Journal of Sociology*, 95(1), 1–37.

Giles, D. (2010). *Psychology of the media*. Palgrave Macmillan.

Giles, D., & Shaw, R. (2009). The psychology of news influence and the development of media framing analysis. *Social and Personality Psychology Compass*, 3(4), 375–393.

Goffman, E. (1974). *Frame analysis: An essay on the organization of experience*. Harvard University Press.

Golan, G. (2006). Inter-media agenda setting and global news coverage. *Journalism Studies*, 7(2), 323–333.

Ha, L., & James, L. E. (1998). Interactivity reexamined: A baseline analysis of early business web sites. *Journal of Broadcasting & Electronic Media*, 42(4), 457–474.

Hennessy, A. (2016, August 19). Theresa May should expel Saudi Arabia from the UN Human Rights Council, but that's not enough to absolve the UK. *The Independent*. Retrieved from http://www.independent.co.uk/voices/saudi-arabia-un-human-rights-council-theresa-may-expel-she-should-enough-a7199066.html

Harvey, N. (2012). *Why do some conflicts get more media coverage than others?* Retrieved from https://newint.org/features/2012/09/01/media-war-coverage/.

Harvey, D. (1989). *The condition of post-modernity*. Basil Blackwell.
Hashim, L., Hasan, H., & Sinnapan, S. (2007). Australian online newspapers: A website content analysis approach to measuring interactivity. In *18th Australasian Conference on Information Systems (ACIS)* (pp. 533–542). Toowoomba.
Hester, A. (1973). Theoretical considerations in predicting volume and direction of international information flow. *Gazette, 19*(4), 238–247.
Hincks, J. (2016). *What do you need to know about the crisis in Yemen?* Retrieved from http://time.com/4552712/yemen-war-humanitarian-crisis-famine/.
Iyengar, S. (1991). Is anyone responsible? In *How television frames political issues*. University of Chicago Press.
Junne, G. (2013). *The role of media in conflict transformation*. Retrieved from http://www.irenees.net/bdf_fiche-analyse-1002_en.html
Kitzinger, J. (2000). Media templates: Patterns of association and the (re)construction of meaning over time. *Media, Culture & Society, 22*(1), 61–84.
Kinder, D. R. (1998). Communication and opinion. *Annual Review of Political Science, 1*(1), 167–197.
Krippendorff, K. (2004). *Content analysis: An introduction to its methodology* (2nd ed.). Sage.
Krippendorff, K. (2013). *Content analysis: An introduction to its methodology* (3rd ed.). Sage.
Landis, J. R., & Koch, G. G. (1977). The measurement of observer agreement for categorical data. *Biometrics, 33*, 159–174.
Li, Z., & Khalaf, T. (2012). Picturing terrorism through Arabic lenses: A comparative analysis of Aljazeera and Al Arabia. *Asian Journal of Communication, 22*, 433–348.
Masmoudi, M. (1979). The new world information order. *Journal of Communication, 29*(2), 172–179.
Mccombs, M., & Shaw, D. (1972). The agenda-setting function of mass media. *Public Opinion Quarterly, 36*, 176–187.
McMillan, S. J. (2000). *Interactivity is in the eye of the beholder: Function, perception, involvement, and attitude toward the web site*. Paper presented to Proceedings of the 2000 Conference of the American Academy of Advertising, East Lansing, Michigan State University.
Mohammadi, A. (1997). *International communication and globalization*. Sage.
Muin, M. (2011). *Agenda-setting theory and the role of the media in shaping public opinion for the Iraq War*. Retrieved from http://ndc.gov.bd/lib_mgmt/webroot/earticle/1665/Role_of_the_Media_in_Iraq_War.pdf.
Nevens, K. (2011). *Yemen's Youth revolution in the Arab Spring: Implications for British policy*. Conservative Middle East Council.

OCHA Yemen. (2017). *Humanitarian needs overview: People in needs*. Retrieved from https://docs.unocha.org/sites/dms/Yemen/YEMEN%202 017%20HNO_Final.pdf.
Pavelka, J. (2014). *The factors affecting the presentation of events and media coverage of topics in mass media*. Retrieved on March 4th 2017 from www.sci encedirct.com. https://doi.org/10.1016/j.sbspro.2014.04.482.
Puddepphatt, A. (2006). *Voices of war: conflict and the role of the media*. Retrieved from https://www.mediasupport.org/wp-content/uploads/2012/ 11/ims-voices-of-war-2006.pdf.
Rosendale, J. A., & Longcore, A. (2015). *On hard versus soft news: A content analysis of reporting by three nationally-televised evening news programs*. Retrieve from http://www.scirp.org/journal/jss, https://doi.org/10.4236/ jss.2015.311008
Ryan, C. (1991). *Prime time activism: Media strategies for grassroots organizing*. South End Press.
Saif, A. (2015). *Yemen Crisis: What role for the EU*. Retrived from http:// www.europarl.europa.eu/RegData/etudes/IDAN/2015/534990/EXPO_I DA(2015)534990_EN.pdf. Accessed on March 13, 2017.
Scheufele, A. D. (2000). Framing as a theory of media effects. *Journal of Communication, 49*, 103–122.
Semetko, H. A., & Valkenburg, P. M. (2000). Framing European politics: A content analysis of the press and television news. *Journal of Communication, 50*, 93–109.
Shoemaker, P. J., Chang, T. K., & Brendlinger, N. (1986). Deviance as a predictor of newsworthiness: Coverage of international events in the U.S. Media. *Communication Yearbook, 10*, 348–365.
Sharp, J. M. (2017). *Yemen: Civil War and regional intervention*. Retrieved from https://fas.org/sgp/crs/mideast/R43960.pdf.
Smith, P. M. (1991). *How CNN fought the war*. Birch Lane Press.
Summers, H. G. (1995). *The Persian Gulf War Almanac*. Facts on File.
Syria's civil war explained from the beginning. (2018, March 4). Retrieved from https://www.aljazeera.com/news/2016/05/syria-civil-war-explained-160505084119966.html.
SWI swissinfo (2015, October 29). *Swiss 'shocked' at targeting of hospitals*. Retrieved from https://www.swissinfo.ch/eng/breaking-war-rules_swiss-sho cked-at-targeting-of-hospitals/41748650
SWI swissinfo.ch. (2015, September 30). *Swiss donations for Syrian crisis swell to CHF20 million*. Retrieved from https://www.swissinfo.ch/eng/helping-hand_swiss-donations-forsyrian-crisis-swell-to-chf20-million/41692362
SWI. (2016, June 16). *UAE says its war in Yemen "practically over*. Retrieved from http://www.swissinfo.ch/eng/.

SWI. (2016, August 24). *Kerry to discuss Yemen, Syria with Gulf Arab states.* Retrieved from http://www.swissinfo.ch/eng/kerry-to-discuss-yemen--syria-with-gulf-arab-states/42396304..

SWI (2016, July 27). *U.N. calls for humanitarian truce in Yemen's Taiz province.* Retrieved from https://www.swissinfo.ch/...calls-for-humanitarian-truce-in-yemen...taiz-province/423.

SWI. (2016, December 6). *Emaciated Yemeni woman now smiles but recovery patchy.* Retrieved from http://www.swissinfo.ch/eng/emaciated-yemeni-woman-now-smiles-but-recovery-patchy/html.

SWI. (2016, December 7). *U.S. urges Yemen to accept U.N.-drafted roadman for peace talk.* Retrieved from https://www.swissinfo.ch/eng/reuters/u-s--urges-yemen-to-accept-u-n--drafted-roadmap-for-peace-talks/42738248.

The Guardian. (2014, August 4). Is western media coverage of the Ukraine crisis anti-Russian? Retrieved from https://www.theguardian.com/world/2014/aug/04/western-media-coverage-ukraine-crisis-russia

The Independent. (2015, April 11). Ceasefire aimed at ending Yemeni forgotten war disrupted by violence. Retrieved on April 28,2017 http://www.independent.co.uk/news/world/middle-east/ceasefire-aimed-at-ending-yemens-forgotten-war-dispruted-by-violence-a6979581.html.

The Independent. (2016a, October 9). Britain and US pile pressure on Saudi Arabia over Yemen funeral bombing. Retrieved from http://www.independent.co.uk/news/world/middle-east/yemen-sanaa-funeral-bombing-air-strikes-uk-arms-sales-us-saudi-arabia-coalition-latest-a7353231.html.

The Independent. (2016b, October 9). Saudi-led coalition in Yemen accused of 'genocide' after airstrike on funeral hall kills 140. Retrieved from http://www.independent.co.uk/news/world/middle-east/yemen-air-strike-bomb-kills-140-saudi-arabia-usa-white-house-a7352386.html.

The Independent. (2016, October 13). Russia 'bombed four hospitals in Syria in four hours', report finds. Retrieved from https://www.independent.co.uk/news/world/middle-east/russia-syria-bomb-hospitals-war-kurds-putin-assad-idlib-a9153786.html

The Independent. (2016, October 21). Experts say Saudi coalition violated international humanitarian law in Yemen attack. Retrieved from http://www.independent.co.uk/news/world/middle-east/un-saudi-arabia-yemen-air-strikes-violated-international-law-a7372936.html.

The Independent. (2016, December 1). In Yemen's war, trapped families ask: Which child should we save? Retrieved from http://www.independent.co.uk/news/world/middle-east/yemen-civil-war-trapped-families-ask-which-children-to-save-a7448996.html.

The Independent. (2016, December 7). The world has forgotten the Yemen war, says senior UN humanitarian official. Retrieved from http://www.ind

ependent.co.uk/news/world/middle-east/yemen-war-saudi-arabia-world-forgotten-houthi-rebels-conflict-un-official-comments-a7460081.html.

Tomlinson, J. (1997). *Cultural globalization and cultural imperialism*. In K. Thompson (Ed.), *Media and cultural regulation*. The Open University.

Vreese, D. C.H. (2002). *Framing Europe. Television news and European integration*. Oxford University Press.

Vreese, D. C. H. (2004). The effects of frames in political television news on issue interpretation and frame salience. *Journalism & Mass Communication Quarterly, 81*, 36–52.

Weber, R. P. (1990). *Basic content analysis* (2nd ed.). Sage.

Warrens, M. J. (2012). Cohen's quadratically weighted kappa is higher than linearly weighted kappa for tridiagonal agreement tables. *Statistical Methodology, 9*, 440–444.

Withnall, A. (2015, September 30). *Aylan Kurdi's story: How a small Syrian child came to be washed up on a beach in Turkey*. Retrieved from https://www.independent.co.uk/news/world/europe/aylan-kurdi-s-story-how-a-small-syrian-child-came-to-be-washed-up-on-a-beach-in-turkey-10484588.html.

Yemen's Houthis form own government in Sana'a. (2015, February 7). Retrieved from http://www.aljazeera.com/news/middleeast/2015/02/yemen-houthi-rebels-announce-presidential-council-150206122736448.html.

CHAPTER 7

Conclusion

Moosa Elayah

If you are reading this book, you are likely to be one of many who care about devising an effective peacebuilding process in fragile and conflict-torn countries. The main proposition in the book is the concept of National Dialogue and political reconciliations as the only safe methods to avert civil wars, which are wide threats to regional and international security. One of the many internal conflicts presented in this book was the case of Afghanistan, where terrorist groups affect both domestic and regional security. The activities of these groups have also been exported outside the country, thereby threatening the security of regional and international countries. This has led the US and other western countries to gather and declare what they call the "War on Terror" campaign, while we are left pondering over what else can be done to handle the severe security threats in some conflict-ridden countries.

This book presents a sophisticated analysis of cases, such as Ethiopia and Afghanistan that have achieved a level of success with their National Dialogues and attempted to combat the negative impact of the conflicts. This is due to a number of essential reasons. Firstly, it was the strong will of the political forces to continue negotiations, regardless of the upcoming challenges, to save their countries from receding into the swamp of past failures. Secondly, the simultaneous international support for the political and developmental processes helped these countries continue their negotiations on the path to democracy. In addition, public awareness of the importance of the National Dialogues created support and motivation for the continuation of the political processes, accompanied by public solidarity in advocating the ongoing process.

However, some unsuccessful cases were also analysed in this book such as the case of Iraq, wherein nothing could be done to cease the conflict and to build peace. Iraq's religious conflicts were not the only weakening factors contributing to the incomplete national reconciliation, although they had a great impact. There was also a conflict among the Iraqi elite groups, alongside a policy of revenge that attempted to win the scene and the authority—based on *zero-sum* game theory. In addition, the state of poverty and social division in Iraq fuelled terrorist groups and offered them a chance to recruit and militarise huge numbers of Iraqis; a huge number accepted due to financial constraints. In any peacebuilding process, including the Iraqi situation, improvement of the economic condition of the country or state must go hand in hand with political reconciliation.

The peacebuilding processes and dialogues in Yemen faced tribal, sectarian, Jihadist, and secessionist threats. The Yemeni National Dialogue shares important features with National Dialogues in Afghanistan (2002) and Iraq (2008), but with lesser emphasis on reconciliation (Afghanistan) and resource distribution (oil rents in Iraq). There were also differences with Tunisia's 2013 "Quartet" dialogue, which was initiated by strong civil society groups in the country (including workers and employers) instead of being imposed by foreign powers. It tackled fewer issues in a more private setting, after a trust-building exercise. The Arab uprising that started in both Tunisia and Yemen in early 2011 motivated us to conduct an in-depth analysis comparing the two cases more extensively than the other presented cases in this book.

YEMEN AND TUNISIA: PROMISING BEGINNINGS BUT DIFFERENT ENDINGS

The process of National Dialogue in both Tunisia and Yemen illustrates the extent of the discrepancy in the design of an effective dialogue with practical aspects. In Yemen, the National Dialogue focused on the dialogue process, but unlike the Tunisian case, it did not focus on resolution. There are many factors that controlled the political change in Tunisia, which made the Tunisian National Dialogue more effective compared to the situation in Yemen. The factors are mostly linked to the security and military forces' position and their role in the political process. The Tunisian military forces are considered the least in number in the Arab World as there are about 40,500 soldiers for a total population of 11 million. Also, those forces have not been engaged in a big war before (Ghriwal, 2016). In addition, the Tunisian Military forces did not support the regime (ruling party) during the revolution, which played an important role in making the revolution successful because the Tunisian military forces avoided internal politics since independence, and so they did not respond to the orders of regime or fire at the protestors, but rather guarded the public institutions (Mahmoud, 2016). If this is compared to the case in Yemen, the Tunisian military institution's effect was limited. The military forces in Yemen were divided between former president Ali Abdullah Saleh and General Ali Mohsen al-Ahmar, the former second man in Yemen. This division was one of the reasons that made the military forces weak and not professional enough, as the nomination of the leaders of the military units was based on affiliation, not experience and efficiency (ACRPS, 2011).

Furthermore, the two powerful parties allied with non-official militants. Subsequently, Ali Mohsen al-Ahmar allied with some Salafi movements and the Muslim Brotherhood Party, and some influential Sheiks, whereas Ali Saleh allied with Jihadists and Ansar al-Sharia. Consequently, the military forces were supposed to save the citizens and foster social unity, but unfortunately, they did the opposite by siding with their own leaders. The Gulf Initiative called for a rehabilitation of the Yemeni forces and an end to their defection,[1] but their loyalty remained with effective figures, not to their homeland (Alshargbi, 2013).

The nature of Tunisian society is entirely different. There are not multiple sectarian or tribal affiliations, which is why the revolution was successful, because there is alignment of goals. If the same thing had happened in another country that has multiple sects and tribes, the situation would have been different.

Yemeni society contains two main religious groups, the Shia related to the Zaidi sect in the north of the country, and the Sunni related

---

[1] GCC Initiative states that: Within five days of Initiative entry into force, the Vice President during the transitional period forms a Military Affairs Committee and its Presidency to achieve stability and put an end to the division within the armed forces and its causes.

to the Alshafei sect, in southern and eastern Yemen. The religious division in Yemen used to be limited. Throughout history, Yemen has never had internal conflicts supported by political, economic, sectarian, or tribal interventions. If such conflicts coincided with the eruption of some religious conflicts, they are not considered the main causes of conflict, as religious mergers are natural for Yemenis.

But recently, particularly after the Arab Spring revolutions in 2011, sectarian dissent has increased and Yemeni society has been reformulated based on sects, and the relations between people are formed on false foundations. In short, the sectarian conflicts in Syria, Iraq, and Lebanon finally penetrated Yemen's borders (Musalami, 2015).

The Tunisian society played an important role as they urged the people to demand change, unlike the civil society organisations in Yemen. The latter focused on quantity but not quality and most of them are just names without real entities backing them. Due to the conflict between the regime and the opposition, the opposition tried to attract them and get the benefits of their activities for individual interests. Each party realised that their role was not significant as they did not participate effectively in defending human rights and development (Al-Qurashi, 2014).

It is worth mentioning that the public atmosphere also plays an important role in the success or the failure of the political dialogues. In this regard, there are points that we assumed helped Tunisian NDC to restore order in the country, while not in the case of Yemeni NDC:

The dominant political culture: The Tunisian society enjoys a great deal of openness due to its relationship with Europe, especially France. Conversely, the Yemeni society is ruled by a closed tribal culture, which played a negative role in managing the National Dialogue, political forgiveness, and building political agreements.

The political dignitaries (Elites): Larry Diamond claims that the political features of dignitaries play a role in forming the democratic process such as courage and creation (Bellin, 2015). In Tunisia, the National Dialogue could not have happened without a secret meeting in Paris on 15 August 2013 between "The two Sheiks"— Al-Bāġī Qāʾid as-Sibsī and Rashid Al Ghannushi—who responded to the meeting under the patronage of businessmen supported by some European capitals. Political parties such as Nidaa Tounes and Ennahda did not expect that to happen. As-Sibsī was successful in convincing his opponent to participate in the dialogue sponsored by the four organisations. Without those procedures, the situation could have been different (Alhadad, 2015).

The situation in Yemen was different. Some political figures were invited by the presidency committee, yet they did not have the courage to show up and they boycotted the dialogue. There were no secret rooms or any prior meetings that brought together all rival parties and ensured effectiveness in highlighting all the woes in the dialogues, putting public interests before personal and party interests.

Islam and State: In the summer of 2013, Egyptian military forces staged a coup against the leader of the Muslim Brothers, President Mohammed Morsi. Tunisia benefitted from this experiment as the Ennahda Islamic party agreed to nominate a technocrat government in an attempt to please the opposition. They moved the regime to a non-partisan government and fulfilled the demands of demonstrators who were not happy with the political assassinations against secular people as well as the economic crisis. The Ennahda party was successful in forming a kind of moderate political imagination and showed an interest in moderating some points of view related to women and Islamic Shariah (Holzapffel, 2014).

In contrast, some National Dialogue members in Yemen disbelieved some religious Fatwas—a ruling on a point of Islamic law given by a recognised authority—because of article No. 4 in the constitution, especially the item related to marriage of underage girls, and about the rights of Yemeni women to be nominated in some positions in the government by implementing a 30% gender quota.

Education level: Based on UNESCO reports, the average illiteracy level in Tunisia is about 18%, whereas in Yemen it is more than 30% and this great gap affects the level of political awareness and affiliation, either in the elections or in different political and carnival practices (Sawa, 2016).

Two main factors that played a decisive and important role in drawing the map of the transitive period were the continuation of the security apparatuses, and the ability of the effective figures to reach to a minimum agreement on the political process that formed the political transition. Unlike Tunisia, the Yemeni dignitaries (Elites) only fought for their personal interests and their affiliated parties, and not for the benefits of their homeland or to serve Yemen's population. The slogans and signs that were raised by the Yemeni parties and political entities disappeared once they were about to be applied in reality (Sabahi, 2015).

HISTORY OF NATIONAL DIALOGUES

This book has also looked into whether National Dialogues have merely delayed the outbreak of civil wars in Yemen. Historically, dialogue processes for peacebuilding in Yemen were, with one notable exception, directly followed by a civil war. It can be concluded that the Yemeni dialogues as a gateway to resolve political crises and armed conflicts were not the right tool for several reasons.

Firstly, in historical dialogues in Yemen, we have seen that building an environment of trust between the warring factions before embarking on the agenda of the dialogue is imperative for the effectiveness of the overall peace process. It important to make some concessions that refer to the goodwill of the various factions. This is especially because the peacebuilding process represents a place of encounter where concerns about both the "past" and the "future" can rendezvous and converge. Therefore, investment in trust-building among negotiating groups prior to a dialogue or peacebuilding process allows space to articulate experiences of loss and to acknowledge related feelings. The recommendation is to have a "slow start" to provide some space to build basic levels of trust between the incumbent and new factions. While a trust-building phase before initiating formal negotiations is important, it is unclear whether trust-building should be a separate phase, or can be part of a reconciliation stage, which the literature on dialogues singles out as highly conducive to success.

Secondly, in many cases, external/regional actors greatly influenced the course of the conflict and the dialogue, which made the dialogues less feasible. Weaker factions tried to establish links with some external powers in order to get more weight internally. The solution is direct involvement of outsiders in the negotiations and discussions of a dialogue process as they are part of the conflict in Yemen, as well as calling upon international economic, technical, and logistical support. Therefore, the Yemeni case showed that to have successful dialogues, a large sense of local ownership is only by definition or theory an important precondition; empirical evidence has shown that international and regional involvement is also essential as external bodies are one of the causes of internal conflict in Yemen.

As previously argued, we found that in the case of distrust among conflicting factions as well as non-positive external interventions, there is no common view or shared objectives in a dialogue because the agenda of the conflicting factions is different and externally driven. Even if there is a margin of inclusiveness to embrace the different segments of society at the dialogue table, this would not create an environment conducive to successful dialogue. Because of the imbalance of power in the community, the deep state/traditional actors would control everything in society. In a historical moment, these actors can use a dialogue process as a tactic to overcome temporary unrest to reorder their power means and try to retain power. This is what happened in the National Dialogue Conference of 2013.

GROUND REFLECTIONS ON DESIGNING A NATIONAL DIALOGUE IN A FRAGILE SETTING

In this book, to add to Lederach's model for peacebuilding in divided contexts, we assert the importance of incorporating information on the implicit and explicit local knowledge of a non-democratic society (Elayah, 2014). There is vital need for more investigation about the direct and indirect/formal and informal actors and their external and internal sources of power, as it will be helpful to distinguish who can change the course of a conflict and who has the potential to resolve a conflict. Those actors can be found at three levels: top formal and informal leadership (elite), middle-range formal and informal leadership, and grassroots formal and informal leadership (Lederach, 1997). This pattern of local knowledge is very important for a realistic analysis of the situation and for devising appropriate strategy to deal with conflict, thereby facilitating peace.

Attention must be paid to the circumstances under which National Dialogues or peacebuilding process could lead to successful results. Several criteria are considered, of which building an environment of trust and the ownership of external interventions seem to be the most significant. A trust-building phase before entering into formal negotiations is important, but it is unclear whether this should be a separate phase, or can be part of a reconciliation stage, which the literature on dialogues singles out as highly conducive for success. Local ownership is an important precondition for success in Lederach's theoretical discourse, but (direct) international and regional involvement is required, as all selected cases have shown, especially the Yemeni case, that external bodies are often the cause of internal conflicts in Yemen.

The authors concur with Lederach that it is crucial to make strategic use of economic support alongside political support. Carrot-and-stick tactics, where willingness to enter into dialogue is loosely tied to funding for economic investments, have been applied in Afghanistan and Iraq with some success. In Yemen, the (re)building of the economy did not receive similar impetus during the dialogue period. Improving economic prospects, at the right time, should enhance the "peace dividend" for the dialoguing partners.

Consider the potential role economic actors could play in the dialogue. The Tunisian "Quartet" included representatives of business and workers, which is considered one of the factors that contributed to its success. None of the other dialogues included groups based on their economic function. However, it is yet unproven whether this would work in countries where economic actors, or civil society organisations in general, do not enjoy the same level of involvement as in the Tunisian case.

Since the threat of violence derails power balance, carrying out offensive targeted operations to "neutralize and disarm" rebel movements and armed groups before the official dialogue starts is imperative. In Yemen, for example, the issue of withdrawing weapons from armed groups is still a priority for the success of any future peace negotiations, which requires genuine guarantees of implementation. Even if there is consensus in any negotiations, there needs to a guarantor force that ensures implementation of the outputs. These guarantees can be placed at either regional or international levels, especially from those regional countries that are encouraging the local factions for intransigence and hegemony.

There is a need to take greater care in the selection of participants, to include intellectual elites and provincial leaders, and ensure broader representation from all levels of leadership. Furthermore, more effort is needed to involve the government (bureaucracy) in the dialogue, to avoid a lack of support during implementation (the weak role for the PM of the transition government in Yemeni NDC 2013 backfired). A complete roadmap for the National Dialogue, including a more streamlined agenda and implementation schedule, must be drawn up, which may require pre-agreements on key issues (to narrow decision frame) and a focus on high-level decisions only, to be worked out in smaller assemblies afterwards. Civil society groups should be invited, conditional on grassroots consultation, and their internal coordination should be stimulated.

Another recommendation is to appreciate the revolutionary aspect of having women and youth represented in the political arena in Afghanistan and Yemen, while allowing traditional players some time to come to terms with these new entrants in the political game. A "slow start" could provide some space to build basic levels of trust between incumbent and new factions. A trust-building phase before entering into formal negotiations was successfully tried in Tunisia, although participation of women in political affairs historically enjoyed a relatively high level of acceptance in this context. It is unclear whether trust-building should be a separate phase or part of a reconciliation stage, which the literature on National Dialogues singles out as highly conducive for success. Reconciliation was part and parcel of the Iraqi dialogue, albeit in a deeply flawed manner.

Furthermore, it is important to be aware of the risk of competing loyalties of marginalised groups that are granted reservations (via quotas) in the dialogue. The Yemeni experience revealed that some women occupying reserved seats did not (at least not primarily) represent women's voices but were guided by their political or clan affiliation instead. Preventing such forced or willing co-optation by the political elite requires "deep" knowledge of local (family-tribal and social class) structures.

Then, contemplate the long-term implications of excluding actors with a (real or perceived) terrorist hallmark. Exclusion of the Taliban from the Afghan National Dialogue is widely considered a strategic mistake, as also witnessed by the strong resurgence of Taliban forces today. It remains to be seen whether the Yemeni dialogue drew the right demarcation line between eligible (Houthi) and non-eligible (Al-Qaeda) factions. However, their respective degrees of local embeddedness and popular support seem more useful inclusion criteria than the degree to which they are perceived by foreign actors as a threat to international security. In fact, peaceful civil society participants should also be scrutinised for having a 'grassroots' constituency to safeguard their legitimacy.

Finally, it is important to anticipate that a country may need a sequence of dialogues (with intermittent "relapses" into armed strife) to wean itself off a tendency to settle grievances through violence. The history of dialoguing in Yemen is a testament (a series of dialogue events were clustered within relatively short time spans). A relapse does not automatically imply that local actors perceive the dialogue as an outright failure, or that "no dialogue" would have been better than a "failed dialogue," as long as the dialogue delivers some negotiated outcomes that can be picked up in the next round of dialogue.

It is likely that the National Dialogues will remain a prevalent tool in the coming years and therefore worthy of further study and research, especially in fragile countries, which will suffer from multiple wars and conflicts. The historical experience of the countries that managed to build strong democratic systems have shown that the basic condition for the establishment and continuity of such systems is the ability of the diverse political parties to organise dialogues to reach consensus of various kinds. As in the space of dialogues and negotiation mechanism, there are no losers or winners, but the process is done through wide-open and transparent discussions among all conflicting factions without preconceived ideas, down to the compatibility between multiple views, which requires parallel, equal, mutual compromise, without adhering to the utmost goals, or putting down preconditions, or threatening in order to persuade, but instead adopting flexibility in dealing with the objectives as well as in the methods used.

Humanitarian Aid and Peacebuilding

To bolster our analysis of the cases chosen for this book, we also looked at the rationale of Humanitarian Aid and the effectiveness of the EU's peace interventions in the regional setting. For this exploration, we looked at the historical context of aid from the period following World War II. As governments began to accept the need for international intervention, the need for HA grew. Relief efforts grew internationally with the growth in technology, transport, and telecommunication which resulted in a shift of focus from Europe to lesser or under-developed countries, laying the foundation for the current HA scenario.

The main challenges in the conflict zone, within the ambit of HA, is the question of accommodating universalism within diversity. Globalisation and modernity clash with fundamentalism and tradition which has contributed to the development of war economies (Barnett, 2011). War economies have brought about festering long-term issues, by making political governance systems unstable and eventually falling apart. This, in turn, only exacerbates conflict.

A proposed alternative to food-based aid, which is contributing to the war economy dynamic, is cash-based aid which grants people the power and dignity to choose what to purchase based on their life priorities. This infuses satisfaction and power back into the hands of the public and minimises the growth and proliferation of war economies. However, the final outcome of such a switch is yet to be realised as organisations hesitate to implement the system. The chapter also discusses other challenges faced by these organisations with regard to food-aid distribution and food-aid diversion. The chapter proposes how cash-based interventions are a potential solution for these challenges and a means to transform the notion of the political and economic situation on ground, thereby leading to a truer portrayal in media, in place of the embellished depiction by international media outlets.

European Media and Framing Conflict

In today's world, technology and media and the way people communicate influence debates on issues that concern the international community (Harvey, 1989 cited in Tomlinson, 1997). The role of media in a democracy is to provide a platform for the multitudinous nature of the public's views on current issues. It is not restricted to providing news and current affair updates, it is also to shape opinion on worldly issues and in turn shape policy decisions and conflict resolution. A free media must not resort to censorship or inciting propaganda, or misrepresentations of sensitive situations as it can contort the approach of an international intervention as is apparent in the case HA in the Arab region.

This chapter compared the media coverage of wars in Yemen and Syria by four European media outlets (The Independent, United Kingdom; NRC Handelsblad, the Netherlands).

In the case of Yemen, it is noticed that there is little empirical data and only a few studies available on the media coverage of the Saudi Arabian-led intervention in Yemen war that was launched in March 2015, and it is assumed that the Yemeni war is underreported as compared to the case of Syria. This chapter comprises empirical observations that allow explorative assumptions as a starting point for future research. It examines and compares the amount of news coverage devoted to the Saudi-led coalition military intervention in Yemen and Russian military intervention in Syria by European media over a period of one year. The analysis initiates research into the nature of news coverage by the European media of both Saudi-Yemen war and Syrian war. As a result, the researchers are able to prove that the Saudi-Yemen war is underreported or receives little attention by the media and international agenda especially in Europe as it is one of the serious crises that engulfed the Middle East similar to Syria. The chapter also examines the news frames that were used to present both conflicts.

As we can see from this exploration, international media has the power and resources to attract global attention to certain conflicts or crises. However, the portrayal can depend on a variety of factors depending on the relationship of the country of the media outlet with the conflicted region along with the monetary aspect. This creates a subsequent imbalance in the reportage of conflicts around the world. This imbalance is delineated in the tables in Chapter 6 based on these news frames—Conflict, Consequences, Attribution of Responsibility, Morality, Human Interest, and Others.

From the study we can glean that the Yemeni war was portrayed as a sectarian conflict between Shia and Sunni groups. However, the atrocities meted out to the people in Yemen are on a level as violent as Syria, yet the media coverage devoted to the Yemen does not indicate that due to the involvement of actors such as Iran, Turkey, US, Hezbollah, and Russia backing the Syrian regime. For future studies, it is recommended that a comparative analysis of coverage devoted to Yemen by other media outlets be compared with other cases in the Middle East region.

As we sum up, we can reflect on the insights provided by the analysis carried out in this book and discern that the two main objectives are being met—(1) to offer a multilevel analytical framework for National Dialogues in fragile settings; and (2) to provide empirical evidence that helps those engaged in the implementation of these processes internally and externally. Furthermore, the book presents a radical contrast between the on-ground reality of the conflicts in the region, which are characterised by various social, political, economic, geographic, and humanitarian elements, and the portrayal of the suffering and challenges faced by the people in European online media. This demonstrates that Chapter 6 is working against the preceding chapters proving that European media somehow fails to provide a true, clear, or holistic image of the conflict in the Arab region and devotes negligible coverage especially to the conflict and violence in Yemen.

With its distinctive analytical approach, we have a greater understanding of the geopolitical situation in Yemen, its on-ground reality versus the negligible abstract portrayal in European media.

References

ACRPS. (2011). *The army and popular revolution in Yemen.* Arab Center for Research and Policy Studies. http://english.dohainstitute.org/release/82eaa6e3-772b-4e9e-b08b-0c6bae9b76df

Alhadad, M. (2015). *Peace Nobel for Tunisian consensus experience.* Life Press.

Al-Qurashi, A. (2014). *Civil society organizations in Yemen quantity without quality, views around the Gulf No. (106).* http://araa.sa/index.php?view=article&id=1618:2014-07-14-07-22-37&Itemid=172&option=com_content

Alshargbi, A. (2013). *Restructuring the Yemeni Army.* Arab Centre for Research and Policy Studies.

Barnett, M. (2011). *Empire of humanity: A history of humanitarianism.* Cornell University Press.

Bellin, E. (2015). *Drivers of democracy: Lessons from Tunisia.* Crown Center for Middle East Studies. http://www.alhayat.com/Opinion/Writers/11613334/

Elayah, M. (2014). *Donors-promoted public sector reform in developing countries and the local knowledge syndrome.* Leiden University and Smart Print.

Ghriwal, S. (2016). *Quiet revolution: Tunisian army after Bin Ali.* Carnegie Peace Center. http://carnegie-mec.org/2016/02/24/ar-62830/iud4

Holzapffel, P. (2014). Peace work, Yemen's transition process between fragmentation and transformation. *Yale Review of International Studies.*

Lederach, J. (1997). *Building peace: Sustainable reconciliation in divided societies.* Institute of Peace Press.

Mahmoud, A. A. (2016). *Tunisia revolution reasons, success factors, results.* General Body for Research. http://www.sis.gov.eg/Newvr/34/8.htm

Musalami, F. (2015). *Sectarianism between Sunnis and Shiites in Yemen.* Kareingi Center for Peace. http://carnegie-mec.org/2015/12/29/ar-63107/iwb3

Sabahi, A. (2015). *Corruption of elites prolongs Yemen conflict.* http://www.albayan.co.uk/Article2.aspx?id=4550#sthash.eCERWt0G.dpuf

Sawa. (2016). *The Backwardness in the Arab world.* Newspaper article: http://www.radiosawa.com/content/international-literacy-day/280417.html

Tomlinson, J. (1997). Cultural globalization and cultural imperialism. In K. Thompson (Ed.), *Media and cultural regulation.* The Open University & Sage.

REFERENCES

Aalen, L. (2006). Ethnic federalism and self-determination for nationalities in a semi-authoritarian state: The case of Ethiopia. *International Journal on Minority and Group Rights, 13,* 243.

Aalen, L., & Tronvoll, K. (2009). The end of democracy? Curtailing political and civil rights in Ethiopia. *Review of African Political Economy, 36*(120), 193–207.

Abdelaty, M. (2021). *Democratization and extremism: The case of Tunisia* [Master's Thesis, the American University in Cairo]. AUC Knowledge Fountain. https://fount.aucegypt.edu/etds/1671

Abdel Shafi, E. (2014). Egypt and Tunisia: Unfair comparison. *Centre Island for Studies.*

AbdelMoula, L. (2013). Spotlight on Tunisia's experience in democratic transition. *Al Jazeera Center For Studies.*

Abdulmajid, A. (2021). *Extremism in the digital era: The media discourse of terrorist groups in the Middle East.* Springer.

Abdul-Muna'im Ibrahim, T. (2019). The dialectical relationship between human and cultural diversity in building a civil state in Iraq research in cultural anthropology on the possibility of presenting a strategy of national dialogue and peaceful coexistence. *Journal of Al-Frahedis Arts* مجلة آداب الفراهيدي *11*(39 I), 519–548.

Acemoglu, D., & Robinson, J. A. (2012). *Why nations fail: The origins of power, prosperity, and poverty.* Crown Publishers.

ACRPS. (2011). *The army and popular revolution in Yemen.* Available at: http://english.dohainstitute.org/release/82eaa6e3-772b-4e9e-b08b-0c6bae9b76df

ACRPS. (2014a). *Outcomes of Yemen's National Dialogue Conference: A step toward conflict resolution and state building?*

ACRPS. (2014b). *The Comprehensive National Dialogue Conference draft in Yemen: A step on the way of crisis solving and building state.*

ActionAid. (2003). *Human security policy briefing note 1 food aid: An action aid briefing paper (2003).* Retrieved from http://www.actionaid.org.uk/doc_lib/food_aid_background_briefing_paper.pdf

Adams, L. & Winahyu, R. (2006). *Learning from cash based responses to the Tsunami: Case studies.* Overseas Development Institute (ODI).

Aguilar, S. L. C. (2021). Ethnic conflicts and peacekeeping. In *Risks, identity and conflict* (pp. 157–183). Palgrave Macmillan.

Ahmed, S. (2014, February). Women's voices in the New Yemen. *Yemen Polling Center.*

Arabic Media Network. (2015). *Who is the quartet sponsor of the dialogue.* www.moheet.com/2015/10/09/2326163

Aryal, A. (2012). Theories of change in peacebuilding: Learning from the experiences of peacebuilding initiatives in Nepal. *CARE International UK and International Alert.* https://www.care.at/images/_care_2013/expert/pdf/COE_Resources/Programming/Theories_of_Change_in_Peacebuilding.pdf

Al-Akhali, R. (2014). The challenge of federalism in Yemen. *Rafik Hariri Center for the Middle East, Atlantic Council.*

Al-Asbahi, A. (2013). *The path of a political settlement in Yemen; Model of resolving internal conflicts.* ASSECAA. http://www.assecaa.org/Arabic/ArabicPublictions/A_workPaperPeacemeeting2013.htm

Al-Ashmlay, M. (2004). *The unity and political conflict; the study of the historical and political configuration of the State of Yemeni unity 1820–2003.* Alnhar Center for Political Studies.

Albakeeri, N. (2013). *Success and failure indicators of the national dialogue in Yemen.* www.aljazeera.net//knowledgdgate/opinions/14l2l2013

Al Batati, S. (2015, March 29). Who are the Houthis in Yemen. *Al Jazeera.* https://www.aljazeera.com/news/middleeast/2014/08/yemen-houthis-hadi-protests-201482132719818986.html

Al-Dawsari, N. (2012). *Tribal governance and stability in Yemen* (p. 24). Carnegie Endowment for International Peace.

Alexander, N. M. (2009). *International and comparative mediation: legal perspectives* (Vol. 4). Kluwer Law International BV.

Aleya-Sghaier, A. (2012). The Tunisian revolution: The revolution of dignity. *The Journal of the Middle East and Africa,* 3(1), 18–45.

Al-Faqih, A. (2012). *Identity and political reform: The case of the Hashemites, Hashed, and Bakeel in Yemen, Part III.* Open access at http://dralfaqih.blogspot.com/2012/11/19-21-2012_5.html. Date of visit 28 December 2015.

Al-Fraah, H. (2005). *Yemen multi-party elections, parliamentary and presidential 1993–2003*. Ebadi Center for Publishing and Distribution.

Alhadad, M. (2015). *Peace nobel for Tunisian consensus experience*. Life Press.

Alhaidosi, A. (2013). *A list of the parties concerned to participate in the national dialogue*. Available at: www.hakaekonline.com/?p=38865.

Al Hammadi, K. (2014). Yemen: Yemen's consensus government faces some threats of withdrawing trust and the parliament giving more days to pass the insuperable conditions. *Al-Quds-Al-Arabi*. Available at: www.alquds.co.uk/?p=171982

Alhalali, A. (2013). *The government recognizes urgent action to win back southerners*. Marib Press. www.marebpress.net/mobile/news_details.php?sid=59290

Al-Harbi, A. (2013). *Yemen: The past that refuses to go around and the future hindered his coming*. Ebadi Center for Studies and Publications.

Aljawrash, S. A. (2016). National dialogue in Tunisia. *SWI swissinfo.ch*. www.swissinfo.ch/ara/37576704

Al Janahi, A. (1992). *The national movement in Yemen from the revolution to the unity*. El-Amal Center for Studies and Publishing.

Al-jadbe, J. (2014). *Five agreements in the five years of dialogues between the GPC and JMP*. Yemeni Foreign Ministry. Open access at: http://www.mofa.gov.ye/mota.htm

Al Jazeera. (2018). *Syria's Civil War*. https://www.aljazeera.com/program/featured-documentaries/2018/3/15/syrias-war-seven-years-seven-documentaries

Allahi, F., Taheri, S., Kian, R., Sabet, E., De Leeuw, S., Cianci, R., & Revetria, R. (2019). Cash-based interventions to enhance dignity in persistent humanitarian refugee crises: A system dynamics approach. *IEEE Transactions on Engineering Management*.

Alley, A. L. (2013). Tracking the "Arab Spring": Yemen changes everything... and nothing. *Journal of Democracy*, 24(4), 74–85.

Almagro, M. M. (2021). Indicators and success stories: The UN sustaining peace agenda, bureaucratic power, and knowledge production in post-war settings. *International Studies Quarterly*, 65(3), 699–711.

Al Majdhoub, F. (2016). Framing the ISIL: A content analysis of the news coverage by CNN and Aljazeera. *Malaysian Journal of Communication*, 32, 335–364.

Al-Maqtari, A. (2010). The influence of the political factors on the economic reform policy in the Republic of Yemen. *Center for Arab Unity Studies*.

Al-mikhlafi, A. (2013). *Report of the Technical Committee for the preparations for the national dialogue*.

Almzehagi, M. (2016). *Laws of transitional justice in Yemen: Manipulating the truth and muting the voices of the victims*. A study available at: www.legal-agenda.com/print.php?id=261&folder=articles&lang=ar

Alnoaman, M. (2013). The southern Hirak forces rejected the Yemeni dialog: It demands the retake of the south state. *The Global Center of Rapprochement between Islamic Sects*. Study available at: www.taghrib.org/pages/content.php?tid=174

Al-Qurashi, A. (2014). *Civil society organizations in Yemen quantity without quality, views around the Gulf No. 106*. Available at: https://araa.sa/index.php?view=article&id=1618:2014-07-14-07-22-37&Itemid=172&option=com_content

Amiri, A. (2011). The humanitarian challenge in the Middle East. *Humanitarian Practice Network (HPN), 51*, 2–9. Available at: https://odihpn.org/wpcontent/uploads/2011/09/humanitarianexchange051.pdf. Accessed 1 June 2020.

Antoine, L., & Johannes, S. (2013). *Tunisian political parties organize national dialogue*. https://www.wsws.org/en/articles/2013/10/15/tuni-o15.html

Aryal, A. (2012). *Theories of change in peacebuilding: Learning from the experiences of peacebuilding initiatives in Nepal*. CARE International UK and International Alert. Available at: https://www.care.at/images/_care_2013/expert/pdf/COE_Resources/Programming/Theories_of_Change_in_Peacebuilding.pdf

Alshamary, M. R. (2021). Religious peacebuilding in Iraq: Prospects and challenges from the Hawza. *Journal of Intervention and Statebuilding, 15*, 1–16.

Alshargbi, A. (2013). *Restructuring the Yemeni Army*. Arab Centre for Research and Policy Studies.

Al-smadi, Z. (2016). *Resolving conflicts—A revised version of the Jordanian perspective, international peace studies program*. United Nations Peace University.

Al-Saqqaf, F. (1998). *The national reconciliation in Yemen and its dimensions and perspectives, a series of symposia of the future studies*. Center for Future Studies.

Alsoswa, A. A. A., & Brehony, N. (Eds.). (2021). *Building a New Yemen: Recovery, transition and the international community*. Bloomsbury.

Al-Shamiri, S. (2012). *The sociology of the popular revolution of Yemen*. Ebadi Center for Studies and Publishing.

Alwazir, A. Z. (2012). Youth inclusion in Yemen: A necessary element for success of political transition. *Arab Reform Initiative. Arab Reform Brief, 64*.

Alwazir, A. Z. (2013). Yemen's independent youth and their role in the National Dialogue Conference: Triggering a change in political culture. *Stiftung*

Wissenschaft und Politik: German Institute for International and Security Affairs.

Al-Wazier, Z. (2011). *Reading the texts and documents of the Khmer national conference.* The Union of Yemeni Popular Forces. The Committee of Information.

Andrieu, K. (2016). Confronting the dictatorial past in Tunisia: Human rights and the politics of victimhood in transitional justice discourses since 2011. *Human Rights Quarterly, 38,* 261.

Annan, K. (2004). The causes of conflict and the promotion of durable peace and sustainable development in Africa. *African Renaissance, 1*(3), 9–42.

Asim, M. M. (2015). Examining the role of emotion as a dimension of affective agenda setting. *International Journal of Humanities and Management Sciences (IJHMS), 3,* 6.

Autesserre, S. (2017). International peacebuilding and local success: Assumptions and effectiveness. *International Studies Review.*

Avis, W. (2020). *International actors' support on inclusive peace processes.* K4D Helpdesk Report. Brighton, UK: Institute of Development Studies.

Axelrod, A. (2009). *Selling the great war: The making of American Propaganda.* Martin's Press.

Ayoob, M. (2002). Humanitarian intervention and state sovereignty. *The International Journal of Human Rights, 6*(1), 81–102.

Ballentine, K., & Nitzschke, H. (2005). The political economy of civil war and conflict transformation. *Berghof Research Center for Constructive Conflict Management, 39*(3), 430–455.

Bandsom, K. (2018). *Fighting hunger with cash.* Retrieved from https://www.welthungerhilfe.org/our-work/countries/yemen/fighting-hunger-with-cash/

Banerjee, A. (2017). *Violence and female inclusion: Elections and female political participation in Afghanistan.* Georgetown University.

Barash, D. P., & Webel, C. P. (2016). *Peace and conflict studies.* Sage.

Baron, A. (2015). Civil War in Yemen: Imminent and avoidable. *European Council on Foreign Relations.*

Barnett, M. (2011). *Empire of humanity: A history of humanitarianism.* Cornell University Press.

Barnett, M., & Snyder, J. (2011). The grand strategies of humanitarianism. In *Humanitarianism in question* (pp. 143–171). Cornell University Press.

Barrett, C., & Maxwell, D. (2005). *Food aid after fifty years.* Routledge.

Barrington, L. (2020, April 9). *WFP to halve food aid in Houthi Yemen as funding drops.* Retrieved from https://www.reuters.com/article/yemen-security-aid/wfp-to-halve-food-aid-in-houthi-yemen-as-funding-drops-idUSL5N2BX4YH

Bar-Siman-Tov, Y. (2004). *From conflict resolution to reconciliation.* Oxford University Press.

Basurrah, S. (2012). *The Gulf initiative and executive mechanism between the pros and cons*. The Gulf of Academic Development Center.
Bates, M. J., & Lu, S. (1997). An exploratory profile of Personal Home Pages: Content, Design. *Metaphors. Online and CD-Rom Review, 21*(6), 331–340.
Battera, F., & Ieraci, G. (2019). *Party system and political struggle in Tunisia*. EUT Edizioni Università di Trieste.
Baum, M., & Zhukov, Y. M. (2016). *Media ownership and news coverage of international conflict*. Retrieved on April 14, 2017 from https://www.hks.harvard.edu/fs/mbaum/documents/BaumZhukov_MediaOwnershipAndWar-WORKINGDRAFT.pdf.
BBC Arabic. (2010). *President Hamid Karzai inaugurates the work of the Peace Council for Dialogue in Afghanistan*. Available at: http://www.bbc.com/arabic/lg/worldnews/2010/10/101007_karzai_tc2.shtml
BBC. (2017, March 28). *"Yemen Crisis: Who is fighting whom?"*. Retrieved on April 10,2017 from http://www.bbc.com/news/world-middle-east-293 19423
BBC. (2019, June 21). *Yemen crisis: UN partially suspends food aid*. Retrieved from https://www.bbc.com/news/world-middle-east-48716258
Bélair, J. (2016). Ethnic federalism and conflicts in Ethiopia. *Canadian Journal of African Studies / Revue canadienne des études africaines, 50*, 295–301. https://doi.org/10.1080/00083968.2015.1124580
Benchoff, P. N. (2012). *Yemen: Preventing the next Afghanistan*. Army War Coll Carlisle Barracks.
Benomar, J. (2013). s Yemen a new model? *Journal of International Affairs, 67*(1), 197–203.
Bellamy, A. J. (2004). The 'next stage' in peace operations theory? *International Peacekeeping, 11*(1), 17–38.
Bellin, E. (2015). Drivers of democracy: Lessons from Tunisia. *Crown center for Middle East Studies*. Available at: http://www.alhayat.com/Opinion/Writers/11613334/
Ben Salem, M. (2016). The national dialogue, collusive transactions and government legitimacy in Tunisia. *International Spectator, 51*(1), 99–112.
Benthall, J. (2003). Humanitarianism and Islam after 11 September. *Humanitarian Action and the 'Global War on Terror'* (pp. 37–47).
Bercovitch, J., & Houston, A. (1996). The study of international mediation: Theoretical issues and empirical evidence. *Theory and Practice of International Mediation: Selected Essays*.
Bercovitch, J., Jackson, R., & Jackson, R. D. W. (2009). *Conflict resolution in the twenty-first century: Principles, methods, and approaches*. University of Michigan Press.
Berdal, M. (2016). A mission too far? NATO and Afghanistan, 2001–2014. *Politics, 18*, 3.

Berdal, M. (2019). NATO's landscape of the mind: Stabilisation and state-building in Afghanistan. *Ethnopolitics, 18*(5), 526–543.

Berg, M., Mattinen, H., & Pattugaian, G. (2013). *Examining protection and gender in cash and voucher transfers.*

Bettye, P., & Thomas, P. (2007). Democratic dialogue—A handbook for practitioners. *International IDEA.* Available at: http://www.idea.int/es/pub lications/democratic_dialogue/loader.cfm?csmodule=security/getfile&pag eid=19459

Bird, T., & Marshall, A. (2011). *Afghanistan: How the West lost its way.* Yale University Press.

Binder, M. (2015). Paths to intervention: What explains the UN's selective response to humanitarian crises? *Journal of Peace Research, 52*(6), 712–726.

Blanchard, C. M., Humud, C. E., & Nikitin, M. B. D. (2014). *Armed conflict in Syria: Overview and US response.* Library of Congress Washington DC Congressional Research Service.

Blunck, M., et al. (2017). *National dialogue handbook.* Berghof Foundation Operations.

Boege, V. (2011). Potential and limits of traditional approaches in peacebuilding. *Berghof handbook II: Advancing conflict transformation* (pp. 431–457).

Bollinger, S. (2015). *Navigating Yemen to safe shores: Prospects for national dialogue and reconciliation.* Oxford Research Group.

Boone, C. (2011). Politically allocated land rights and the geography of electoral violence: The case of Kenya in the 1990s. *Comparative Political Studies, 44*(10), 1311–1342.

Boutros-Ghali, B. (1992). An agenda for peace: Preventive diplomacy, peacemaking and peace-keeping. *International Relations, 11*(3), 201–218.

Brehony, N. (2015). Yemen and the Huthis: Genesis of the 2015 crisis. *Asian Affairs, 46*(2), 232–250.

Breslau, D. (1997, December). The political power of research methods: Knowledge regimes in U.S. labor-market policy. *Theory and Society, 26*(6):869–902.

Brown, M. E. (1996). *The international dimensions of internal conflict* (Vol. 10). MIT Press.

Burton, J. W. (2010). *Systems, states, diplomacy and rules.* Cambridge University Press.

Burton, J. (2020). "Doing no harm" in the digital age: What the digitalization of cash means for humanitarian action. *International Review of the Red Cross, 102*(913), 43–73.

Cabot Venton, C. (2014). *Value for money of cash transfers in emergencies.* Ethiopia Case Study (annexA), United Kingdom Department for International Development.

Call, C., & Cousens, E. (2008). Ending wars and building peace: International responses to war-torn societies. *International Studies Perspectives,* 9(1), 1–21.
CaLP. (2020). Available at: https://www.calpnetwork.org/wp-content/uploads/2020/07/SOWC2020-Full-Report.pdf
Camaj, L. (2010). Media framing through stages of a political discourse: International news agencies' coverage of Kosovo's status negotiations. *International Communication Gazette,* 72(7), 635–653.
Caparini, M. (2016). Challenges to contemporary peace support operations in Africa. *Journal of Military and Strategic Studies,* 17(2).
Cappella, J. N., & Jamieson, K. H. (1997). *Spiral of cynicism. The press and the public good.*
Carlman, A., & Svedlund, A. I. (2013). *Peace journalism, How media reporting affects wars and conflicts.* The Kvinna till Kvinna Foundation.
Carter, D. B. (2010). The strategy of territorial conflict. *American Journal of Political Science,* 54(4), 969–987.
Cash for Work: Promoting Livelihood Opportunities for Urban Youth in Yemen. (2020, March 3). Retrieved from https://en.unesco.org/news/cash-work-promoting-livelihood-opportunities-urban-youth-yemen
Castaneda, D. (2012). *The European Union in Colombia: Learning how to be a peace actor.* L'Institut de Recherche Stratégique de l'École Militaire.
Castillo, J. G. (2021). Deciding between cash-based and in-kind distributions during humanitarian emergencies. *Journal of Humanitarian Logistics and Supply Chain Management,* 11(2), 272–295.
Chang, T. K., Shoemaker, P., & Brendlinger, N. (1987). Determinants of international news coverage in the US media. *Communication Research,* 14, 396–414.
Chang, T. K. (1998). All countries not created equal to be news: World system and international communication. *Communication Research,* 25, 528–566.
Cheng-Hopkins, J. (2010). *UN peacebuilding: An orientation.* United Nations.
Christopher, A. (2005). *Authoritarianism and civil society in Tunisia.* MER205. http://www.merip.org/mer/mer205/authoritarianism-civil-society-tunisia
Citha, M. (2006). National reconciliation in Afghanistan conflict History and search for an Afghan approach. *International Asienforum,* 37(1–2), 5–35.
CIVICUS—World Alliance for Citizen Participation. (2010). *Civil Society Index Analytical Country Report for Zambia.* http://civicus.org/downloads/CSI/Zambia.pdf
CIVICUS—World Alliance for Citizen Participation. (2011). *Bridging the gaps: Citizens, organizations and dissociation.* http://www.civicus.org/downloads/Bridging%20the%20Gaps%20-%20Citizens%20%20Organisations%20and%20Dissociation.pdf
Clapham, C. (1998). Rwanda: The perils of peacemaking. *Journal of Peace Research,* 35(2), 193–210.

Clay, E. (2005). *The development effectiveness of food aid—Does tying matter?* Organisation for Economic Co-operation and Development.
Collén, C. (2014). *National dialogue and internal mediation processes perspectives on theory and practice*. The Ministry for Foreign Affairs.
Concern Worldwide. (2011). *Hard cash in hard times: cash transfers versus food aid in rural Zimbabwe*. Brief. Concern Worldwide.
Connelly, A. (2016, September 20). The Iraqi constitutional process. *The Michigan Journal of Public Affairs, 13*, 69–81.
Cottle, S. (2006). *Mediatized conflict: Developments in media and conflict studies*. McGraw-Hill Education.
Crocker, C. A., Hampson, F. O., & Aall, P. R. (1999). *Herding cats: Multiparty mediation in a complex world*. US Institute of Peace Press.
Crowe, M. (2015). *Tunisia's historic step towards democracy*. Carnegie Center for Peace. Available at: http://carnegie-mec.org/2015/01/14/
CRT Fund. (2012). *The Yemen National Dialogue and constitutional reform trust fund (YNDCRTF)*.
Cunliffe, P. (2018). From peacekeepers to praetorians—How participating in peacekeeping operations may subvert democracy. *International Relations, 32*(2), 218–239.
Currie-Alder, B., Ravi, K., David, M., & Rohinton, M. (2014). *International development: Ideas, experience, and prospects*. Oxford University Press.
Dandeker, C. (2020). What "success" means in Afghanistan, Iraq, and Libya. In *How 9/11 changed our ways of war* (pp. 116–148). Stanford University Press.
Dahlgren, S., & Augustin, A. L. A. (2015). The multiple wars in Yemen. *Middle East Research and Information Project, 18*.
D'Angelo, P. (2002). News framing as a multi-paradigmatic research program: A response to Entman. *Journal of Communication, 52*, 870–888.
Day, S. W. (2014). The 'Non-Conclusion' of Yemen's National Dialogue. *Foreign Policy, 27*.
de Jongh, S., & Kitzen, M. (2021). The conduct of lawfare: The case of the Houthi insurgency in the Yemeni civil war. In *The Conduct of War in the 21st Century*, 249–264. Routledge.
Del Castillo, G. (2008). *Rebuilding war-torn states: The challenge of post-conflict economic reconstruction*. Oxford University Press.
DeLozier, E., (2019). In Damning Report, *UN panel details war economy in Yemen* [online] The Washington Institute. Available at: https://www.washingtoninstitute.org/policy-analysis/view/in-damning-report-un-panel-details-war-economy-in-yemen. Accessed 31 March 2020.
Deng, F. M., Kimaro, S., Lyons, T., Rothchild, D., & Zartman, I. W. (2010). *Sovereignty as responsibility: conflict management in Africa*. Brookings Institution Press.

Dessu, M. K., & Yohannes, D. (2020). National dialogues in the horn of Africa: Lessons for Ethiopia's political transition. *ISS East Africa Report, 2020*(32), 1–24.

Development Initiatives' Report. (2019). Available at: http://devinit.org/wp-content/uploads/2019/09/GHA-report-2019.pdf

Diouf, S. P. (n.d.). *Food assistance: Cash and in-kind.* Retrieved July 10, 2020, from https://www.wfp.org/food-assistance

Dirksen, N. (2019). *Afghanistan's altercation: Media influence in Western conflict interventions.*

Dimitrova, D., Kaid, L., Williams, A., & Sweetser, K. (2005). War on the web: The immediate news framing of Gulf War II. *Harvard International Journal of Press-Politics, 10,* 22–44.

Dialogue. Dictionary.com Retrieved from: https://www.dictionary.com/browse/dialogue

Doocy, S. (2017). The effectiveness and value for money of cash-based humanitarian assistance: A systematic review. *Journal of Development Effectiveness, 10*(1), 121–144.

Doll, M. E. (2021). *Interpreting peace journalism in East Africa: Individual, organizational, and professional influences* (Doctoral dissertation). University of Washington.

Donais, T., & McCandless, E. (2017). International peace building and the emerging inclusivity norm. *Third World Quarterly, 38*(2), 291–310.

Donini, A. (2004, Autumn). Western aid agencies don't have a humanitarian monopoly. *Humanitarian Affairs Review,* 12–15.

Doyle, M., & Sambanis, N. (2000). International peacebuilding: A theoretical and quantitative analysis. *The American Political Science Review, 94*(4), 779–801. https://doi.org/10.2307/2586208

Dudouet, V. (2006). *Transitions from violence to peace: Revisiting analysis and intervention in conflict transformation.*

Durac, V. (2011). The joint meeting parties and the politics of opposition in Yemen. *British Journal of Middle Eastern Studies, 38*(3), 343–365.

Durac, V. (2012). Yemen's Arab Spring—Democratic opening or regime maintenance? *Mediterranean Politics, 17*(2), 161–178.

Eaton, T. (2018). *Libya's war economy. Predation, Profiteering and State Weakness.* Chatham House Research Paper. Disponível em https://www.chathamhouse.org/sites/files/chathamhouse/publications/research/2018-04-12-libyas-war-economy-eaton-final.pdf

Edwards, A. (2019). Yemen: Civil War and humanitarian Catastrophe. *Political Insight, 10*(2), 14–16.

Egeland, J. (2016, August 30). *They all had a name.* Retrieved from https://www.nrc.no/perspectives/2016/they-all-had-a-name/

Elayah, M. (2014). Donors-promoted public sector reform in developing countries and the local knowledge syndrome. *Leiden University and Smart Print*.
Elayah, M. A. A. (2015). [Foreign aid effectiveness between the strategic objectives of, and the internal influences within, donor countries] [In Arabic]. *Siyasat Arabiyah [Arab Policies Journal], 14*, 141–158.
Elayah, M. A. A., van Kempen, L. A. C. M., & Schulpen, L. W. M. (2016). *Civil society's diagnosis of the 2013 National Dialogue Conference (NDC) in Yemen: (Why) did it fail?* [Policy brief].
Elayah, M. A. A., Schulpen, L. W. M., Abu-Osba, B., & Al-Zandani, B. (2017). *Yemen: A forgotten war and an unforgettable country*.
Elayah, M., Schulpen, L., van Kempen, L., & Aglan, M. M. (2018). *The role of the United Nations and its special envoys in the current Yemeni War: Floundering in a tragic reality*.
Elayah, M. (2016). Lack of foreign aid effectiveness in developing countries between a hammer and an anvil. *Contemporary Arab Affairs, 9*(1), 82–99.
Elayah, M., & Verkoren, W. (2020). Civil society during war: The case of Yemen. *Peacebuilding, 8*(4), 476–498.
Elayah, M. (2021). Humanitarian aid and war economies: The case of Yemen. *Economics of Peace and Security Journal, 16*(1), 52–65.
Elayah, M. (2021). Arab conflicts today: Statistics and trends. In I. Fraihat (Ed.), *The rooting and marketing of conflict science in the Arab world*. Arab Center for Research and Policy Studies.
Elayah, M., Al-Daily, W., & Alkubati, M. (2021). The women, peace, and security (WPS) agenda between rhetoric and action in the MENA region: A case study of Yemen and Libya. In *Female pioneers from ancient Egypt and the Middle East* (pp. 129–143). Springer.
Elayah, M., & Fenttiman, M. (2021). Humanitarian aid and war economies: The case of Yemen. *The Economics of Peace and Security Journal, 16*(1), 52–65.
Elayah, M., Schulpen, L., van Kempen, L., Almaweri, A., AbuOsba, B., & Alzandani, B. (2020). National dialogues as an interruption of civil war—The case of Yemen. *Peacebuilding, 8*(1), 98–117.
Elayah, M., van Kempen, L., & Schulpen, L. (2020). Adding to the controversy? Civil society's evaluation of the National Conference Dialogue in Yemen. *Journal of Intervention and Statebuilding, 14*(3), 431–458.
Elbadawi, I. (2000). *External interventions and the duration of civil wars*.
Entman, R. M. (1993). Framing: Towards clarification of a fractured paradigm. *McQuail's reader in mass communication theory* (pp. 390–397).
Emily, P & Thomas, D. (2007). *Conflict and human rights: A theoretical framework*. University of Birmingham. Available at: http://shur.luiss.it/files/2008/10/shurwp01-07.pdf

Erica, G. (2014). *Process lessons learned in Yemen's National Dialogue*. United States Institute of Peace.
Esfandiary, D., & Tabatabai, A. (2016). Yemen: An opportunity for Iran-Saudi dialogue? *The Washington Quarterly, 39*(2), 155–174.
Eshaq, A., & Al-Marani, S. (2016). Assessing the EU's conflict prevention and peacebuilding interventions in Yemen. *WOSCAP Case Study Report*.
Estefan, L. F., Armstead, T. L., Rivera, M. S., Kearns, M. C., Carter, D., Crowell, J., & Daniels, B. (2019). Enhancing the national dialogue on the prevention of intimate partner violence. *American Journal of Community Psychology, 63*(1–2), 153–167.
European Peacebuilding Liaison Office. (2013). *National dialogue processes in political transitions*.
Fahmy, S. S. (2020). Virtual theme collection: Journalism and mass communication research in the MENA region. *Journalism & Mass Communication Quarterly, 97*(3), 590–593.
Farahat, G. (2014). The end of the national dialog on Yemen..... start of wars, *Bydayat Magazine* (7). Available at: www.bidayatmag.com/node/145
Farhadi, A. (2020). *Countering violent extremism by winning hearts and minds*. Springer.
Fazilat, S. M. (2020). *Afghanistan civil war and ethnic conflicts: 1992–2018* (Doctoral dissertation).
Feierstein, G. (2017). Is there a path out of the Yemen conflict? Why it matters. *Prism, 7*(1), 16–31.
Fetherston, A. B. (2000). Peacekeeping, conflict resolution and peacebuilding: A reconsideration of theoretical frameworks. *International Peacekeeping, 7*(1), 190–218.
Findley, M. G. (2018). Does foreign aid build peace? *Annual Review of Political Science, 21*, 359–384.
Fischer, M. (2011). *Transitional justice and reconciliation: Theory and practice advancing conflict transformation*. The Berghof Handbook. Available at: http://www.berghof-foundation.org/fileadmin/redaktion/Publicati ons/Handbook/Articles/fischer_tj_and_rec_handbook.pdf
Fisher, R. J. (2001). *Methods of third-party intervention*. Available at: https://www.berghof-foundation.org/fileadmin/redaktion/Publications/ Handbook/Articles/fisher_handbookII.pdf
Fisher, R. J. (2011). *Methods of third-party intervention*. Available at: https://www.berghof-foundation.org/fileadmin/redaktion/Publications/ Handbook/Articles/fisher_handbookII.pdf
Fiseha, A. (2015). *Dealing with territorial cleavages in constitutional transitions: Case study of Ethiopia*. Available at: http://www.constitutionnet.org/ files/dealing_with_territorial_cleavages_in_constitutional_transitions_-_confer ence_outline_24_september.pdf

Fisher, R., & Ury, W. (1981). *Getting to yes: Negotiating agreement without giving in.* Houghton Mifflin.
Fisher, R. J., & Keashly, l. (1991). The potential complementarity of mediation and consultation within a contingency model of third party intervention. *Journal of Peace Research, 28*(1), 29–42.
Forsythe, D. P. (2005). *The humanitarians: The international committee of the Red Cross* (p. 16). Cambridge University Press.
Fox, J. (1998). The effects of religion on domestic conflicts. *Terrorism and Political Violence, 10*(4), 43–63, 43.
Fraihat, I. (2016). *Unfinished revolutions.* Yale University Press.
Francis, D. J. (2017). *Uniting Africa: Building regional peace and security systems.* Routledge.
France24. (2015). *What is the Quartet Dialogue that culminated in the Nobel Peace Prize.* www.france24.com/ar/20151009
France24. (2015, March 26). *Saudi could not allow Houthis to take control of Yemen.* Retrieved on April 22,2017 from http://www.france24.com/en/201 50326-saudi-arabia-coalition-military-intervention-yemen-houthi-rebels.
France24. (2015, April 12). *France voices support for Saudi campaign in Yemen.* Retrieved on April 22,2017 from http://www.france24.com/en/20150412-france-fabius-support-saudi-campaign-yemen-houthis.
France24. (2015, April 25). *Former Yemen president calls for dialogue to end war.* Retrieved from http://www.france24.com/en/20150425-yemen-saleh-dialogue-talks-houthi-saudi.
France24. (2015, April 27). *Saudis pound Houthi targets as UN picks new mediator.* Retrieved on March 30, 2017 from http://www.france24.com/en/201 50427-saudis-pound-houthi-targets-un-mediator-yemen.
France24. (2015, August 8). *UN official warns of 'deliberate starvation' in Yemen.* Retrieved from http://www.france24.com/en/20150812-un-official-warns-deliberate-starvation-yemen.
France24. (2016, February 11). *Human smugglers on trial over Syrian toddler Aylan Kurdi's death.* Retrieved from https://www.france24.com/en/201 60211-turkey-syria-aylan-kurdi-toddler-human-traffickers-trial-refugees-death
France24. (2016, March 13). *Worst year yet for child deaths in Syria war, says UNICEF 3).* https://www.france24.com/en/20170313-worst-year-yet-child-deaths-syria-war-says-unicef
France24. (2016, April 11). *Warring sides pledge to respect Yemen ceasefire.* Retrieved from w.france24.com/en/20160411-yemen-warring-sides-pledge-respect-ceasefire-un.
France24. (2016, April 22). *UN-backed Yemen peace talks begin in Kuwait.* Retrieved from http://www.france24.com/en/20160422-un-backed-yemen-peace-talks-begin-kuwait.

France24. (2016, May 3). *Shelling by rebels in Syria's Aleppo kills more than a dozen people*. Retrieved from https://www.france24.com/en/20160503-Shelling-rebels-Syrias-Aleppo-kill-more-dozen-people.
France24. (2017, December 15). *Three UN envoys who tried and failed in quest for Syria peace*. Retrieved from https://www.france24.com/en/20190115-three-un-envoys-who-tried-failed-quest-syria-peace
Frankel, J. R., & Wallen, N. E. (2009). *How to design and evaluate research in education* (7th ed.). McGraw-Hill.
Gamson, W. A., & Modigliani, A. (1989). Media discourse and public opinion on nuclear power: A constructionist approach. *American Journal of Sociology*, 95(1), 1–37.
Garallah, M. A. (2013). *Successful separationists in a unity fan society: Al-Hirak Al-Janubi social movement in the Republic of Yemen*. Naval Postgraduate School Monterey, CA, Defense Analysis Deptartment.
Garrett, S. (2019). *Tunisia's Ennahda Party: Developing a framework for interpreting political decision-making in historical context*.Undergraduate Dissertation, Georgetown University.
Gaston, E. (2014). *Process lessons learned in Yemen's National Dialogue*. United States Institute of Peace.
Gedamu, Y. (2021). *The politics of contemporary Ethiopia: Ethnic federalism and authoritarian survival*. Routledge.
Gerges, F. A. (2017). *ISIS: A history*. Princeton University Press.
Gerhards, J., & Schäfer, M. S. (2014). International terrorism, domestic coverage? How terrorist attacks are presented in the news of CNN, Al Jazeera, the BBC, and ARD. *International Communication Gazette*, 76(1), 3–26. https://doi.org/10.1177/1748048513504158
Gerring, J. (2007). The case study: What it is and what it does. In *The Oxford handbook of comparative politics*.
Gerring, J. (2007). *Case study research: Principles and practices*. Cambridge University Press.
Ghafarzade, B. (2015). Yemen: Post-conflict federalism to avoid disintegration. *New York University Journal of International Law and Politics*, 48, 933.
Ghanim, D. (2011). *Iraq's dysfunctional democracy*. ABC-CLIO.
Ghannouchi, R. (2014). The Tunisian experience. *The Cairo Review of Global Affairs*, 13, 98.
Ghriwal, S. (2016). *Quiet revolution: Tunisian army after Bin Ali*. Carnegie Peace Center. Available at http://carnegie-mec.org/2016/02/24/ar-62830/iud4
Gibelman, M., & Gelman, S. R. (2001). Very public scandals: Nongovernmental organizations in trouble. *Nonprofit and Voluntary Sector Quarterly*, 12(1), 49–66.

Giessmann, H. J., & Wils, O. (2011). *Seeking compromise? Mediation through the eyes of the conflict parties.* Berghof Foundation.
Gilboa, E. (2006). Media and international conflict. *The Sage handbook of conflict communication: Integrating theory, research, and practice* (pp. 596–626).
Gilboa, E., Jumbert, M. G., Miklian, J., & Robinson, P. (2016). Moving media and conflict studies beyond the CNN effect. *Review of International Studies*, 42(4), 654–672.
Girke, N. C. (2015). A matter of balance: The European Union as a mediator in Yemen. *European Security*, 24(4), 509–524.
Gitlin, T. (1980). *The whole world is watching: The mass media in the making and unmaking of the left.* University of California Press.
Ginsberg, R. H. (1999). Conceptualizing the European Union as an international actor: Narrowing the theoretical capability-expectations gap. *JCMS: Journal of Common Market Studies*, 37(3), 429–454.
Giustozzi, A., & Ibrahimi, N. (2017). From new dawn to quicksand: The political economy of statebuilding in Afghanistan. In *Political Economy of Statebuilding* (pp. 246–262). Routledge.
Gobe, E., & Salaymeh, L. (2016). Tunisia's "revolutionary" lawyers: From professional autonomy to political mobilization. *Law & Social Inquiry*, 41(2), 311–345.
Goffman, E. (1974). *Frame analysis: An essay on the organization of experience.* Harvard University Press.
Golan, G. (2006). Inter-media agenda setting and global news coverage. *Journalism Studies*, 7(2), 323–333.
Goodson, L. P. (2011). *Afghanistan's endless war: State failure, regional politics, and the rise of the Taliban.* University of Washington Press.
Giles, D. (2010). *Psychology of the media.* Palgrave Macmillan.
Giles, D., & Shaw, R. (2009). The psychology of news influence and the development of media framing analysis. *Social and Personality Psychology Compass*, 3(4), 375–393.
Grewal, S., & Hamid, S. (2020, January). *The dark side of consensus in Tunisia: Lessons from 2015–2019.* Brookings Report. Available at https://www.brookings.edu/research/the-darkside-of-consensus-in-tunisia-lessons-from-2015-2019
Gulf initiative between GPC and its allies and JMP partners signed on 23 November. (2011). Document available at: www.almotamar.net/news/95152.htm.
Gunter, F. R. (2013). *The political economy of Iraq: Restoring balance in a post-conflict society.* Edward Elgar.
Ha, L., & James, L. E. (1998). Interactivity reexamined: A baseline analysis of early business web sites. *Journal of Broadcasting & Electronic Media*, 42(4), 457–474.

Haddad, S. (2013). Yemen's National Dialogue: The need for a contingency plan. *Saferworld*. http://www.saferworld.org.uk/resources/view-resource/756-yemens-national-dialogue

Habtu, A. (2003). Ethnic federalism in Ethiopia: Background, present conditions and future prospects. *International Conference on African Development Archives, 57*. https://scholarworks.wmich.edu/africancenter_icad_archive/57

Haider, H. (2019). *National dialogues: Lessons learned and success factors*. K4D Helpdesk Report, Institute of Development Studies, Brighton, UK.

Halliday, F. (2013). *Arabia without sultans*. Saqi.

Hamidi, H. (2015). A comparative analysis of the post-Arab spring national dialogues in Tunisia and Yemen. *African Journal on Conflict Resolution, 15*(3), 11–35.

Hamoudi, H. A. (2013). *Negotiating in civil conflict: Constitutional construction and imperfect bargaining in Iraq*. University of Chicago Press.

Hartmann, H. (2017). *National Dialogues and development* (National Dialogue Handbook Background Paper, 3).

Harvey, N. (2012). *Why do some conflicts get more media coverage than others?* Retrieved from https://newint.org/features/2012/09/01/media-war-coverage/

Harvey, D. C. (1989). *The condition of post-modernity*. Basil Blackwell.

Harvey, D. C. (2012). *The invisible genocide: An analysis of ABC, CBS, and NBC television news coverage of the 1994 genocide in Rwanda* (Electronic Thesis and Dissertation Repository).

Harvey, P. (2005, February). *Cash and vouchers in emergencies* (Discussion Paper). Humanitarian Policy Group, Overseas Development Institute, London. http://www.odi.org.uk/hpg/papers/cash_discussion_paper.pdf

Harvey, P. (2007) *Cash based responses in emergencies*. HPG Report 24. Overseas Development Institute (ODI), London.

Hassan, A. S. (2014). Yemen National Dialogue conference: Managing peaceful change? *Legitimacy and Peace Processes: From Coercion to Consent. Accord: International Review of Peace Initiatives, 25*, 50–54.

Hashim, L., Hasan, H., & Sinnapan, S. (2007). Australian online newspapers: A website content analysis approach to measuring interactivity. In *18th Australasian Conference on Information Systems (ACIS)* (pp. 533–542). Toowoomba, Australia.

Haugbølle, R. H., Ghali, A., Yousfi, H., Limam, M., & Mollerup, N. G. (2017). *Tunisia's 2013 National Dialogue*. Berghof Foundation Report. Şubat.

Heathershaw, J. (2008). Unpacking the liberal peace: The dividing and merging of peacebuilding discourses. *Millennium, 36*(3), 597–621.

Heathershaw, J. (2013). *Towards better theories of peacebuilding: Beyond the liberal peace debate*.

Hedlund, K., Majid, N., Maxwell, D., & Nicholson, N. (2013). *Final evaluation of the unconditional cash and voucher response to the crisis 2011–12 in southern and central Somalia*. Executive Summary, Humanitarian Outcomes and United Nations Children's Fund, Somalia, UNICEF.
Hennessy, A. (2016, August 19). Theresa May should expel Saudi Arabia from the UN Human Rights Council, but that's not enough to absolve the UK. *The Independent*. Retrieved from http://www.independent.co.uk/voices/saudi-arabia-un-human-rights-council-theresa-may-expel-she-should-enough-a7199066.html
Hertog, K. (2010). *The complex reality of religious peacebuilding: Conceptual contributions and critical analysis*. Lexington Books.
Hester, A. (1973). Theoretical considerations in predicting volume and direction of international information flow. *Gazette, 19*(4), 238–247.
Higgins, J. W. (2011). Peace-building through listening, digital storytelling, and community media in cyprus. *Global Media Journal: Mediterranean Edition, 6*(1), 1–13.
Hill, G. (2017). *Yemen endures: Civil war*. Oxford University Press.
Hill, G., Salisbury, P., Northedge, L., & Kinninmont, J. (2013). *Yemen: corruption, capital flight and global drivers of conflict*. Chatham House.
Hincks, J. (2016). *What do you need to know about the crisis in Yemen?* Retrieved from http://time.com/4552712/yemen-war-humanitarian-crisis-famine/.
Hoelscher, K., Miklian, J., & Nygård, H. M. (2017). Conflict, peacekeeping, and humanitarian security: Understanding violent attacks against aid workers. *International Peacekeeping, 24*(4), 538–565.
Hoelman, M. (2009). *Social audit in development sector*. Retrieved from https://www.changemakers.com/
Holper, A., & Kirchhoff, L. (2021). Peace mediation as a balancing act between methodology, power and politics. *Peace Mediation in Germany's Foreign Policy*
Holzapffel, P. (2014). Peace work, Yemen's transition process between fragmentation and transformation. *Yale Review of International Studies*.
Houlihan, E. C., & Bisarya, S. (2021). *Practical considerations for public participation in constitution-building what, when, how and why?* (International IDEA Policy Paper No. 24). International Institute for Democracy and Electoral.
Human Rights Watch. (2008). *Iraq events of 2008*. https://www.hrw.org/world-report/2009/country-chapters/iraq
Humphreys, M. (2003). *Economics and violent conflict* (p. 31). Harvard University Press
Hyder, M. (2007). Humanitarianism and the Muslim world. *The Journal of Humanitarian Assistance*.
ICG. (2012). *The persistence of conflicts and threats to the transition process* (Middle East Report, 125). International Crisis Group. Available at: http://www.crisisgroup.org/~/media/Files/Middle%20East%20North%20Africa/Iran%20Gulf/Yemen/Arabic%20translations/125-yemen-enduring-conflicts-threatening-transition-arabic.pdf

ICG. (2012). *Yemen: Conflict continuity and threats to the transition process.* International Crisis Group.

ICG. (2013). *Yemen's Southern question: Avoiding a breakdown.* http://responsibilitytoprotect.org/Yemen%20-%20ICG%20report%2009_13.pdf

ICG. (2014). *The Huthis: From Sadaa to Sanaa* (Middle East Report No. 154). https://d2071andvip0wj.cloudfront.net/the-huthis-from-saada-to-sanaa.pdf

ICG. (2014). *Houthis from Saddah to Sana'a international crisis group.*

Institute of International and Development Studies. (2015). *Peace and inclusive transition initiative, summary of national dialogue.* Geneva. Available at: http://www.inclusivepeace.org/sites/default/files/IPTI-National-Dialogues-Arabic.pdf

Incerti-Thery, I. (2016). Dialogue as a tool in peacebuilding: Theoretical and empirical perspectives. *UiT The Arctic University of Norwy.*

International Crisis Group. (2002). *The Loya Jirga: One small step forward?* Available at: http://www.crisisgroup.org/en/regions/asia/south-asia/afghanistan/B017-the-loya-jirga-one-small-step-forward.aspx

Irrera, D. (2021). Non-state actors and conflict management in Proxy Wars. In *Oxford Research Encyclopedia of International Studies.*

Issaev, L., & Zakharov, A. (2021). The chaotic federalism: Yemen. In *Federalism in the Middle East*, 71–93. Springer.

Island Center for studies. (2014). *Mechanisms and prospects.* Study available at : www.studies.aljazeera.net/ar/files/discussionstrategytosolvearabworldconflict/2014/02/201426105920985479

Iyengar, S. (1991). Is anyone responsible? In *How television frames political issues.* University of Chicago Press.

Jinping, Z. (2013). National Dialogue Conference and political transition in Yemen. *West Asia and Africa.*

Joenniemi, P. (2015). *Russia's approach to arms control, peace mediation and National Dialogues.* Tampereen yliopisto.

Johnson, T. H. (2010). Religious figures, insurgency, and jihad in southern Afghanistan. *Who speaks for Islam* (pp. 41–65).

Jones, S. G. (2008). The rise of Afghanistan's insurgency: State failure and Jihad. *International Security, 32*(4), 7–40.

Jost, P., & Koehler, C. (2021). Who shapes the news? Analyzing journalists' and organizational interests as competing influences on biased coverage. *Journalism, 22*(2), 484–500.

Jun, H. W., & Reiterer, M. (2021). Preventive diplomacy and crisis management in EU–Korea security relations. In *EU–Korea Security Relations*, 98–120. Routledge.

Junne, G. (2013). *The role of media in conflict transformation.* Retrieved from http://www.irenees.net/bdf_fiche-analyse-1002_en.html

Juneau, T. (2013). Yemen and the Arab Spring: Elite struggles, state collapse and regional security. *Orbis*, *57*(3), 408–423.

Kacowicz, A. M. (1997). 'Negative' international peace and domestic conflicts, West Africa, 1957–96. *The Journal of Modern African Studies*, *35*(3), 367–385.

Kamal, O. (2021). *After the collapse of the Taliban: A study of the US statebuilding failure* (Doctoral dissertation, Webster University).

Karlsrud, J. (2017). *The UN at war: Peace operations in a new era*. Springer.

Kasimbazi, E., & Bamwine, F. (2021). Resolving the grand Ethiopian renaissance dam conflict through the African Union Nexus approach. In *Nile and grand Ethiopian renaissance dam* (pp. 61–78). Springer.

Katzman, K. (2004). *Iraq: US regime change efforts and post-Saddam governance*. Library of Congress Washington DC Congressional Research Service.

Kenkel, K. M. (2013). Five generations of peace operations: From the "thin blue line" to "painting a country blue." *Revista Brasileira De Política Internacional*, *56*(1), 122–143.

Kendall, E. (2021). Jihadi militancy and Houthi insurgency in Yemen. In *Routledge handbook of US counterterrorism and irregular warfare operations*, 83–94. Routledge.

Kent, R. C. (1987). *Anatomy of disaster relief: The international network in action* (pp. 137–8). London: Pinter.

Kestemont, E. (2018). *What role(s) for the European Union in national dialogues? Lessons learned from Yemen* (EU Diplomacy Paper 05/2018).

Khan, H. U., & Rahman, G. (2020). Pakistan's aid to Afghanistan since 2001 and its prospects for state building in Afghanistan. *FWU Journal of Social Sciences*, *14*(3).

Khan, D. (2021). Political economy of uneven state spatiality: Conflict, class, and institutions in the postcolonial state of Pakistan. *Rethinking Marxism*, *33*(1), 52–70.

Kiley, S., Sirgany, S. E., & Lainé, B. (2019, May 20). *CNN exposes systematic abuse of aid in Yemen*. Retrieved from https://edition.cnn.com/2019/05/20/middleeast/yemen-houthi-aid-investigation-kiley/index.html

Kim, J. Y. (2017). *Rethinking development finance*. World Bank.

Kimball, A. M., & Jumaan, A. (2020). Yemen: The challenge of delivering aid in an active conflict zone. *Global Security: Health, Science and Policy*, *5*(1), 65–67.

Kinder, D. R. (1998). Communication and opinion. *Annual Review of Political Science*, *1*(1), 167–197.

Kirmanc, Ş. (2013). *Identity and nation in Iraq*. Lynne Rienner Publishers.

Kitzinger, J. (2000). Media templates: Patterns of association and the (re)construction of meaning over time. *Media, Culture & Society*, *22*(1), 61–84.

Kohler, M. H. (2015). *Agents of democracy: Political parties in the success and failure of Tunisia and Egypt*. Western Illinois University.
Korostelina, K. (2007). *Social identity and conflict: Structures, dynamics, and implications*. Palgrave Macmillan US.
Koser, K. (2007). Addressing internal displacement in peace processes, peace agreements and peace-building. *IDP Newsletter*.
Krause, K. (1998). Cross-cultural dimensions of multilateral non-proliferation and arms control dialogues: An overview. *Contemporary Security Policy, 19*(1), 1–22.
Kriesberg, L. (2007). *Constructive conflicts: From escalation to resolution*. Rowman & Littlefield.
Krippendorff, K. (2004). *Content analysis*. Sage.
Kristiina, R., Karam, K., & Charlotta, C. (2014). National dialogue and internal mediation processes: Perspectives on theory and practice. *Minister for Foreign Affairs*.
Kronenfeld, S., & Guzansky, Y. (2014). Yemen: A mirror to the future of the Arab Spring. *Military and Strategic Affairs., 6*(3), 79–99.
Kumar, C. (2012). *Building National infrastructures for peace: UN assistance for internally negotiated solutions to violent conflict*. Available at:http://www.pnud.org/content/dam/undp/library/crisis%20prevention/UNDP_BCPR_Chetan%20Kumar_UN%20Support%20to%20internal%20solutions.pdf
Kurze, A. (2015). *Tunisian National Dialogue Quartet wins nobel peace prize*.
Lackner, H. (2016). Yemen's peaceful transition from autocracy: Could it have succeeded? *IDEA*: http://www.idea.int/sites/default/files/publications/yemens-peaceful-transition-from-autocracy.pdf
Lackner, H. (2019). *Yemen in crisis: Road to war*. Verso Books.
Lackner, H. (2020). The role of the United Nations in the Yemen crisis. In *Global, regional, and local dynamics in the Yemen Crisis* (pp. 15–32). Palgrave Macmillan.
Lamont, C. K., & Boujneh, H. (2012). Transitional justice in Tunisia: Negotiating justice during transition. *Politička Misao: Časopis Za Politologiju, 49*(5), 32–49.
Lamont, C. (2015). *The Tunisian National Dialogue Quartet: A model for Asia?*
Landis, J. R., & Koch, G. G. (1977). The measurement of observer agreement for categorical data. *Biometrics, 33*, 159–174.
Larson, A. (2021). *Democracy in Afghanistan: Amid and beyond conflict*.
Laub, Z., & Robinson, K. (2016). Yemen in crisis. *Council on Foreign Relations, 19*, 1–7.
Lederach, J. (1997). *Building peace: Sustainable reconciliation in divided societies*. Institute of Peace Press.
Lee, S. T., & Maslog, C. C. (2005). War or peace journalism? Asian newspaper coverage of conflicts. *Journal of Communication, 55*(2), 311–329.

Lehmann, C. and Masterson, D. (2014) *Emergency economies: The impact of cash assistance in Lebanon, an impact evaluation of the 2013–14 Winter cash assistance program for Syrian refugees in Lebanon*. International Rescue Committee.
Lehti, M. (2019). Inclusivity in track one mediation and national dialogues. In *The era of private peacemakers* (pp. 165–177). Palgrave Macmillan.
Lemay-Hébert, N. (2009). Statebuilding without nation-building? Legitimacy, state failure and the limits of the institutionalist approach. *Journal of Intervention and Statebuilding*, 3(1), 21–45.
Lempereur, A., Salzer, J., Colson, A., Pekar, M., & Kogan, E. B. (2021). *Mediation: Negotiation by other moves*. Wiley.
Lerougetel, A., & Stern, J. (2013). Tunisian political parties organize national dialogue. https://www.wsws.org/en/articles/2013/10/15/tuni-o15.html
Levine, S., & Chastre, C. (2004, July). *Missing the point: An analysis of food security interventions in the Great Lakes* (Network Paper. 47). Humanitarian Practice Network, Overseas Development Institute, London. http://www.odi hpn.org/documents/networkpaper047.pdf.
Lewis, A. (2015). Divide and rule: Understanding insecurity in Yemen. In *Security, clans and tribes: Unstable governance in Somaliland, Yemen and the Gulf of Aden*, 65–91. Palgrave Pivot.
Li, Z., & Khalaf, T. (2012). Picturing terrorism through Arabic lenses: A comparative analysis of Aljazeera and Al Arabia. *Asian Journal of Communication*, 22(5), 433–348.
Liotta, P. H., & Owen, T. (2006). Why human security. *Whitehead Journal of Diplomacy and International Relations* 7, 37.
Loschi, C. (2019). Local mobilisations and the formation of environmental networks in a democratizing Tunisia. *Social Movement Studies*, 18(1), 93–112.
Loh, F. K. W. (2021) Ethnic diversity and the nation-state in the 21st century: Lessons from Malaysia and Myanmar. *International Journal of Asian Christianity*, 4(1), 28–49.
Llewellyn, J. J., & Philpott, D. (2014). *Restorative justice, reconciliation, and peacebuilding*. Oxford University Press.
Lynch, J. (2013). *A global standard for reporting conflict*. Routledge.
Lyons, T. (2006). Ethiopia in 2005: the beginning of a transition? *CSIS Africa Notes*, 25.
Mancini, F., & Vericat, J. (2016, November). *Lost in transition: UN mediation in Libya, Syria, and Yemen*.
Magure, B. (2008). The state, labour and the politics of social dialogue in Zimbabwe 1996–2007: Issues resolved or matters arising? *African and Asian Studies*, 7(1), 19–48.

Mahmoud, A. A. (2016). Tunisia revolution reasons, success factors, results. *General Body for Research*. Available at: http://www.sis.gov.eg/Newvr/34/8.htm
Mao, J., & Gady, A. A. A. (2021). The legitimacy of military intervention in Yemen and its impacts. *Beijing Law Review, 12*(2), 560–592.
Maaß, C. D. (2006). National reconciliation in Afghanistan. Conflict history and the search for an Afghan Approach. *Internationales Asienforum, 37*(1/2), 5.
Margolies, M., & Hoddinott, J. (2014) Costing alternative transfer modalities. *Journal of Development Effectiveness*.
Mark, J. (2010). Reintegration and reconciliation in Afghanistan. *Miltary Review*.
Masadykov, T., Giustozzi, A., & Page, J. M. (2010). *Negotiating with the Taliban: Toward a solution for the Afghan conflict* (Crisis States Research Centre Working Paper 66, Series 2). London: London School of Economics.
Masmoudi, M. (1979). The new world information order. *Journal of Communication, 29*(2), 172–179.
Matanock, A. M. (2017). *Electing peace: From civil conflict to political participation*. Cambridge University Press.
Mattinen, H., & Ogden, K. (2006). Cash-based interventions: Lessons from southern Somalia. *Disasters, 30*(3), 297–315.
Maweu, J., & Mare, A. (2021). Introduction. Changing the tide: Re-examining the interplay of media, conflict and peacebuilding in Africa. In *Media, Conflict and Peacebuilding in Africa* (pp. 1–16). Routledge
McAuliffe, P. (2017). Transitional opportunity? How peace negotiations and power-sharing impede root cause approaches. In *Transformative transitional justice and the malleability of post-conflict states*. Edward Elgar.
McCandless, E. (2013). Wicked problems in peacebuilding and statebuilding: Making progress in measuring progress through the new deal. *Global Governance, 19*, 227.
Mccombs, M., Llamas, J., López-Escobar, E., & Rey Lennon, F. (1997). Candidate images in Spanish elections: Second-level agenda-setting effects. *Journalism & Mass Communication Quarterly, 74*, 703–717.
Mccombs, M., & Shaw, D. (1972). The agenda-setting function of mass media. *Public Opinion Quarterly, 36*, 176–187.
McCombs, M., & Valenzuela, S. (2020). *Setting the agenda: Mass media and public opinion*. Wiley.
McMillan, S. J. (2000). The microscope and the moving target: The challenge of applying content analysis to the world wide web. *Journalism and Mass Communication Quarterly, 77*(1), 80–98.
McMillan, S. J. (2000). *Interactivity is in the eye of the beholder: Function, perception, involvement, and attitude toward the web site*. Paper presented to Proceedings of the 2000 Conference of the American Academy of Advertising, East Lansing, Michigan State University.

MEM. (2020, April 22). *Yemen: WFP slams Houthis' misuse of food aid*. Retrieved from https://www.middleeastmonitor.com/20200422-yemen-wfp-slams-houthis-misuse-of-food-aid/
Mengistu, M. M. (2015). Ethnic federalism: A means for managing or a triggering factor for ethnic conflicts in Ethiopia. *Social Sciences, 4*(4), 94–105.
Merdjanova, I. (2016). Overhauling interreligious dialogue for peacebuilding. *Occasional Papers on Religion in Eastern Europe, 36*(1), 3. Available at: http://digitalcommons.georgefox.edu/ree/vol36/iss1/3
Mia, M. (2016). National Dialogue Quartet in democratic transition of Tunisia: An analysis. *Asian Studies, 19781*, 125.
Mihalka, M. (2017). Conclusion: values and interests: European support for the intervention in Afghanistan and Iraq. In *Old Europe, New Europe and the US* (pp. 281–304). Routledge.
Mikha'el, K., Michael, K., Kellen, D., & Ben-Ari, E. (Eds.). (2009). *The transformation of the world of war and peace support operations*. Greenwood Publishing.
Millar, G. (2021). Trans-scalar ethnographic peace research: Understanding the invisible drivers of complex conflict and complex peace. *Journal of Intervention and Statebuilding, 15*, 1–20.
Miller, L. E., & Aucoin, L. (2010). *Framing the state in times of transition: Case studies in constitution making*. US Institute of Peace Press.
Mirkan, H. H. (2021). Potential challenges and opportunities in Iraq's future. In *From territorial defeat to global ISIS: Lessons learned*, 24–40. IOS Press.
Mitchell, R., & Hancock, E. (2012). *Local peacebuilding and national peace: Interaction between grassroots and Elite processes*. Continuum.
Mohammad, S. (2008). *Thwarting Afghanistan's insurgency: A pragmatic approach toward peace and reconciliation*. United States Institute of Peace.
Mohammadi, A. (1997). *International communication and globalization*. Sage.
Morales, A. J. M., Ramírez, A. O. M., Trejo, E. M., González, G. O., López, O. A. R., & Angulo, P. S. (2020). *Progress, death and conflict: An Ethiopian possible future*.
Moremi, P. R. (2013). *Legal dimension of the role of African Union and United Nations in conflict resolution in Africa* (Doctoral dissertation). The Open University of Tanzania
Morrissey, A. (2021). *Iraqi Militias, state management, and security* (Doctoral dissertation).
M'rad, H. (2015). *National dialogue in Tunisia: Nobel peace prize 2015*. Éditions Nirvana.
Mubarak, S. (2020). *Political settlement and national reconciliation: The right diplomacy for ending the war in Afghanistan* (Doctoral dissertation). Indiana University

Muin, M. (2011). *Agenda-setting theory and the role of the media in shaping public opinion for the Iraq War.* Retrieved from http://ndc.gov.bd/lib_mgmt/webroot/earticle/1665/Role_of_the_Media_in_Iraq_War.pdf.

Mukhammadsidiqov, M. (2020). The importance of regulating the relationship between the state and religion in ensuring the stability of society. *The Light of Islam, 2020*(2), 12–17.

Murphy, R. (2007). *UN peacekeeping in Lebanon, Somalia and Kosovo: Operational and legal issues in practice.* Cambridge University Press.

Murray, C. (2013). *Yemen's National Dialogue Conference.* Department of Public Law.

Murray, C. (2014). National dialogues in 2013. In *Constitution building: A Global Review* (pp. 11–15). IDEA.

Murray, C. (2017). *National dialogues and constitution making* (National Dialogue Handbook Background Papers, 2).

Murray, T. (2007). Police-building in Afghanistan: A case study of civil security reform. *International Peacekeeping, 14*(1), 108–126.

Murray, E., & Stigant, S. (2021). *National dialogues in peacebuilding and transitions – Creativity and adaptive thinking.* United States Institute of Peace, June 2021, No. 173. https://www.usip.org/sites/default/files/pw_173-national_dialogues_in_peacebuilding_and_transitions_creativity_and_adaptive_thinking.pdf.

Musalami, F. (2015). Sectarianism between Sunnis and Shiites in Yemen. *Kareingi Center for Peace.* Available at: http://carnegie-mec.org/2015/12/29/ar-63107/iwb3

Mwagiru, N. (2016). *An inquiry into the nature of effective dialogue and discourse and peacebuilding through leadership.*

Nan, A., Zachariah, M., & Andrea, B. (2012). *Peacemaking: From practice to theory.* Praeger, 1&2.

Nagar, M. F. (2021). The emergence of an empire and evolution of federal democracy in Ethiopia. *The road to democratic development statehood in Africa,* (pp. 97–115). Palgrave Macmillan.

Ndekwo, R. (2020). *National dialogue as a strategy for intra-state conflict resolution in Africa: the case study of Anglophone Cameroon* (Doctoral dissertation). University of Nairobi.

Nevens, K. (2011). Yemen's youth revolution. *The Arab Spring: Implications for British policy* (pp. 24–27). Conservative Middle East Council. https://cmec.org.uk/sites/default/files/field/attachment/October%202011%20CMEC-Arab-Spring.pdf.

Nohrstedt, S. A., & Ottosen, R. (2014). *New wars, new media and new war journalism: professional and legal challenges in conflict reporting.* Nordicom.

Norberg, J. (2016). *Progress—Ten reasons to look forward to the future.* Oneworld Publications.

Nsia-Pepra, K. (2016). *UN robust peacekeeping: Civilian protection in violent civil wars*. Springer.

Nunzio, M. D. (2014). 'Do not cross the red line': The 2010 general elections, dissent, and political mobilization in urban Ethiopia. *African Affairs, 113*(452), 409–430.

OCHA. (2017). *Humanitarian Needs Overview: Yemen*. https://www.unocha.org/sites/dms/Yemen/YEMEN%202017%20HNO_Final.pdf

Odendaal, A. (2011). *The role of political dialogue in peacebuilding and statebuilding: An interpretation of current experience* (Working Group on Political Dialogue of the International Dialogue on Peacebuilding and State-Building).

Olaifa, O. (2017). Curbing violent extremism through peace building in Nigeria. *Journal of US-China Public Administration, 14*(4), 221–223.

Omairan, H. (2021). *Regional and International influence on the Yemen Crisis and the failure of the peace process*.

Omri, M. S. (2015). No ordinary union: UGTT and the Tunisian path to revolution and transition. *Workers of the World, 1*(7), 14–29.

Omri, M. (2016). *Confluency (tarafud) between trade unionism, culture and revolution in Tunisia*. Tunisian General Labour Union.

Overseas Development Institute (ODI) and the Center for Global Development (CGD). (2015). *Doing cash differently: How cash transfers can transform humanitarian aid*.

Özerdem, A., Akgül-Açıkmeşe, S., & Liebenberg, I. (Eds.). (2021). *Routledge handbook of conflict response and leadership in Africa*. Routledge.

Paakkinen, E., & Turtonen, O. (2017). *National dialogues conference: The third conference on national dialogues*. http://nationaldialogues.fi/wp-content/uploads/2017/09/NDC-2017-Conference-Report-final.pdf

Paden, J. N. (2015). *Religion and conflict in Nigeria*. US Institute of Peace.

Paffenholz, T. (2009). Understanding peacebuilding theory: Management, resolution and transformation. *Journal of Peace Research and Action, 14*(2), 4–6.

Paffenholz, T. (2013). *International peacebuilding goes local: analyzing Lederach's conflict transformation theory and its ambivalent encounter with 20 years of practice Peacebuilding*. https://doi.org/10.1080/21647259.2013.783257

Paffenholz, T., & Ross, N. (2016). Inclusive political settlements: New insights from Yemen's National Dialogue. *Prism, 6*(1), 199–210.

Paffenholz, T., & Ross, N. (2015). Managing complexity in negotiations: All inclusive national dialogues: The cases of Congo and Egypt. In *Conference paper for Academic Conference on International Mediation*. Pretoria(pp. 2–4).

Paffenholz, T., Zachariassen, A., & Helfer, C. (2017). *What makes or breaks national dialogues?* Inclusive Peace & Transition Initiative, Graduate Institute of International and Development Studies.

Palik, J. (2017). "Dancing on the heads of snakes": The emergence of the Houthi movement and the role of securitizing subjectivity in Yemen's civil war. *Corvinus Journal of International Affairs, 2*(2–3), 42–56.

Papagianni, K. (2006). National conferences in transitional periods: The case of Iraq. *International Peacekeeping, 13*(3), 316–333.

Papagianni, K. (2013). *National dialogue processes in political transitions* (Civil Society Dialogue Network Discussion Paper No. 3).

Papagianni, K. (2014). *Civil society dialogue network discussion* (Paper No. 3). National Dialogue.

Paragi, B. (2019). *Foreign aid in the Middle East: In search of peace and democracy*. Bloomsbury.

Paulmann, J. (2013). Conjunctures in the history of international humanitarian aid during the twentieth century. *Humanity: An International Journal of Human Rights, Humanitarianism, and Development, 4*(2), 215–238.

Pavelka, J. (2014). The factors affecting the presentation of events and the media coverage of topics in the mass media. *Procedia-Social and Behavioral Sciences, 140*, 623–629.

Pearson, J. (1997). Mediating when domestic violence is a factor: Policies and practices in court-based divorce mediation programs. *Mediation Quarterly, 14*(4), 319–335.

Pelham, S., Göth, T., Kamminga, J., Alkadri, H., Ehsan, M., & Tonelli, A. (2021). *'Leading the way': Women driving peace and security in Afghanistan*. The Occupied Palestinian Territory and Yemen.

Pettersson, T., Högbladh, S., & Öberg, M. (2019). Organized violence, 1989–2018 and peace agreements. *Journal of Peace Research, 56*(4), 589–603.

Pettersson, T., & Wallensteen, P. (2015). Armed conflicts, 1946–2014. *Journal of Peace Research, 52*(4), 536–550.

Phillips, C. (2016). *The battle for Syria*. Yale University Press.

Pia, E., & Diez, T. (2007). *Conflict and human rights: A theoretical framework*.

Planta, K., Prinz, V., & Vimalarajah, L. (2015). Inclusivity in national dialogues. *Guaranteeing social integration or preserving old power hierarchies*.

Pongracz, S. (2015). *Value for money of cash transfers in emergencies: Lebanon case study*. DFID.

Pondy, L. (1967). Organizational conflict: Concepts and models. *Administrative Science Quarterly* (pp. 296–320). Sage. https://doi.org/10.2307/2391553

Potter, A., & Centre for Humanitarian Dialogue. (2005). *We the women: Why conflict mediation is not just a job for men*. HD Centre for Humanitarian Dialogue.

Presidential Decree (No.13- 2012). *For forming a communication commission*. Available at: www.hiwar-watani.org/uploads/1/5/2/3/15238886/decree_13-2012_form_contact_committee.docx

Presidential Decree (No.30–2012). *For establishing technical committee to prepare comprehensive National Dialogue Conference*. Available at: www.hiwar-watani.org/uploads/1/5/2/3/15238886/rep-decree30_form_tc_ar.docx

Processes in Political Transitions. Available at: http://www.hdcentre.org/uploads/tx_news/National-Dialogue-Processes-in-Political-Transitions.pdf

Price, M. E., Al Marashi, I., & Stremlau, N. A. (2009). Media in the peace-building process: Ethiopia and Iraq. *Departmental Papers (ASC)*, 149.

Pruitt, B., & Thomas, P. (2007). *Democratic dialogue—A handbook for practitioners*. International IDEA.

Project on Middle East Political Science (POMEPS). (2013, March 19), *Arab uprisings, Yemen's National Dialogue, foreign policy, the Middle East channel*. POMEPS Briefings. http://www.idea.int/es/publications/democratic_dialogue/loader.cfm?csmodule=security/getfile&pageid=19459

Puddepphatt, A. (2006). *Voices of war: conflict and the role of the media*. Retrieved from https://www.mediasupport.org/wp-content/uploads/2012/11/ims-voices-of-war-2006.pdf

Pugh, M., Cooper, N., & Goodhand, J. (2005). War economies in a regional context: Challenges of transformation. *African Security Review, 14*(4), 128.

QAsem, A. (2013). Five barriers to youth engagement, decision-making, and leadership in Yemen" s political parties. *Resonate Yemen and Saferworld, 5*, 5.

Qassim, A., Amin, L., Transfeld, M., & Strzelecka, E. (2020). *The role of civil society in peacebuilding in Yemen*.

Quie, M. (2012). Peace-building and democracy promotion in Afghanistan: The Afghanistan peace and reintegration programme and reconciliation with the Taliban. *Democratization, 19*(3), 553–574.

QUNO. (2015). Reconciliation—Transforming relationships in divided societies. *UNITAR Workshop on Reconciliation & Peacebuilding*.

Ramsbotham, O., & Woodhouse, T. (2013). *Peacekeeping and conflict resolution*. Routledge.

Rantanen, T. (2004). European news agencies and their sources in the Iraq War coverage. In *Reporting War* (pp. 311–324). Routledge.

Regan, P. M. (2002). *Civil wars and foreign powers: Outside intervention in intrastate conflict*. University of Michigan Press.

Redissi, H., & Boukhayatia, R. (2016). *The national constituent assembly of Tunisia and civil society dynamics* (Working Paper, No. 2).

Resta, V., Cavatorta, F., & Storm, L. (2018). Leftist parties in the Arab region before and after the Arab uprisings: unrequited love? *Political parties in the Arab world. Continuity and change* (pp. 23–48).

Riad, H. (2015). *Concept development of peace-building: Study on the theory and approaches*. Available at: http://guelma.moontada.net/t5709-topic

Richmond, O. P. (2008). Reclaiming peace in international relations. *Millennium, 36*(3), 439–470.

Richmond, O. P. (2010). A genealogy of peace and conflict theory. In *Palgrave advances in peacebuilding* (pp. 14–38). Palgrave Macmillan.

Richmond, O. P. (2013). The legacy of state formation theory for peacebuilding and statebuilding. *International Peacekeeping, 20*(3), 299–315.

Rodt, A. P., & Okeke, J. M. (2013). AU-EU "strategic partnership": Strengthening policy convergence and regime efficacy in the African peace and security complex? *African Security, 6*(3–4), 211–233.

Ropers, N. (2004). From resolution to transformation: The role of dialogue projects. *Transforming Ethnopolitical Conflict* (pp. 255–269). VS Verlag für Sozialwissenschaften.

Ropers, N. (2011). *A systemic approach: Reflections on Sri Lanka*. Handbook article. Berghof Foundation.

Ropers, N. (2017). *Basics of dialogue facilitation*. Berghof Foundation. Available at https://www.berghof-foundation.org/fileadmin/redaktion/Publications/Other_Resources/Ropers_BasicsofDialogueFacilitation.pdf

Rosato, S. (2021). *Intentions in great power politics: Uncertainty and the roots of conflict*. Yale University Press.

Rosendale, J. A., & Longcore, A. (2015). *On hard versus soft news: A content analysis of reporting by three nationally-televised evening news programs*. Retrieve from http://www.scirp.org/journal/jss, https://doi.org/10.4236/jss.2015.311008

Rosenthal, C. (2015). *Reconsidering agenda setting and intermedia agenda setting from a global perspective: a cross-national comparative agenda setting test*. Londres: Media@ LSE.

Rose-Ackerman, S., & Palifka, B. J. (2016). *Corruption and government: Causes, consequences, and reform*. Cambridge University Press.

Rotberg, R. I. (2010). One. The failure and collapse of nation-states: Breakdown, prevention, and repair. In *When states fail* (pp. 1–50). Princeton University Press.

Rozanov, A., Kharlamova, J., & Shirshikov, V. (2021). *The role of fake news in conflict escalation: A theoretical overview*. Available at SSRN 3857007.

RT-Arabic. (2009). *July 29th Afghanistan and the Taliban. Prepping for elections*.

Rupesinghe, K. (1995). Non-governmental organizations and the agenda for peace. *The Ecumenical Review, 47*(3), 324–327.

Ryan, C. (1991). What's newsworthy? In *Prime time activism: Media strategies for grassroots organizing* (pp. 31–52). South End Press.

Rysaback-Smith, H. (2016). History and principles of humanitarian action. *Turkish Journal of Emergency Medicine, 15*, 5–7.

Sabahi, A. (2015). *Corruption of Elites Prolongs Yemen conflict*. Available at http://www.albayan.co.uk/Article2.aspx?id=4550#sthash.eCERWt0G.dpuf

Sadiq, I. (2021). *Origins of the Kurdish Genocide: Nation Building and Genocide as civilizing and de-civilizing processes*. Rowman & Littlefield.

Saif, A. (2015). *Yemen crisis: What role for the EU*. Accessed on March 13, 2017 from http://www.europarl.europa.eu/RegData/etudes/IDAN/2015/534990/EXPO_IDA(2015)534990_EN.pdf

Salameh, M. (2015). *Civil society organizations in Yemen East Afro-mountain region*. Report funded by Critical Ecosystem Partnership Fund.

Saleem, N., & Hanan, M. A. (2014). Media and conflict resolution: Toward building a relationship model. *Journal of Political Studies, 21*(1), 179.

Salisbury, P. (2015). *Federalism, conflict and fragmentation in Yemen*. Saferworld

Sargent, W. M. (2016). *Civilizing peace building: Twenty-first century global politics*. Routledge.

Sassoon, J. (2012). *Saddam Hussein's Ba'th Party: Inside an authoritarian regime*. Cambridge University Press.

Sawa. (2016). *The Backwardness in the Arab World*. Newspaper article available at: http://www.radiosawa.com/content/international-literacy-day/280417.html

Sarkin, J., & Sensibaugh, H. (2011). Why achieving reconciliation in Iraq is possible: Suggestions for mechanisms and processes including a truth and reconciliation commission. *The Fletcher Journal of Human Security, XXIII–2008*, 1–28.

Sassoon, J. (2016). Iraq's political economy post 2003: From transition to corruption. *International Journal of Contemporary Iraqi Studies, 10*(1–2), 17–33.

Schaefer, C. D. (2010). Local practices and normative frameworks in peacebuilding. *International Peacekeeping, 17*(4), 499–514.

Scheufele, D. A. (2000). Agenda-setting, priming, and framing revisited. Another look at cognitive effects of political communication. *Mass Communication & Society, 3*, 297–316.

Schirch, L. (2004). *The little book of strategic peacebuilding*. Good Books.

Schmitz, C. (2014). *Yemen's National Dialogue* (MEI Policy Paper). Middle East Institute. http://www.mei.edu/sites/default/files/publications/Schmitz%20Policy%20Paper.pdf

Schulpen. L., & Habraken, M. (2014). *Southern civil society in perspective: A literature review, policy report*. Radboud University Press.

Schwab, B. (2019). Comparing the productive effects of cash and food transfers in a crisis setting: Evidence from a randomized experiment in Yemen. *The Journal of Development Studies, 55*(sup1), 29–54.

Schwartz, M. (2016). *War without end: the Iraq war in context*. Haymarket books.

Seale, P. (2013). Yemen seeks to talk its way out of Chaos. *Washington Report on Middle East Affairs, 32*(2), 24.

Semetko, H. A., & Valkenburg, P. M. (2000). Framing European politics: A content analysis of press and television news. *Journal of Communication*, 50(2), 93–109.

Sharp, J. (2017). Yemen: Cholera outbreak. *CRS INSIGHT*. https://fas.org/sgp/crs/mideast/IN10729.pdf

Sharqieh, I. (2013). *A lasting peace? Yemen's long journey to national reconciliation*. Brookings Doha Center Analysis, 7.

Shoemaker, P. J., Chang, T. K., & Brendlinger, N. (1986). Deviance as a predictor of newsworthiness: Coverage of international events in the U.S. media. In M. L. McLaughlin (Ed.), *Communication yearbook*(p. 10). Sage.

Shoemaker, P.J., & Reese, S.D. (1995). *Mediating the message: Theories of influences on mass media content*.

Shuker, H. & Alrdisi, H. (2015). *Presidential elections in Tunisia between competition and consensus*. Arab Reform Web, Political Alternatives. Available at: www.arab-reform.net/sites/default/files

Siebert, H. (2014). National dialogue and legitimate change. *Accord*, 25, 36.

Siebert, H. (2016). Beyond mediation: Promoting change and resolving conflict through authentic national dialogues. In *Interventions in conflict* (pp. 153–162). Palgrave Macmillan.

Singer, H. W. (1988). Food aid: Pros and cons. *Intereconomics*, 23(2), 79–83.

Smet, S. (2010). Freedom of expression and the right to reputation: Human rights in conflict. *American University International Law Review*, 26, 183.

Smith, L. (2007). *Political violence and democratic uncertainty in Ethiopia*. United States Institute of Peace.

Smith, P. M. (1991). *How CNN fought the war*. Birch Lane Press.

Sobel, M. R., & Riffe, D. (2015). US linkages in *New York Times* coverage of Nigeria, Ethiopia and Botswana (2004–13): Economic and strategic bases for news. *International Communication Research Journal*, 50(1), 3–23.

Spence, R. (2006). *Post-conflict peacebuilding: Who determines the peace? Governance and stability in the Pacific*. University of the Sunshine Coast.

Spencer, G. (2005). *The media and peace. From Vietnam to the war on terror*. Palgrave.

Sphere Project. (2004). *Humanitarian charter and minimum standards in disaster response*. Sphere Project.

Stanekzai, M. M. (2008). *Thwarting Afghanistan's insurgency*. US Institute of Peace.

Stavenhagen, R. (2016). *Ethnic conflicts and the nation-state*. Springer.

Steele, D. (2008). *Reconciliation strategies in Iraq*. Institute of Peace. Available at: http://www.usip.org/sites/default/files/sr213.pdf

Steenkamp, C. (2017). The crime-conflict nexus and the civil war in Syria. *Stability: International Journal of Security and Development*, 6(1), 11.

Stigart, S & Murray, E. (2015). *National dialogue, a tool for conflict transformation*. Institute of Peace. http://www.usip.org/sites/default/files/PB194-National-Dialogues.pdf

Suhrke, A. (2007). Reconstruction as modernisation: The 'post-conflict' project in Afghanistan. *Third World Quarterly, 28*(7), 1291–1308.

Sukhoparava, I. (2014). *Tunisia: Success story?* Available at: www.rt.com/op-edge/tnisia-arab-spring-democratic-transition-579

Summers, H. G. (1995). *Persian Gulf War Almanac*. Facts on File.

Svensson, I., & Brounéus, K. (2013). Dialogue and interethnic trust: A randomized field trial of 'sustained dialogue' in Ethiopia. *Journal of Peace Research, 50*(5), 563–575.

SWI swissinfo.ch. (2015, September 30). *Swiss donations for Syrian crisis swell to CHF20 million*. Retrieved from https://www.swissinfo.ch/eng/helping-hand_swiss-donations-forsyrian-crisis-swell-to-chf20-million/41692362

SWI swissinfo. (2015, October 29). *Swiss 'shocked' at targeting of hospitals*. Retrieved from https://www.swissinfo.ch/eng/breaking-war-rules_swiss-shocked-at-targeting-of-hospitals/41748650

SWI. (2016, June 16). *UAE says its war in Yemen "practically over"*. Retrieved from http://www.swissinfo.ch/eng/

SWI. (2016, July 27). *U.N. calls for humanitarian truce in Yemen's Taiz province*. Retrieved from https://www.swissinfo.ch/...calls-for-humanitarian-truce-in-yemen...taiz-province/423

SWI (2016, August 24). *Kerry to discuss Yemen, Syria with Gulf Arab states*. Retrieved from http://www.swissinfo.ch/eng/kerry-to-discuss-yemen--syria-with-gulf-arab-states/42396304

SWI (2016, December 6). *Emaciated Yemeni woman now smiles but recovery patchy*. Retrieved from http://www.swissinfo.ch/eng/emaciated-yemeni-woman-now-smiles-but-recovery-patchy/html

SWI. (2016, December 7). *U.S. urges Yemen to accept U.N.-drafted roadman for peace talk*. Retrieved from: https://www.swissinfo.ch/eng/reuters/u-s--urges-yemen-to-accept-u-n--drafted-roadmap-for-peace-talks/42738248

Syria's civil war explained from the beginning. (2018, March 4). Retrieved from https://www.aljazeera.com/news/2016/05/syria-civil-war-explained-160505084119966.html

Tamburini, F. (2021). The ghost of the constitutional review in Tunisia: Authoritarianism, transition to democracy and rule of law. *Journal of Asian and African Studies*.

Taylor, B. C., & Bean, H. (Eds.). (2019). *The handbook of communication and security*. Routledge.

The Diary of Sheikh Abdullah bin Hussein al-Ahmar. (2009). *Unknown history: Egyptian-Saudi bloody intervention in Yemen, the Yemeni scene* (p. 24). Open access at http://www.almashhad¬alyemeni.com/print.php?Id=31815, Date of visit 5 January 2016.

The Guardian. (2014, August 4). Is western media coverage of the Ukraine crisis anti-Russian? Retrieved from https://www.theguardian.com/world/2014/aug/04/western-media-coverage-ukraine-crisis-russia

The Independent. (2015, April 11). Ceasefire aimed at ending Yemeni forgotten war disrupted by violence. Retrieved on April 28, 2017 http://www.independent.co.uk/news/world/middle-east/ceasefire-aimed-at-ending-yemens-forgotten-war-dispruted-by-violence-a6979581.html

The Independent (2016, October 9). Britain and US pile pressure on Saudi Arabia over Yemen funeral bombing. Retrieved from http://www.independent.co.uk/news/world/middle-east/yemen-sanaa-funeral-bombing-air-strikes-uk-arms-sales-us-saudi-arabia-coalition-latest-a7353231.html

The Independent. (2016, October 13). Russia 'bombed four hospitals in Syria in four hours', report finds. Retrieved from https://www.independent.co.uk/news/world/middle-east/russia-syria-bomb-hospitals-war-kurds-putin-assad-idlib-a9153786.html

The Independent. (2016, December 7). The world has forgotten the Yemen war, says senior UN humanitarian official. Retrieved from http://www.independent.co.uk/news/world/middle-east/yemen-war-saudi-arabia-world-forgotten-houthi-rebels-conflict-un-official-comments-a7460081.html

The Independent. (2016, October 9). Saudi-led coalition in Yemen accused of 'genocide' after airstrike on funeral hall kills 140. Retrieved from http://www.independent.co.uk/news/world/middle-east/yemen-air-strike-bomb-kills-140-saudi-arabia-usa-white-house-a7352386.html

The Independent (2016, October 21). *Experts say Saudi coalition violated international humanitarian law in Yemen attack*. Retrieved from http://www.independent.co.uk/news/world/middle-east/un-saudi-arabia-yemen-air-strikes-violated-international-law-a7372936.html

The Independent. (2016, December 1). In Yemen's war, trapped families ask: Which child should we save? Retrieved from http://www.independent.co.uk/news/world/middle-east/yemen-civil-war-trapped-families-ask-which-children-to-save-a7448996.html

The Presidential Decree No. (2013, November). *The formation and naming members of the National Dialogue Conference*. Available at: https://arabic.rt.com/news/32501

Thomas, K. (1992). Conflict and Conflict Management: Reflections and Update. *Journal of Organizational Behavior*, 13(3), 265–74. Available at: http://www.jstor.org.citytech.ezproxy.cuny.edu:2048/stable/2488472

Thomassen, A. (2015). *How do trade unions contribute to democratisation?* (Master's thesis). The University of Bergen.

Tidwell, A. (2001). *Conflict resolved?: A critical assessment of conflict resolution*. A&C Black.

Tomlinson, J. (1997). Cultural globalization and cultural imperialism. In K. Thompson (Ed.), *Media and cultural regulation*. The Open University & Sage.

Transfeld, M. (2016). Political bargaining and violent conflict: Shifting elite alliances as the decisive factor in Yemen's transformation. *Mediterranean Politics, 21*(1), 150–169.

Trotskovets, I. V. (2021). *The role of media in hybrid wars: Ukrainian experience* (Doctoral dissertation). National Aviation University

Tschirgi, N. (2015). Bridging the Chasm between domestic and international approaches to peacebuilding: Conceptual and institutional tools. *RCCS Annual Review. A Selection from the Portuguese journal Revista Crítica de Ciências Sociais,* (7).

Tuğal, C. (2015). Elusive revolt: The contradictory rise of middle-class politics. *Thesis Eleven, 130*(1), 74–95.

Turkoglu, O. (2021). Supporting rebels and hosting refugees: Explaining the variation in refugee flows in civil conflicts. *Journal of Peace Research*, 0022343321989786.

Unger, T. (2010). *The European union and transitional justice.* TMC Asser Institute.

UK National Audit Office. (2011). *Transferring cash and assets to the poor.* Report by the Comptroller and Auditor General. HC 1587, Session 2010–2012.

UN. (2019, July 31). *Implementing a cash transfer project in Yemen.* Retrieved from https://yemen.un.org/en/19047-implementing-cash-transfer-project

United Nations Office for the Coordination of Humanitarian Affairs (OCHA). 2020. Global humanitarian overview. (2020). *United Nations-Coordinated Support to People Affected by Disaster and Conflict* (pp. 4–85). OCHA.

Unruh, J. D. (2015). The structure and function of keywords in the development of civil wars: Opportunities for peace building? *Peace and Conflict: Journal of Peace Psychology, 21*(4), 621.

Urlacher, B. (2007). *Third parties and the tacit mediation of intra-state conflict: Negotiating with an elephant in the next room.* University of Connecticut.

UNDP. (2004). *Security with a human face: Challenges and responsibilities.* Afghanistan National Human Development Report. Available at: http://hdr.undp.org/sites/default/files/afghanistan_2004_en.pdf

UNDP. (2009). *Why dialogue matters for conflict prevention and peacebuilding.* Available at http://www.undp.org/content/dam/undp/library/crisis%20prevention/dialogue_conflict.pdf

UNDP. (2019, December 22). *Supported cash-for-work initiative helps deal with mounting solid waste crisis in Hodeidah: UNDP in Yemen.* Retrieved from https://www.ye.undp.org/content/yemen/en/home/stories/undp-supported-cash-for-work-initiative-helps-deal-with-mounting.html

UNESCO. (2019, November 12). *Yemen: Cash for work.* Retrieved from https://en.unesco.org/news/yemen-cash-work

UNICEF. (2019). *Emergency cash transfer project*. Retrieved from https://www.unicef.org/yemen/emergency-cash-transfer-project

UNPF. (2014). *What is peacebuilding?* Available at: http://www.unpbf.org/application-guidelines/what-is-peacebuilding/#fnref-1937-3

USAID. (2007). *Yemen: Civil society sector assessment*. United States Agency for International Development.

USAID. (2011). *The 2011 civil society organization sustainability report for the Middle East and North Africa*. United States Agency for International Development

USAID. (2018, January). *Success stories report*.

Van Nieuwkerk, A. (2021). Peacekeeping and security through the African Union. In *Conflict resolution and global justice* (pp. 148–167). Routledge.

Van Tongeren, P. (2013). Potential cornerstone of infrastructures for peace? How local peace committees can make a difference. *Peacebuilding, 1*(1), 39–60.

Veen, E. (2014). *From the struggle for citizenship to the fragmentation of justice: Yemen from 1990 to 2013*. CRU Report. Netherlands Institute for International Relations.

Verjee, A. (2021). Political transitions in Sudan and Ethiopia: An early comparative analysis. *Global Change, Peace & Security, 33*, 1–18.

Vicenç, F. (2014). *Yearbook of peace processes*. School of Culture of Peace. http://peacemaker.un.org/sites/peacemaker.un.org/files/YearbookPeaceProcesses-ECP-2014.pdf

Vicente, P. N. G. (2013). *International News Reporting in the Multidimensional Network: The socio-demographics, professional culture and newswork of foreign correspondents working across Sub-Saharan Africa* (Doctoral dissertation). Universidade NOVA de Lisboa (Portugal).

Visoka, G., & Doyle, J. (2016). Neo-functional peace: The European Union way of resolving conflicts. *JCMS: Journal of Common Market Studies, 54*(4), 862–877.

Vladisavljević, N. (2015). *Media framing of political conflict: A review of the literature*. Media, Conflict and Democratisation (MeCoDEM).

Vogel, B., Tschunkert, K., & Schläpfer, I. (2021). The social meaning of money: Multidimensional implications of humanitarian cash and voucher assistance. *Disasters*.

Vreese, de C. H. (2002). *Framing Europe*. Aksant Academic Publishers.

Vreese, de C. H. (2004). The effects of frames in political Television News on issue interpretation and frame salience. *Journalism & Mass Communication Quarterly, 81*, 36–52.

Waldman, M. (2015). *Opportunity in crisis navigating Afghanistan's uncertain future*. Royal Institute of International Affairs.

Warrens, M. J. (2012). Cohen's quadratically weighted kappa is higher than linearly weighted kappa for tridiagonal agreement tables. *Statistical Methodology, 9*, 440–444.

WB. (2013). *Yemen civil society organizations in transition: A mapping and capacity assessment of development-oriented civil society organizations in five governorates.* https://openknowledge.worldbank.org/bitstream/handle/10986/16638/810950WP0ENGLI0Box0379828B00PUBLIC0.pdf?sequence=1

Weber, R. P. (1990). *Basic content analysis* (2nd ed.). Sage.

Weldemariam, A. (2009). *Conflict management in the Ethiopian multi-national federation.* European University Center for Peace Studies. Available at: http://epu.ac.at/fileadmin/downloads/research/Weldemariam.pdf

Westley, F. (1991). Bob Geldof and live aid: The affective side of global social innovation. *Human Relations, 44*(10), 1011–1036.

Whalan, J. (2013). *How peace operations work: Power, legitimacy, and effectiveness.* Oxford University Press.

Wildeman, J., & Swan, E. (2021). What lies ahead? Canada's engagement with the Middle East peace process and the palestinians: An introduction. *Canadian Foreign Policy Journal, 27*(1), 1–20.

Williams, P., Sommadossi, T., & Mujais, A. (2017). A legal perspective on Yemen's attempted transition from a unitary to a federal system of government. *Utrecht Journal of International and European Law, 33*, 4.

Wils, O., Hopp, U., Ropers, N., Vimalarajah, L., & Zunzer, W. (2006). *The systemic approach to conflict transformation: Concept and fields of application.* Berghof Foundation for Peace Support Krisenprävention, Zivile Konfliktbearbeitung, Friedensförderung.

Wimmer, A. (2003). Democracy and ethno-religious conflict in Iraq. *Survival, 45*(4), 111–134.

Winright, T., & Johnston, L. (2015). *Can war be just in the 21st century?* Orbis Books.

Winter, B. (2016). Women's human rights and Tunisian upheavals: Is 'democracy' enough? *Global Discourse, 6*(3), 513–529.

Withnall, A. (2015, September 30). *Aylan Kurdi's story: How a small Syrian child came to be washed up on a beach in Turkey.* Retrieved from https://www.independent.co.uk/news/world/europe/aylan-kurdi-s-story-how-a-small-syrian-child-came-to-be-washed-up-on-a-beach-in-turkey-10484588.html

Wodajo, M. R., & Mengesha, O. (2021). Contested politics in Ethiopia, Post of 2018: Challenges and prospects of the ruling party. *SSRN Electronic Journal.* https://doi.org/10.2139/ssrn.3829270

Wolff, S. (2007). *Ethnic conflict: A global perspective.* Oxford University Press.

Wolfsfeld, G., & Gadi, W. (1997). *Media and political conflict: News from the Middle East* (Vol. 10). Cambridge University Press.

Wood, E. J. (2003). Review Essay: Civil Wars: What we don't know.

World Bank. (2018a). *The World Bank Yemen emergency crisis response project—Third additional financing report 2018*. The World Bank.

World Bank. (2018b, May 29). *Yemen food imports: A focus on critical challenges and priority interventions*. Retrieved from https://www.worldbank.org/en/country/yemen/publication/securing-imports-of-essential-food-commodities-to-yemen

Yadav, S. P. (2015). The "Yemen Model" as a failure of political imagination. *International Journal of Middle East Studies, 47*(1), 144–147.

Yamao, D. (2011). National reconciliation as a tool of political struggles: An inquiry into nation building in post-War Iraq. *Third Global International Studies Conference* Available at: http://www.wiscnetwork.org/porto2011/papers/WISC_2011-500.pdf

Yawanarajah, N. (2021). Informality and the social art of mediation: How pure mediators create conditions for making peace. *New England Journal of Public Policy, 33*(1), 10.

Yemeni Center for Strategic Studies. (2013). *Strategic Report of Yemen*.

Yemen's Houthis form own government in Sana'a. (2015, February 7). Retrieved from http://www.aljazeera.com/news/middleeast/2015/02/yemen-houthi-rebels-announce-presidential-council-150206122736448.html

Yemen might return 50 years back. *Radfan Press*. Available at: http://rdfanpress.com/news_details.php?lang=arabic&sid=8796

Yin, R. K. (2009). *Case study research: Design and methods* (4th ed.). Sage.

Yousfi, H. (2017). *Trade unions and Arab revolutions: The Tunisian case of UGTT*. Routledge.

Yusuf, S. (2019). Drivers of ethnic conflict in contemporary Ethiopia. *Institute for Security Studies Monographs, 2019*(202), 46.

Zachariassen, A. (2015). *Dialogues in peace and mediation processes: Definitions, types, goals, and success factors for sustainability, Inclusive peace, transition imitative*. Available at: http://www.inclusivepeace.org/sites/default/files/IPTI-National-Dialogue-12-pager.pdf

Zachariassen, A., Ross, N., Paffenholz, T., & Hawana, F. (2016). *Dialogues in peace and mediation processes: definitions, types, goals, and success factors for sustainability*. Geneva, Inclusive Peace and Transition Initiative (IPTI). https://www.inclusivepeace.org/content/dialogues-peace-and-me-diation-processes-definitions-types-goals-and-suc-cess-factors

Zambaka, C. (2016). *Six factors for successful national dialogues*. The Fletcher forum of world affairs. Available at: www.fletcherforum.org/2016/02/18/zambakari-5/

Zartman, I. W. (1989). *Ripe for resolution: Conflict and intervention in Africa*. Oxford University Press.

Zyck, S. A. (2014). *Mediating transition in Yemen: Achievements and lessons*. International Peace Institute.

Index

A
Afghanistan, 2, 3, 5, 17–19, 21, 27, 33, 68, 76–78, 81, 82, 94–100, 103–106, 113, 119, 120, 153, 192, 201, 202, 208, 209
Agenda setting, 19, 64, 65
Arab Spring, 19–22, 24, 25, 34, 77, 120, 124, 126, 153, 154, 157, 204
Attribution of Responsibility, 66, 179, 180, 182, 187, 188

C
Cash-aid, 69–72, 165–169
Change peacebuilding theory, 33, 54, 56, 57
civil conflicts, 2, 48, 54
civil society organisations, 53, 121, 131, 204, 208
Conflict management, 33, 56, 57
Conflict transformation, 4, 6–8, 12, 57–60
Consequences, 1, 10, 31, 65, 66, 120, 122, 179, 180, 182, 185, 186

constitution, 4, 9, 24, 28, 30, 95, 96, 98, 103, 107, 108, 110, 121, 129, 133, 134, 136, 205
Crisis, 5, 9–11, 19, 21, 24, 28, 29, 31, 52, 64, 68, 69, 78, 127–130, 133, 143, 149, 150, 154, 157, 158, 160, 167, 169, 174, 177, 180, 181, 186, 188, 190, 192, 193, 205

D
Discourse, 5, 10, 52, 66, 143, 175, 208
Divided societies, 53, 57, 60, 120, 149

E
Economic reform, 108, 109, 111, 120
Educational infrastructure, 99
Efficiency, 59, 203
Ethiopia, 2, 3, 6, 18, 19, 21, 27, 28, 33, 70, 76–78, 81, 82, 94,

106–113, 119, 120, 152, 192, 201
European Union (EU), 3, 5, 6, 8, 18, 19, 21, 24, 25, 32, 33, 51, 61, 71, 74, 80, 94–97, 100, 120, 129, 160

F
federal (composite) system, 99, 109, 123
Food-aid, 34, 67, 69–71, 151, 152, 161–164, 166–168
framing conflict, 35, 211
France24, 7, 19, 35, 80–82, 176, 179, 182–187, 189, 190

H
Houthi movement, 23, 24, 71, 157, 158, 188
Human interest, 64, 66, 179, 181–183, 188
Humanitarian aid (HA), 18, 19, 34, 35, 60, 66–71, 73, 75, 76, 82, 143, 149, 150, 152–158, 162, 165, 167–169, 175, 180, 184, 187, 189, 190, 192, 210, 211
Humanitarianism, 66, 67, 152

I
Independent, 7, 16, 19, 30, 35, 61, 77, 81, 82, 132, 133, 137, 159, 175, 176, 181, 182, 211
International Non-governmental Organisations (INGOs), 69–72, 143, 151, 156, 159, 161
Iraq, 2, 3, 6, 18, 19, 21, 31, 33, 34, 64, 69, 76–78, 81, 119–125, 149, 156, 192, 202, 204, 208

L
Lessons learned, 6, 19–21, 81, 82, 94, 104, 111, 119, 124, 126, 142

M
media framing theory, 32, 63, 81
mediation, 10, 13, 15–17, 51, 52, 58, 94, 139
Middle East and North Africa (MENA), 3, 21, 33, 34, 63, 64, 66, 74, 81, 119, 149, 150, 190
military campaign, 191, 192
Morality, 66, 179, 180, 182, 183, 189, 191

N
National Dialogue, 2–10, 12, 15, 19–22, 24, 27, 31–35, 48, 52, 53, 55, 58, 59, 74, 76, 77, 81, 93, 94, 96–100, 102–105, 107, 109, 111, 112, 119–137, 140, 142, 143, 149, 169, 174, 184, 201, 202, 204–210, 212
National Dialogue Conferences (NDCs), 20, 21, 24–26, 33, 34, 76–78, 81, 94, 101, 113, 132–135, 137, 140, 142, 204, 208
negotiation, 3, 8, 10, 12–15, 17, 51, 52, 54, 55, 94, 97, 107, 124, 128, 139, 142, 149, 180, 201, 206–210
News frame, 7, 19, 21, 65, 81, 176, 180, 183, 190, 212
Non-governmental Organisations (NGOs), 19, 34, 49, 50, 58, 69–71, 73, 74, 143, 151, 152, 154, 160–163, 165–168
NRC Handelsblad, 7, 19, 35, 80, 81, 175, 176, 211

P

Peacebuilding, 2, 5, 6, 9, 12, 15, 16, 32, 33, 47–61, 66, 71, 74, 77, 93, 94, 108, 119, 124, 201, 206, 207
Peace intervention, 33, 34, 82, 119, 177, 210
peacekeeping, 48–50, 52, 93
peace-making, 47, 48, 51, 52, 93, 104
peace process, 7, 11, 20, 35, 52, 55, 105, 124, 149, 184, 206
Political culture, 204
political elite, 11, 12, 16, 24, 55, 62, 99, 100, 112, 129, 132, 209

Q

Qualitative approach, 22, 71
Quartet Dialogue, 128, 130

R

Reconciliation, 5, 6, 9, 19, 27, 28, 31–33, 52–55, 57–59, 94, 95, 99, 105–108, 110–112, 120–122, 124–126, 134, 140, 201, 202, 206, 207, 209
reconciliation policy, 54
Religious conflicts, 122, 202, 204

S

Saudi-Yemen war, 5, 7, 22, 176, 178, 179, 190, 191, 211
Social harmony, 4
SWIswissinfo.ch, 7, 19
Syria, 5, 7, 18, 23, 31, 32, 35, 74, 79–81, 124, 153–155, 169, 175, 176, 178, 182, 184–186, 188, 189, 191–193, 204, 211, 212

T

Traditional elites, 99, 109, 123
Transitional Justice (TJ), 107, 108, 134, 135, 140, 141
tribal clans, 121
trust-building, 9, 135, 202, 206, 207
Tunisia, 3, 6, 18–20, 23, 28–30, 33, 34, 61, 76–78, 81, 120, 126–128, 130, 141, 142, 149, 157, 192, 202, 204, 205, 209

V

violence, 5, 8, 24, 49–51, 57, 122–127, 153, 154, 158, 173, 174, 184, 191, 193, 208, 209, 212

W

War economy, 18, 34, 153, 155